'NEW WORLD A-COMING'

Inside Black America

BY ROI OTTLEY

A Life-in-America
Prize Book

HOUGHTON MIFFLIN COMPANY · BOSTON
The Riverside Press Cambridge

To

GLADYS

TARR

OTTLEY

The Riverside Press

CAMBRIDGE · MASSACHUSETTS

PRINTED IN THE U.S.A.

Foreword

        This book, I believe, might very well be named *Inside Black America*. For it is an intimately detailed story of Negro life. Harlem, the most complex of Negro communities, is used as a sort of test tube in which the germs of Negro thought and action are isolated, examined, and held up to full glare to reflect Black America.

It is a reporter's job, relating the Negro's search for democracy, which after all is the essential drive and ultimate goal. Sometimes, in the journey, we are led into curious, entertaining, and often bizarre corners. In the telling, my approach is one of relating affairs in this segregated corner in terms of their broadest meanings and implications to the white community.

By and large, I am concerned with the mass, not individuals. Although the book is built on personalities, they are used only in so far as they reveal the influence of broad social factors.

Events abroad have lifted the 'Negro problem' out of its limited orbit of a strictly domestic issue. Today, more and more, race and color questions are being thrown into the public scene. The Negro's future — and what he thinks it should be — is of greatest consequence. A year ago it seemed that his problem would be lost in the raging global conflict. Now he cannot be neglected or ignored. Black men in this country — a group larger than some nations involved in the war — are feeling a great resurgence of racial kinship to other colored peoples of the world. And this is acutely the concern of white America.

Race, indeed, is the most compelling force in Negro life today. To a certain extent this book is a study of black nationalism (and indeed black chauvinism). I have explored its ramifications in Negro life, its progress in very recent years, its vagaries, and its effect upon the Negro's thinking as he views the future cast of the world — waiting for the new world a-coming.

The bulk of what appears in this book is first-hand knowledge gathered from personal observation and individual testimony. Two rich sources of information were the Negro newspapers and the records of Negro organizations. I am particularly indebted to a number of people, who contributed to this work in a variety of ways.

R. O.

Contents

Chapter I

Well, son, I'll tell you:
Life for me ain't been no crystal stair.
— LANGSTON HUGHES

CAPITAL OF BLACK AMERICA

HARLEM, a bite off Manhattan Island, is called the Negro
capital. But it is more — it is the nerve center of advancing
Black America. It is the fountainhead of mass movements.
From it flows the progressive vitality of Negro life. Harlem is,
as well, a cross-section of life in Black America — a little from
here, there, and everywhere. It is at once the capital of
clowns, cults, and cabarets, and the cultural and intellectual
hub of the Negro world. By turns Harlem is provincial,
worldly, cosmopolitan, and naïve — sometimes cynical. From
here, though, the Negro looks upon the world with audacious
eyes.

To grasp the inner meanings of life in Black America, one
must put his finger on the pulse of Harlem. To begin with,
the Negro community is a vibrant, bristling black metropolis.
All lights and shadows, it is a place of curious extremes. Huge
granite buildings tower over squat leantos. Thousands exist in
basement dungeons, while others bask in Sugar Hill penthouses. Millions of dollars are invested in brick buildings of
worship, and people huddle in ramshackle tenements. The
Negro community is a great slum, but situated in a beautiful
area of broad highways and wooded parks, surrounded by
swift-moving rivers.

Harlem! The word itself signifies a vast, crowded area teeming with black men. Its population is pushing hard toward a million, and is crammed into two square miles. Some are foreign-born and come from diverse racial, religious, and national origins. Though their skins may be black, brown, yellow, or white, they all are seeking a way out of the impasse of Negro life. To this end, the Negro community is a big forum of soapbox oratory. Day-to-day living seems to be an endless vigil of picket lines, strikes, boycotts, mammoth mass meetings, as well as a series of colorful parades, jazzy picnics, and easy stomping at the Savoy Ballroom. But comes Sunday, everybody praises God — faithfully, noisily.

There is a loud Rotarian pride in Harlem.

Yet the panorama of Negro life passes before a backdrop of tenements. This life is often crude and sinister, with muggers flashing switchblades in the darkened corners. The streets are crowded with shabby loiterers, ragged urchins, and over-dressed strollers. Long flashy-looking automobiles park at the curbs, monuments of showy splendor. Bosomy women drape the tenement windows, as the rising smell of cooking mingles with the mustiness of dark dank hallways. Juke boxes grind incessantly. Heard, too, are the distinctive calls of the street vendors, a transplanted institution of the Old South. Trundling little wagons, they happily hurl their musical cries to the topmost windows, urging housewives to buy deviled crabs, fish cakes, corn pone, and sweet potatoes.

'Hurry, hurry, hurry, 'cause I saved it jes' for you!'

'Why, it ain't nothin' but the same old thing,' comes the indignant retort.

Life in Harlem is bizarre, but always pointed, intense, and vivid. The inhabitants eat, sleep, work and play, bear children, and die. But these characteristics, human and prosaic as they may be, are scorched beyond normal recognition in the crucible of a segregated life. Negroes become slum-shocked. They get distorted perspectives, and become hardened or callous. War is sometimes an intangible peril that is dwarfed by the stern realities of living. Yet, this great dark mass of people of unknown potentialities is loudly assertive of its aspirations. The unbounded optimism once reflected in the popular chant, 'Jesus will lead me, and the Welfare will feed me,' has given way to a surging, compelling movement, set into motion by the war and daily gaining momentum, demanding a place in the sun.

The black man knows what he wants. . . .

Today, his problem can't be swept under the carpet. . . .

Even-handed injustice has done things to him. . . .

He knows the tyranny of white faces.

Negroes may quarrel among themselves about minor issues, but on the question of their *rights* — moral, economic, and political — which to them mean the right to integration in American life, they form a solid bloc, each member of it being fiercely group-conscious. They have learned, and learned well, the lesson taught that no individual can rise far above the condition of his race — the lash of color prejudice cuts deeply, equally.

So, with this quick glimpse of a vast, baffling phenomenon, we enter the Negro metropolis to get a first-hand view of the intimate pattern of life in Black America. First, let's find out why Negroes came to Harlem anyhow and the circumstances of that arrival.

Chapter II

> *Whereas, Our ancestors (not of choice) were the*
> *first successful cultivators of the wilds of Amer-*
> *ica, we their descendants feel ourselves entitled to*
> *participate in the blessings of her luxuriant soil,*
> *which their blood and sweat manured . . .*
>
> — RESOLUTION ADOPTED BY
> FREE NEGROES IN 1817

PASSAGE TO UTOPIA

NEW YORK was nothing more than a Dutch outpost called
New Amsterdam, with thirty white families and a few horses
and cattle, when eleven Negroes were imported sometime in
1626. When these first black men to arrive in this part of the
New World were assigned living quarters in a row of clay
houses on the fringe of the Bowery, not only had New York's
first Negro neighborhood come into being, but also a *way of
life* — and indeed the beginnings of Black America. Within
its rude confines a separate group life evolved; here strong
feelings of solidarity developed, and here the black man
formed patterns of living different from the white community.

Each morning, from their homes in the Bowery, Negroes
went forth to cut timber, clear roads, erect dwellings, and
bring the rich soil under cultivation. After several years of
arduous labor, they succeeded in tearing through the tangled
forests and in building a wagon road to 'Haarlem,' an area
that was to become the Black Metropolis, on an Indian path
known today as Broadway. Beyond their labors, they gained
reputations for predicting the weather, an African heritage

which served to reduce farming hazards. Although the Dutch complained that as domestics Negroes were 'lazy and useless trash,' they nevertheless profited by the slaves' introduction of deep-fat cooking, a characteristic of American cuisine today, by their skill in making baskets, pottery, and cutlery, and by their domestication of animals.

Hard work was a prime necessity, but there were white men who seemed little disposed to exert themselves. If pressed too strongly, they were apt to run off to adjacent territories under English rule, where they might engage in the lucrative fur trade. Consequently Negro labor was much in demand, a fact which was illustrated rather curiously in 1641 when a Negro was alleged to have been killed by one of his own race. Torture, the common expedient, was used as a threat to force statements identifying the murderer. Six Negroes came forward and declared that they, as a group, had committed the crime. Confronted with the loss of six laborers by hanging, the old Dutch magistrates turned to an ancient solution, ordering lots to be drawn to determine which of the Negroes should die. The marked one was drawn by a giant of a fellow named Manuel de Gerritt. He was placed on a ladder in the fort with two ropes about his neck and, at a signal from an official, the hangman pulled the ladder from under him — but both ropes broke and he tumbled to the ground. The whole community, which had turned out to witness the execution, clamored so loudly for his pardon that his life was spared.

Under Dutch rule, Negroes were not 'slaves' as the term is understood today: ownership was of labor, not person, and this was lodged in the hands of the West India Company, a Dutch corporation that virtually owned New Amsterdam. Eighteen years after their arrival, the eleven Negro pioneers, albeit in bondage, boldly demanded freedom! Official tempers flared. But the rank-and-file of colonists recalled the early labors of these black men and supported the petition.

The authorities finally settled the question by liberating the eleven men (who by now had wives), granting each man land on the edge of the settlement, in a tangled swamp known today as Greenwich Village. This status won, free Negroes were considered on equal footing with other free people.

Naturally slaves who sought escape from the neighboring English colonies turned toward liberal New Amsterdam — beginning the *passage to utopia*. This traffic, together with the continued importations of slaves, quickly increased the Negro population, and, in time, the congested Negro neighborhood became one of the colorful attractions of the Dutch metropolis. White folks living in the rural areas often made sallies to the Bowery, where the bulk of black men still lived, to witness newly arrived Africans perform exciting dances done to the rhythms of sheepskin-covered eelpots and three-stringed fiddles, and to enjoy the contagious peals of broad-mouthed laughter which punctuated the noisy merry-making.

When the British flag was hoisted over New Amsterdam in 1664, and the province became New York, Negroes entered upon a period of sustained cruelty. The English introduced chattel slavery: children of slaves were compelled to follow the state and condition of the mother for life. Besides, Negroes were not permitted on the streets at night without a lantern, or to gather in groups of more than three under the penalty of flogging; they were forbidden to own property; separate education for the race was instituted, and blacks were set apart from whites on the theory that to permit them to mingle freely would endanger keeping them enslaved. Incensed by these restrictions, a Negro named Prince angrily assaulted the mayor. He was stripped to the waist, tied to a cart, and drawn through the streets, and at each corner was given eleven lashes on his naked back.

When the small shopkeepers, artisans, and farmers started to emulate the landowning class by having slaves, the demand for Negro labor doubled, and, significantly, brought a new class to support the continued enslavement of blacks. To facilitate trading, the Common Council designated a popular meeting point, Wall Street, as the 'place where Negroes and Indians could be bought, sold, or hired.' Here, not only Negroes but indentured white persons were put on the auction block! Thus the New York *Gazette* of September 4, 1738, was able to carry an advertisement offering for sale 'Englishmen, Cheshire cheese, Negro men, a Negro girl, and a few Welshmen.' By the turn of the eighteenth century, out of a population of some fifteen thousand under the English, there were three thousand Negroes in the province — as against some five hundred under Dutch rule.

Along the current of the city's rapid development, the Negro center moved from the Bowery uptown to Catherine Market, site of the present Chatham Square. Here, despite the restrictions, Negroes met to play and gossip, and not infrequently to plot insurrections. Away from their labors, on stolen time, they sold roots, berries, and herbs for pocket change. Fish was a staple item, too, for most Negroes lived within easy distance of waterways where sturgeon, bass, shad, porgies, clams, or oysters were plentiful. Peddling these wares in baskets balanced on their heads, they became picturesque figures in a city that had become used to the sight of pirates in bizarre costumes gleaming with daggers.

Those slaves who came from households that had large staffs of domestic servants dressed somewhat elaborately, and like the gentlemen of the period, wore powdered wigs and embroidered waistcoats with white ruffles. The women dressed in the handsome hand-me-downs of their white mistresses. Not so lucky were their country cousins — those from Harlem, Brooklyn, Long Island, and New Jersey. They usually wore homespun jackets and shirts, flowered handkerchiefs instead of hats, and, in mild weather, went barefoot. Slaves of the city tradesmen cut even less of a figure, attired in cast-off coats, red flannel shirts, and sometimes old black silk hats.

At Catherine Market Negro dancing and singing was first performed much in the manner as we know it today. The dancers brought along boards, called shingles, upon which they performed. These were usually about five or six feet square, and were kept in place during the dance by four of the dancer's companions. Rarely in his deft 'turning and shying off' did the dancer step from the board. Rhythm was provided by members of the party, who sang and beat time on their thighs, or sometimes on tom-toms. After the country slaves had disposed of their wares, they would hasten to the market to compete with the city Negroes, while amused bystanders stimulated the rivalry by tossing them coins.

Harmless as these goings-on appeared, the colonists nevertheless were apprehensive. Negroes already had fired dwellings, attacked public officials, and one night in a bloody foray swept out of a Maiden Lane orchard and killed a number of white persons. The city awoke uneasily one morning (in 1741) to hear cries that another slave plot had been discovered! Excited business people closed their shops, anxious mothers kept their children from school, and worried preachers prayed for deliverance. The citizenry trembled at the terrifying feeling of a nightmare becoming a reality.

The arrest of a Negro slave named Caesar, who allegedly robbed a prominent merchant, brought the plot to light. It involved a white woman, Mary Burton, who was found with the loot in her possession, and Caesar's white mistress, Peggy Kerry, who was described by court records as the 'Irish beauty.' She had borne him a child and was dependent upon him for her support. Perhaps it was the disclosure of this relationship that caused the Burton woman to expose the plot. In any case she testified that Caesar and thirty other slaves had met nightly and planned the uprising at Hughson's tavern, where, in defiance of the law, free mingling of the races was common. The conspirators, supposedly thousands of them, 'tying themselves to secrecy by sucking ye blood of each other's hands,' were to start a fire in the center of the town — a calamity more dread than hostile Indians. The slaves would attack from ambush when the white people ran out to extinguish the flames. Afterward Caesar was to be made 'governor.' Even while this testimony was being heard, terrible fires broke out in various parts of the city, and shouts went up that the blacks were rising. The upshot was that one hundred and fifty blacks and twenty-five whites, who in one way or another had become involved, were arrested and tried. Eighteen were hanged, fourteen burned alive, and more than seventy deported.

Whether this was a major stroke for freedom or whether Negroes began to fire houses only under provocation of widespread arrests, is impossible to tell — for little slaves' testimony exists. At any rate it was the last slave outbreak in New York. The North's commercial and industrial growth was making slavery increasingly unprofitable, and so the rigid restrictions against slaves were relaxed somewhat. Their occupations became more varied and their movements freer. Some, indeed, were utilized in General Braddock's ill-fated expedition against Fort Duquesne during the French and Indian War.

The issue of who should bear the expense of fighting the French — the colonies or England — started white men talking about freedom from oppression. Negroes, concerned with their own bondage, were stirred by such talk. It was the Quakers, however, who began organized opposition to slavery, and drew into the antislavery ranks such public-spirited citizens as John Jay, Alexander Hamilton, and Thomas Jefferson. Later, the Declaration of Independence, with its engaging slogans of liberty, equality, and the rights of man, accelerated the movement.

The Revolutionary War set implacably into motion those elements (and forces) which were to bring about the end of Northern slavery, and which were eventually to reach into

the South. Free talk of liberty led the black population to believe that *freedom* would be extended to them, especially since
the colonies had agreed to halt the slave trade. I can well
imagine how they felt when, only by a hair's breadth, Jefferson's proposal to outlaw slavery altogether was defeated. The
status of Negroes under the existing order being the lowest,
they were, if anything, more ready than whites for a change.
But, upon the outbreak of the Revolution, the authorities
ordered detachments of soldiers 'to guard against the insurrection of slaves.' To capitalize on the unrest, the commander
of the British forces occupying New York, Sir Henry Clinton,
issued a proclamation promising complete freedom to runaway slaves. No precise records exist, as far as I can find, of
the numbers who went over to the invaders, but Jefferson's
estimate of thirty thousand (from all sections) is sufficiently
indicative of the extent of the defection. Alarmed, the colonials countered by also promising freedom to all slaves who
would serve three years in the Continental Army. Five thousand were in this way induced to join — after they had procured their masters' consent as provided by law — and two
regiments of black men were sent against the British.

Events of the Revolution aroused a fresh wave of antislavery
sentiment. A growing number of people felt increasingly the
inconsistency between talk of universal equality and freedom,
and the glaring fact of slavery. Such a group met in the New
York tavern of a Quaker and formed a 'Society for Promoting
the Manumission of Slaves, and Protecting such of them as
have been or may be Liberated,' with John Jay as its president.
Hamilton, Duane, and Clinton, among other members, set
forth principles which, I believe, should be of contemporary
interest.

They declared it their duty 'to enable them [Negroes] to
Share, equally with us, in that civil and religious liberty with
which an indulgent Providence has blessed these States, and

to which these, our Brethren, are, by Nature, as much entitled as ourselves.' This statement proved to be no mere high-minded abstraction. For the Manumission Society, as the organization was commonly called, with branches in other Northern cities, launched a program designed to end slavery, protect Negroes from kidnapping, and provide education for Negro children. Through its efforts a bill was passed in 1799, beginning the gradual emancipation of slaves in New York State — more than a half-century before Lincoln's proclamation.

The first independent act of Negroes was to sever all connections with the white churches, which had assigned them to sections marked 'B. M.,' meaning black members. The movement, extending to every denomination, began when Negroes broke away from the Methodist Episcopal Church and started the African Methodist Episcopal Zion Church. To the Negro his church was more than sectarianism, more indeed than religion — although outwardly it tended to follow the austere pattern of white churches. It was in reality the center and stronghold of his independent existence; a refuge and a shelter for runaway slaves; a meeting place and platform; it cared for the sick, and gave food and succor to the destitute. Above all, it developed strong and intelligent leaders through whom Negroes learned to stand with self-confidence, united in a common understanding of their destiny.

This destiny, as they saw it, was tied to that of the nation. When the call for volunteers was made during the War of 1812, an unnamed 'citizen of colour,' according to the records of the Common Council, called upon his people to work on the Brooklyn fortifications, because it 'becomes the duty of every coloured man to volunteer.' The response was gratifying. More than a thousand black men worked without pay until the project was completed. The legislature then authorized the raising of two Negro regiments of a thousand men. Privates were paid an enlistment bonus of twenty-five dollars,

the same as that given white men. Slaves who enlisted received
their freedom upon discharge. It is evident that there was a
military band, for provisions were made for Negro musicians.
These activities apparently extended to the Navy. For at a
fête in his honor, Commander James Lawrence said that 'a
full half' of his sailors in the victorious battle over the English
warship *Hornet* had been Negroes; later, Perry made some
laudatory remarks about the Negro sailors under his command.

With the resumption of normal living, Negroes made
determined efforts to move into the stream of American life.
The black population of the city had grown to seven thousand
and was now concentrated in the neighborhood of Bleecker
and Mercer Streets on the lower East Side. On the whole,
they were industrious and thrifty. In checking the membership list of the African Society for Mutual Relief, an organization formed in 1810 and still in existence, there is evidence
of a small business and professional class. Foreign visitors
remarked that these Negroes were 'as decently dressed and as
well-behaved as their skin-proud countrymen.' Yet the great
bulk of the male population were laborers, seamen, coachmen,
caterers, hairdressers, butlers, waiters, and cooks; and the
females were domestics and seamstresses; and there were those
'ragging and boning' on their own. Somehow, Negroes managed to open a Broadway theater in 1821, presenting legitimate drama. The playhouse, known as the African Grove
(sometimes as the Hotel), was situated 'in Mercer Street, in
the rear of the one-mile stone on Broadway.' From all accounts, the performances were well attended by whites as well
as Negroes.

Emancipation of Negroes everywhere in the country now
became the goal of free black men in the North. In this matter their philosophy was simple: slavery was wrong, any effort
to end it was right. Hundreds, like Harriet Tubman, sometimes called 'General Tubman,' whose amazing exploits made

enraged slaveholders offer a reward of forty thousand dollars
for her capture, ventured into the South and urged and assisted slaves to escape. Secrecy and ingenuity characterized
these operations, for agents of the slave-owners prowled everywhere. An additional danger were the Blackbirders, a gang of
cut-throats engaged in the bootleg business of kidnapping and
selling Negroes, slave or free. Thousands of slaves nevertheless
made their escape to freedom, helped along by Negro and
white persons. Runaways hid by day and traveled by night,
often guided only by the North Star. Sometimes it was necessary for them to hide for weeks in the woods, waiting for
friendly voices to raise the signal,

> Steal away, steal away,
> Steal away to Jesus. . . .

This informal, cooperative effort became known as the
Underground Railroad, and took concrete form in New York
with the organization of the Committee of Vigilance, at a
meeting held in the African Methodist Episcopal Zion Church.
It became one of the most fearless of the antislavery groups,
and carried on the serious business of spiriting runaway slaves
from place to place along the Underground route. Its members were called 'practical abolitionists.' Fugitives were referred to as 'parcels,' intermediary stops as 'stations,' and the
committee's agents as 'conductors.' In New York, for example,
runaways were concealed in such 'stations' as the basement of
Plymouth Church, Brooklyn, and its pastor, Henry Ward
Beecher, was a 'conductor.' In this manner, we are told, 'the
best blood of the South drifted this way in search of freedom.'

This wholly surreptitious migration, which white and black
men risked their lives to advance, added considerably to the
city's population. But inability to provide for the thousands
of runaways, or even provide for the unemployed already here,
drove many into the infamous Five Points Neighborhood,
hangout of the city's criminal element. Charles Dickens, after

a visit accompanied by two policemen, made no bones about saying that here all was 'loathsome, drooping, and decayed.' To fight off Blackbirders, fugitive slaves were compelled to band together, and in time became a pretty vicious lot themselves. Black men also formed a controlling part of the Five Points population, it was said, and 'retained more consistency and force of character than whites' — despite their similar condition. Some blacks associated upon equal terms with whites, and many of them either had white wives or mistresses, sometimes both.

The hangout of this crowd was the boisterous Dickens' Place, a joint named after the famous author and run by a Negro named Pete Williams. Forerunner of modern black-and-tan cabarets, it was a basement dive with whitewashed walls situated in Cow Bay Alley, a deadend where Negroes and the police often fought. In the cabaret a Negro band played while a show performed on a rough platform without curtain or scenery. Customers — both white and Negro — were served at little tables by waitresses who doubled as singers and dancers, and often as taxi dancers. When business was exceptionally brisk, women were brought in from the streets. The bawdy entertainment, the rowdy singing and dancing, and the frequent brawls that overflowed into the neighborhoods where respectable Negroes lived occasioned much complaint. But Dickens' Place carried on at full blast, for it also catered to a slumming trade.

Uncertainty of life in New York — to return to the underground movement — was discouraging, perhaps, but the abolitionists went on working with undiminished effort. A heartening display of courage was exhibited when the Vigilance Committee daringly called a convention of fugitive slaves. It was held in Cazenovia, about twenty miles southeast of Syracuse, New York, and was attended by a spirited body of more than thirty ex-slaves. Chief among the business transacted was the preparation of a public letter addressed 'To the American Slaves — from those who have fled American Slavery':

> Afflicted and Beloved Brothers! . . . The chief object [of this letter] is to tell you what circumstances we find ourselves in. . . . We get wages for our labor. We have schools for our children. Some of us take part in the election of civil rulers. . . .
>
> Numerous as are the escapes from slavery, they would be far more so, were you not embarrassed by your misinterpretation of the rights of property. You hesitate to take even the dullest of your masters' horses — whereas it is your duty to take the fleetest. . . . You are taught to respect the rights of property. But no such rights belong to a slaveholder. His right to property is but the robber-right. . . .
>
> We are happy to say that every year is multiplying the facilities for leaving the Southern prison house. . . . Companies of individuals in various parts of the country are doing all they can, and it is much, to afford you a safe and a cheap passage from slavery to liberty.

The director of the Vigilance Committee in this city was a Negro, David Ruggles, who operated from 67 Lispenard Street. He was frequently denounced by the proslavery news-papers as an 'insolent inveigler' and on one occasion at least an attempt was made to kidnap him. He watched for the arrival and departure of vessels suspected as being slavers, through the committee furnished legal aid for alleged fugitives, and provided transportation for runaways whose usual desti-nation was Canada.

Many slaves made their way to his door, including a young, half-starved runaway lad, who was later to become known as Frederick Douglass, the most famous fugitive in the annals of the Underground Railroad. He later grew to be a powerful, militant, and fearless orator and writer, attracting the atten-tion of William Lloyd Garrison. In pursuing his fight against slavery, Douglass was forced to flee to Europe, where he learned much from the great liberals. His lectures and publi-cations in England played a part in arousing British sentiment against the recognition of the Confederacy. He later returned to continue his antislavery struggles. His newspaper, the *North Star*, published from Rochester, where he made his home, had wide influence, and he became the confidant of Garrison, friend and adviser to Lincoln, and acknowledged leader of his people.

Most of the other Negro leaders were former slaves, too, who had somehow escaped, or were brought North by fugitive parents. Many became clergymen and a few managed to secure footholds in other professions. James McCune Smith earned a medical degree at Glasgow University. J. W. C. Pennington, the 'fugitive blacksmith,' succeeded in becoming a minister, as did the ex-slaves Theodore S. Wright, Charles Bennett Ray, and Alexander Crummell, a graduate of Cambridge University. Samuel Ringgold Ward, said to be 'as black as night,' taught school. There was the excitable Henry Highland Garnet, who became a minister, but like others of the church gave most of his time to the emancipation struggle. His one-legged figure became a familiar one on abolitionist platforms. Samuel E. Cornish, another fugitive figure, became coeditor of *Freedom's Journal*, the first Negro newspaper published in the United States.

Much inspiration was gathered from Sojourner Truth, called the 'Libyan Sibyl' because of her alleged gift of prophecy. As a young girl she had experienced the ignominy of being sold three times. After gaining her freedom she came to New York, and one night in a religious meeting she rose suddenly and announced herself to be 'Sojourner Truth.' The Lord had commanded her, she said, to travel throughout the land to declare Truth! She became one of the most effective antislavery speakers, and, later, she took a large part in the movement for women's suffrage.

White people were slow in taking up the struggle to end slavery nationally. One reason was that white abolitionists were not free from prejudice, and differences arose as to

methods by which the Negro's problems were to be solved.
But shortly after William Lloyd Garrison's *Liberator* carried
the famous antislavery Manifesto, white men went into action.
A call was issued in the New York press to 'Friends of Immediate Abolition' for a meeting on October 5, 1833, at Clinton
Hall. Garrison was scheduled as a speaker. The proslavery
Courier and Enquirer promptly demanded: 'Are we tamely to
look on, and see this most dangerous species of fanaticism extending itself through society? . . . Or shall we, by promptly
and fearlessly crushing this many-headed Hydra in the bud,
expose the weakness as well as the folly, madness and mischief
of these bold and dangerous men?'

Editorials, equally vigorous if less mixed in metaphor, appeared in other papers. When inflammatory posters appeared
in barrooms and brothels, the abolitionists warily passed the
word that the meeting place had been changed to the Chatham Street Chapel. As expected, a belligerent mob descended
on Clinton Hall but found the place dark. After shouting
noisily for Garrison, its members stormed through the streets
to Tammany Hall, where a tumultuous meeting was held
until word arrived that the abolitionists were gathered instead
in the Chatham Street Chapel. Meanwhile the New York
Anti-Slavery Society was peacefully and expeditiously organized, resolutions passed, and other necessary business transacted. Its members were on the point of adjourning when the
mob caught up with them. The abolitionists quickly left
through the rear of the building, as the front door was broken
in by the mob. Disappointed upon finding the place empty,
the hoodlums seized an old Negro who was passing outside,
dragged him to the rostrum, and jeeringly called for a speech.

'I am called upon to make a speech,' the old man began.
'You doubtless know that I am a poor, ignorant man, not accustomed to make speeches. But I have heard of the Declaration of Independence, and I have read the Bible. The Declaration says all men are created equal, and the Bible says God has

made us all of one blood. I think, therefore, we are entitled to good treatment, that it is wrong to hold men in slavery, and that ——' Interrupting him by yells and curses, the crowd broke up. As it happened, Garrison was not present at the abolitionist meeting. He had chosen instead to witness the mob at close hand. For hours he roamed the streets in the midst of the howling mob while they searched for him.

Two months later a convention was held in Philadelphia, and a national body was formed, the American Anti-Slavery Society. Sixty Negro and white delegates, representing ten Northern states, adopted a resolution demanding 'immediate and unconditional abolishment' of slavery. New York was selected as headquarters, consequently the city leaped into prominence in the abolitionist movement. The strong pro-slavery sentiment and close commercial connections with the South, as well as the presence of a militant and articulate Negro population — evidenced by an aggressive press and pulpit — made the metropolis a strategic point from which to direct the fight. The society's formal attack on slavery aroused the expected opposition. Abolitionists were denounced as being fanatics and traitors; some, indeed, were the victims of violence. In spite of such manifestations, the society, from its offices in Nassau Street, continued to pour out pamphlets, letters, and newspapers. The famous 'seventy' abolitionist agents were sent on missions throughout the country, and in time the whole nation became abolition-conscious. By 1835 the American Anti-Slavery Society had nearly two thousand branches scattered about the country.

As the stream of runaway slaves grew, ominous rumblings came from Washington. In 1850 Congress passed the Fugitive Slave Law — and things began to happen thick and fast. Unlike the others, this law had firm teeth for enforcement. It denied jury trial to an alleged fugitive, denied him the right to testify or summon witnesses in his own behalf, and provided heavy penalties for anyone helping runaways. When taken before a federal commissioner, five dollars was paid that official for a decision in favor of the Negro and ten for one in favor of the 'owner,' or his agent.

This law brought the slavery question to a furious boiling point in New York as elsewhere. The passion which accompanied division of opinion was illustrated in a riot which occurred in Purdy's National Theatre during the performance of Harriet Beecher Stowe's *Uncle Tom's Cabin*. The play was well started on a long run when a section of the theater was set apart for colored patrons. Proslavery hecklers in the audience cheered Simon Legree and hooted Uncle Tom. The abolitionists were resentful, and bitter fighting broke out. Gentlemen escorted their women to their carriages and returned to battle. The riot overflowed the auditorium and tumbled into the street and near-by alley. Even policemen who came to halt the fracas engaged instead on either side according to their opinions on the slavery issue.

If Uncle Tom was a bone of contention, so too was Dred Scott, a slave suing for his freedom before the United States Supreme Court in 1857. A mighty deluge was unloosed by that body when it ruled by implication that the Negro had no rights which the white man was bound to respect. Then John Brown took matters into his own hands by seizing the United States arsenal at Harper's Ferry. His execution, together with that of his Negro and white comrades, climaxed dramatically the political and sectional differences between North and South. 'The whole land rocked with this great controversy,' Douglass declared. Nothing but blood, it appeared, would settle the issue.

The Civil War was hailed by the abolitionists as a step toward nation-wide emancipation, although the declared objective was to save the Union. Douglass and Radical Republicans not only demanded immediate emancipation but urged enlistment of black men. The administration feared that such a step would transform the conflict into an antislavery war and drive the wavering border states into rebellion. Undaunted, Negroes offered the government three regiments of troops — armed, equipped, clothed, and maintained for the duration by the black population. The offer was declined. While the North thus gingerly handled the problem, the South made effective use of Negroes as laborers, and even as sailors and soldiers.

Finally, black men were allowed to enter the Union Army, but not until the government had made unsuccessful appeals to the border states to accept 'compensated emancipation.' The alternative, according to Lincoln, was 'surrendering the Union and with it the Constitution, or laying strong hands upon the colored element.' The signing of the Emancipation Proclamation, on September 22, 1862, effective January 1, 1863, he called 'a fit and necessary war measure for repressing said rebellion.' It decreed that all persons held as slaves in states in rebellion were to be freed, and those of suitable condition were to be 'received into the armed service of the United States.'

A tumultuous wave of enthusiasm greeted the news. Men, women, and children in New York jammed into the Great Hall at Cooper Union, where they cheered 'Lincoln, our native land, the Stars and Stripes and the abolitionists who for thirty years operated on the heart of the nation.' Hastily composed poems were read and songs sung, one of them to the music of 'John Brown's Body.' The high point of the celebration came when Henry Highland Garnet intoned the proclamation.

Austere was the word for celebrations in the North. Those reported in the South reached the very souls of the people. Though many slaveholders attempted to suppress the news, the glad tidings swept down the 'grapevine telegraph.' Everywhere it was said, 'Marse Lincum done freed us slaves!' To those released, 'Marse Lincum' was 'Gawd an' John de

Baptis' both,' and the phrase 'free at last' was as sweet as any word in the Bible. 'Never was no time like 'em befo' or since,' declared a living ex-slave. 'Niggers shoutin' an' clappin' hands an' singin'! Chillun runnin' all over de place beatin' tins an' yellin'. Ev'rybody happy. Sho' did some cele-bratin'!'

Without scratching of memory, another ex-slave said that when the news came Sister Carrie, who was 'near 'bout a hundred,' started singing:

> Tain't no mo' sellin' today,
> Tain't no mo' hirin' today,
> Tain't no pullin' off shirts today,
> It's stomp down Freedom today.
> Stomp it down!

When Sister Carrie said 'Stomp it down!' all the slaves joined in — shouting, dancing, and singing:

> Stomp down Freedom today —
> Stomp it down!
> Stomp down Freedom today.

A feeling of uneasiness swept over New York on the morning that Negro troops were about to leave for the front. Steps had to be taken to protect their families from proslavery hoodlums. But a picturesque parade took place without disorder, with a large crowd of admiring Negroes on the sidelines, many of them women who carried baskets filled with delicacies for the soldiers. But if the heavy cordon of police that patrolled the streets proved unnecessary, it was not due to James Gordon Bennett's *Herald*. Seizing upon the fact that a flag had been given the troops as 'an emblem of love and honor from the [white] daughters of this great metropolis to her brave cham-pions,' the *Herald* declared acidly: 'This is a pretty fair start for miscegenation. Why, the phrase "love and honor" needs only the little word "obey" to become the equivalent to a marriage ceremony.' But Lincoln afterward wrote, 'Some of the most important battles would have been lost, if the Negro soldiers had not flocked into the Northern Army.'

Beyond the regular Union Army — in which more than two hundred thousand served — Negroes were active throughout the conflict in Union espionage. Harriet Tubman, the intrepid underground conductor, was one of those pressed into service. Numbers of Negro runaways were sent back as agents to the South. A Southern planter wrote a friend in New York that four of his runaway slaves had returned voluntarily after a spell of 'Yankee Freedom.' But several months later he complained bitterly that the same four had run away again — this time taking with them two hundred other slaves. A typical incident was reported in South Carolina, where the white people becoming suspicious of the increasing number of Negro funerals trailed a group of mourners to a cemetery; there it was discovered that the coffin carried so solemnly by the Negroes actually contained arms which were being removed to a hiding place!

High hopes were held for the Reconstruction Period. Had Lincoln not said the Negro had 'demonstrated in blood' his right to the ballot; and that he, Lincoln, had regarded himself as 'the nation's guardian of these people'? But the great man lay dead of an assassin's bullet. Negroes were heartbroken. What appeared in store for them in future years was suggested when Lincoln's remains arrived in New York on the way to Springfield for burial. Vast preparations were made by the City Council for a funeral procession, but when Negroes sought to participate they were rudely barred.

Ratification of the Thirteenth Amendment (1865), ending slavery and involuntary servitude; the Fourteenth (1868), giving the rights of citizenship to Negroes; and the Fifteenth (1871), giving Negroes the vote, gave friends of the Negro a sense of security for the race. Actually, in the next forty years the Negro's status as a citizen steadily declined. The abolitionists were dying off, and the early Negro leaders had grown old, and some weary. The Negro's position was precarious. Fifty strikes had been called in the North by 'lily-white' unions against the employment of Negro working men. In the South, there was the emergence of the Ku Klux Klan, the enactment of Black Laws which sharply restrict the Negro even to this day, and toward the close of the century, the alarming increase in lynching. In addition, the freed slaves had been turned adrift without home or job.

The close of the Civil War, it appeared, had marked only a step, albeit a large step, in the Negro's struggle for integration in American life. Black men were spurred into action — and new leaders came forward. A promising move was made when the Afro-American Council was organized in 1890 for a renewed fight for equal rights. J. C. Price, head of Livingston College, North Carolina, was elected president, and a New York editor, T. Thomas Fortune, secretary. But they were unable to raise sufficient funds to maintain a permanent organization, or to arouse the necessary spirit, and the council soon disbanded.

National leadership fell to Booker T. Washington, principal of Tuskegee Institute, Alabama, and a rising figure in the South. To raise the Negro's economic standards and to win the white man's respect, he sought to make Negroes efficient workers by industrial education; and by encouraging independence through the establishment of Negro business. After a memorable speech at the opening of the Cotton States Exposition in Atlanta, Georgia, he was hailed as the 'economic emancipator' of the Negro — a mighty leap for a man born a slave. 'In all things purely social,' said Washington in his Atlanta address, referring to Negroes and whites, 'we can be as separate as the five fingers and yet as one as the hand in all things essential to mutual progress.'

He succeeded in winning the support of the influential white people in both North and South, thus establishing a strategic place for himself in American life. But in the North, Negroes held his doctrines conciliatory and charged him with a willingness to sanction a lower status for the Negro. Not until the next century were Northern Negroes able to take the helm — and this was coincident with large-scale migration to the North.

Chapter III

*I urgently advised colored people to buy (property).
Had my counsel been heeded, they would now own
Harlem.*

— A. CLAYTON POWELL, SR.

THE NEGRO
PITCHES HIS TENT!

HARLEM was yet a vague, faraway place in the minds of
most Negroes at the turn of this century — though New York's
black population had jumped to sixty thousand, and was
desperately fumbling about for elbowroom. External forces
led the way finally — race riots.

Mass shifts of the Negro population in New York — as elsewhere — have always been accelerated by racial conflicts.
The first great movement followed the Draft Riots on the
lower East Side in the midst of the Civil War, when white
men rioting against the draft law diverted their attack to
Negroes, who were seen as the reason for the conflict. Blacks
were dragged through the streets, beaten, hanged from lampposts, and their homes burned. The riot raged for three days
and nights before it was put down by soldiers summoned
from the front. Four thousand persons, white and black, were
killed and a thousand wounded. Relief had to be given to
ten thousand victims. Two million dollars in property was
destroyed. Thousands of Negroes, in fear of future violence,
moved across the river to Brooklyn and up to midtown Manhattan — a section that came to be called 'Black Bohemia' —
where Negro life began to take the form in which it is seen
today.

Fighting with white men became a part of everyday living in Black Bohemia, as well as in the Tenderloin, Hell's Kitchen, and San Juan Hill areas. The most innocent incident stirred the smoldering ill-feeling between the races. When a Negro, Granville T. Woods, inventor and Edison pioneer, perfected the third rail, and electricity replaced steam on the elevated railway, the white men who lost their jobs as steam engineers attacked Negroes whom they met on the streets because some 'damn nigger' devised the innovation. The Negro who drove one of the first automobiles seen in New York — a white man's chauffeur, no doubt — was beaten, the car smashed, and afterward the homes of other Negroes were stoned.

New York's fourth great race riot, which occurred in 1900, marked the beginning of the wholly turbulent career of Harlem. This disorder was touched off in the Tenderloin by the fatal stabbing of a white man, later found to be a policeman in civilian clothes, who had made unwelcome advances to a Negro woman. Within a short time hundreds of white people poured into the streets, attacking every black man, woman, and child. Houses were sacked and burned, and places that employed Negroes were raided. When Negroes appealed to the police, they were cracked over the head with nightsticks, refused refuge at the police stations, and thrown back to the raging mob.

Demands for an investigation met with excuses and delays, while the buck was shuttled gingerly between city officials and police authorities, with the fine hand of Tammany Hall operating behind the scenes. Negroes took steps to force action. A mass meeting was held at Carnegie Hall, the Citizens' Protective League formed, and funds raised to carry on a vigorous fight. An aroused Negro public brought the league's membership up to five thousand within a few weeks. The organization retained as counsel Israel Ludlow, who brought claims against the city for nearly a half-million dollars; one

in behalf of the poet, Paul Laurence Dunbar, and another for
the well-known pugilist, Joe Walcott. Finally, a police department investigation was held that turned out to be a sham
and whitewash.

The air grew tense. Tempers were at trigger-point. Then,
the Negro pulpit and press began a strange campaign, terrifying in its implications. 'Have your houses made ready,'
ran a typical warning, 'to afford protection against the fury
of white mobs. Carry a revolver. Don't get caught again!'

When the storm cleared, the historic exodus of Negroes
began to the elegant green pastures of Harlem. Certain
strong social factors also contributed to this wholesale movement. The principal Negro neighborhood, Black Bohemia —
wedged between the Tenderloin and San Juan Hill sections —
embodied the newer and more daring phases of Negro life;
and it was here that most of the clubs frequented by the
sporting and theatrical people were situated. While life in
this area was perhaps a little more colorful than in other districts, actually it was no more than a glorified slum. Its
population had increased from three hundred families to
almost five thousand. This human landslide, contained in
three blocks, paid exorbitant rents, and lived in dilapidated,
ill-ventilated, overcrowded lodging-houses. Many lived in
cold-water flats, washtubs in the kitchen furnishing the only
bathing facilities. The Negro, when he worked, averaged five
or six dollars a week, and in the local theaters, comedians
were singing: 'Rufus Rastus Johnson Brown? What you
gwine do when de rent comes roun'?'

The sidewalks were choked with sweaty, irritable pedes-
trians. Disease was rampant. Epidemics were frequent, the
toll of life enormous: two babies in every seven died under the
age of one year. Besides, the area was a notorious red-light
district, with bands of Negro and white whores roving the
streets like hungry wolf packs. To make men follow them,

they would snatch their hats and run into dark hallways, where their victims were robbed by accomplices. Harlots, dressed in 'unbuttoned Mother Hubbards,' stood in front of churches Sunday evenings and openly solicited men as they emerged.

Finally, a delegation of Negro clergymen appealed to Mayor Gaynor, a Tammany Hall politician.

'Don't come down here,' he said, 'bothering me with any more protests about assignation houses until you can bring concrete evidence of such houses. . . . One of your men must pay a woman for the privilege of having intimate relationship with her, and you must bring a witness that she accepted the money.'

Negroes returned to Black Bohemia and attempted to combat these conditions themselves. Under a thirty-day Gospel bombardment, led by the Reverend A. Clayton Powell, Sr., of the Abyssinian Baptist Church, the neighborhood's pimps, prostitutes, and keepers of dives and gambling dens were drawn to the revival meetings, confessed conversion, and were baptized. 'Many of them remained faithful until death,' the Reverend Powell reports, 'but the majority went back to wallowing in the mire because they had no place else to go.' Without official support, efforts to change conditions seemed futile, so it was only natural that Negroes sought escape to the more desirable areas of the city.

The Harlem they first entered, about 1900, was a cheerful neighborhood of broad drives, brownstone dwellings, and large apartment houses, with the streets carefully laid out in the pattern of a gridiron. The white gentry resided here in suburban aloofness. People spoke of the section as an area of 'Brownstone fronts and Saratoga trunks.' Lenox Avenue was used for the showing of thoroughbred horses, and polo was actually being played on the Polo Grounds. The main thoroughfare was a favorite track of many wealthy horsemen toward the close of the last century. Here, any afternoon, the finest trotting stock could be seen driven by such men as Commodore Vanderbilt, Colonel Kip Rhinelander, and Russell Sage. A nice cultural touch was contributed by Oscar Hammerstein, who erected the Harlem Opera House.

Odd street names still commemorated some incident or honored some figure in the earlier life of the city and nation, and vividly recalled the days of Dutch and English occupation. The name Jumel Place, for example, commemorated Stephen Jumel, a wealthy wine merchant who died in 1832, and his wife, generally referred to as Madame Jumel. She added to her fame, or notoriety, by marrying Aaron Burr in 1833. The mansion in which the Jumel family lived still stands as a museum high on a hill overlooking the Polo Grounds — marking the northernmost tip of Harlem — and is in the custody of the Daughters of the American Revolution. It was built in 1765 by Colonel Roger Morris, who gave it to his bride, Mary Philipse, on their wedding day. During the Revolutionary War it was the headquarters of George Washington for a time and of General Henry Clinton and his British officers.

If this bit of almost-forgotten lore had little significance to new Negroes, certainly exciting connotation was attached to Hamilton Place, where Alexander Hamilton had built his beautiful mansion, 'The Grange,' which still stands on the western boundary of Harlem as a historic landmark. Legend has it that the great revolutionary figure, once a slaveholder, was himself a Negro and the father of the Reverend William Hamilton, one of the prominent Negroes in New York at the beginning of the nineteenth century. Some historians say that his fatal duel with Aaron Burr was fought over the accusation that he had Negro blood — no doubt an apocryphal tale. What is a fact, however, is that so convinced were Negro historians of Hamilton's Negro ancestry that one industrious scholar made a trip to his birthplace, Nevis, B.W.I., to check the facts.

In Hamilton's day Harlem was a section of elaborate estates and quiet aloofness, and was said to be 'a community which knew nothing of sensational issues.' Real-estate speculators looked upon this locality as 'a far off country' too remote, without adequate transportation to be available for city lots, and, no doubt, too aristocratic for republican popularity — the Astors nevertheless shrewdly invested in Harlem land, laying the foundation for one of the great American fortunes. The few scattered and less affluent dwellers used stagecoaches to travel downtown. Hostelries dotted the roads at convenient distances.

There were still some Negro oldtimers who remembered that before the Civil War Cato Alexander, a Negro caterer, operated a popular roadhouse at what was then the southernmost end of Harlem — situated at the Beekman Place. His inn had a diminutive sitting-room with a bar, sanded floors, and coarse white walls covered with engravings. It was frequented by those socially prominent people who believed in the marked superiority of colored cooks. Its hospitality was described as 'unbiased by any modern abolition doctrines.' Mr. Alexander, it appears, was a remarkable host — as other records suggest that his place was actually a station of the Underground Railroad and he an active conductor.

The Third Avenue horse-drawn railroad, erected in 1853, took the place of stagecoaches, but it took an hour and twenty minutes to travel from lower Manhattan to Harlem — provided, travelers complained, no horse balked or fell dead across the tracks. It appears that the Harlem Navigation Line, operating boats on the Hudson River, was the more practical means of conveyance, making the journey from Harlem to Wall Street in an hour — and without untoward incident.

In those days Harlem figured but little in the city's annals. The one 'sensational' issue it had to face was the entrance of the first Negro child — daughter of a cook — into the school, causing great consternation among the white parents. Otherwise Harlem still was a quiet country town shut off by a long ride or sail from its 'ruling center.' Finally, the immigrant Irish moved into the lower section, an area that came to be known as 'Goatville,' because of the domestic goats of the Irish squatters who lived in shacks in what is now the northern end of Central Park. The erection of the elevated railway in the nineties accelerated Harlem's development, and the area had a swift change in character.

Appropriately enough, it was the black aristocracy which first took up residence in Harlem — Bert Williams, the famous actor, and Harry T. Burleigh, the composer, were in that vanguard. An enterprising realtor, Philip A. Payton, induced the owners of two houses near Fifth Avenue to rent apartments long vacant to Negroes. Neither Payton nor the white property-owners envisioned the direct outcome. The little colony quickly expanded, spread west across Lenox Avenue and into the fashionable St. Nicholas Park area. The white residents became alarmed, mobilized their forces, and attempted to halt the advance.

A new type of racial warfare broke out with methods that were exceedingly subtle, even insidious. The whites formed the Harlem Property Owners' Improvement Association and brought pressure on financial institutions not to loan money to Negroes, and not to renew mortgages on properties which they occupied. Inflammatory handbills were surreptitiously circulated, which held that the Negro's presence depreciated real estate value. 'This in itself,' shouted the *Indicator*, a local real estate publication, 'is an indication that their presence is undesirable among us. They should not only be disfranchised, but also segregated in some colony on the outskirts of the city, where their transportation and other problems will not inflict injustice and disgust on worthy citizens.'

Massing much of their financial resources into a dummy corporation, the Hudson Realty Company, white people bought up properties that housed Negroes and evicted them.

Enlisting the prestige and influence of the white community, the campaign to drive blacks from Harlem gained compelling momentum. The metropolitan press rose in all its 'yellow' might and denounced the 'black invasion.' Even the liberal old *World* came thundering down the stretch, editorially, and sought by tortuous logic to reconcile its ordinarily progessive policy with bigotry. The Negro was entitled to pitch his tent wherever he wished, it conceded, but wherever he did 'calamitous depreciation' resulted.

'The assimilative ideal is premature,' was the final judgment of that great organ.

Negroes stood alone. But with wonderful zeal they rapidly took counter steps. Dipping into their savings, in what assumed the proportions of a mass demonstration, they organized companies to buy and lease Harlem property. Negro press and pulpit launched blasting campaigns to stimulate (or to shame) black men into swift action, holding that it was a 'race duty' to acquire property, dispossess whites, and rent to members of their own race. Inroads were made and a toehold secured as the profit motive (or avarice) operated to the Negro's advantage. But the largest of these crusading companies, the Afro-American Realty Company — ambitiously capitalized at five hundred thousand dollars though never fully subscribed — was soon defunct. Extermination of the blacks seemed final, irrevocable.

No one figured — certainly not Negroes — on one of those curious ironies of capitalistic progress. About this time, the Pennsylvania Railroad Company was seeking a site for a new central terminal, and chose the area upon which one of the oldest Negro congregations in the city, Saint Philip's Protestant Episcopal Church, had its sprawling plant. An offer was made, but Negroes were reluctant to sell, as Harlem looked none too inviting. The company countered by jacking up the bid to the sufficiently persuasive figure of five hundred and forty thousand dollars in cash. This sum was immediately turned to strategic use: a row of thirteen large apartment houses was purchased in the very heart of Harlem — to be exact, 135th Street near Lenox Avenue. The area quickly became the most fashionable in the country for Negroes and was to become one of the most widely known streets in the world.

White people threw up their hands in despair and in panic fled as from a flood, leaving house after house, and block after block, in yawning vacancy. Properties were sold far below assessed values. The Equitable Life Assurance Society, trying desperately to unload its Harlem holdings quickly, sold some eighty brick houses designed by Stanford White, each of which contained fourteen large rooms, two baths, French doors, and hardwood floors, for an average price of eight thousand dollars apiece. Some were bought for as low as six thousand dollars — five hundred dollars down payment and the balance in small yearly installments. Negroes grabbed up these buys, situated in an area that later was to become fashionable as 'Strivers' Row,' or 'Block Beautiful,' the stronghold of Negro society. The handwriting was clearly on the wall as to the future of Harlem.

Yet, with all the hue and cry, barely a thousand Negroes had moved into the neighborhood. They occupied but three or four blocks. Actually, Harlem did not begin to take shape and character as a Negro community until 1910. The growth thereafter was nothing short of phenomenal. The immediate reason was the mass movement from the South. The United States was preparing to enter the first World War and there was a considerable pressure for increased production. Large numbers of white men left industrial pursuits for military service both in the United States Army and in the armies of their native lands, thereby causing an unprecedented shortage of labor.

A mad race began to draw on the South's reservoir of black

labor. Agents traveled to Southern cities and towns and over the protests of whites, literally gathered up consignments of blacks and shipped them North. The Department of Labor aided and encouraged the migration through its employment service. Acting upon the urgent requests of industry, the Pennsylvania and Erie Railroads picked up trainloads of Negroes 'on the promise of a long, free ride to the North.' James Weldon Johnson saw two thousand persons snatched up in batches of a hundred, tagged, and packed tightly into day coaches, along with their cardboard baggages and lunch boxes. Like cattle, hundreds of others were stuffed into box-cars in the pell-mell journey North.

'Come North, where there is more humanity, some justice and fairness,' cried Northern Negro newspapers. Chain letters repeating the same refrain were dispatched hither and yon. Negroes made the pilgrimage to Harlem on foot, by train, and by boat. Their travels were marked with joy and prayers of thanksgiving. Solemn ceremonies were held as they crossed the Mason-Dixon Line. Men stopped their watches to begin a New Day in the North. Amid tears, the migrants sang the old familiar songs of deliverance. They were glad, glad, glad to escape a pattern of life in which competing groups of the white race wielded ruthless power to preserve racial inequalities. They were fed up with the abuses of the tenant farm system, lack of schooling, and miserable living conditions — legends of urban freedom were alluring.

This migration was in fact a flight from a feudal to a modern way of life — a surging mass movement that was to drive on unabated. Into this exodus to Harlem swept a largely unnoticed element — the dark-skinned immigrants. So desperate was the demand for black labor that its pull had reached down into the islands of the Caribbean and even to a certain extent into faraway Africa. Actually, though, Negro immigrants had been settling in New York since the Civil War — no doubt attracted by the conspicuous liberality of the

United States in freeing the slaves. Before the turn of the century more than fifty thousand had entered the country. But just prior to the first World War, they came in mighty droves. By 1920 New York's black population had jumped to one hundred and fifty thousand — and conservative estimates put the total Negro ownership of Harlem property at two hundred million dollars.

The developments of the period extended to sterner affairs. For back in the summer of 1908, the country was shocked by a race riot in Springfield, Illinois — the home of Lincoln — in which scores of Negroes were killed or wounded and thousands of others driven from the city. A white woman of wealth and influence, Mary White Ovington, was moved to approach other liberal white people to form 'a large body of citizens' to revive the 'spirit of [the] abolitionists.' In a little room of a New York apartment in 1909, the National Association for the Advancement of Colored People was born, an organization which has ever since been in the struggle for the rights of the Negro.

Oswald Garrison Villard, grandson of William Lloyd Garrison, the abolitionist, and then publisher of the New York *Evening Post*, later issued a call which brought to the movement such white persons as Charles Edward Russell, Jane Addams, John Dewey, Lillian D. Wald, Rabbi Stephen S. Wise, the Reverend John Haynes Holmes, and William Dean Howells; and the Negroes Bishop Alexander Walters, Ida Barnett and the Reverend Francis J. Grimke. A prominent Boston lawyer, Moorfield Storey, was elected president, offices were established at 20 Vesey Street (now at 69 Fifth Avenue), and W. E. B. Du Bois, already an outstanding figure, was called from his professorship at Atlanta University to become director of publicity and research, and later editor of the organization's official organ, *The Crisis* — considered the most effective and best-written propagandist periodical in the United States.

Du Bois, bearded, scholarly, and ornate, was born in Great
Barrington, Massachusetts and educated at Harvard and
Heidelberg, and had come to the fore in 1903 with his attack
on Booker T. Washington's conciliatory philosophy. Du Bois
held that 'The Negro race, like all races, is going to be saved
by its exceptional men.' This group he called the 'Talented
Tenth,' or educated Negro élite. 'The best and most capable
of the [Negro] youth,' he declared, 'must be schooled in the
colleges and universities of the land.... Not too many college-
bred men, but enough to leaven the lump, to inspire the
masses, to raise the talented tenth to leadership.' He criticized
Washington's speech at Atlanta, Georgia, later termed the
'Atlanta Compromise,' because the Southern leader had distinctly asked colored people to give up, at least for the present,
political rights, insistence on civil rights, and higher education
for Negro youth. Under Du Bois's leadership a conference was
held in 1903 at Buffalo, New York, and the Niagara Movement was launched to abolish all distinctions based on race,
class, or color. Hampered as it was by a lack of funds, and by
a membership confined to one race, the movement died an
early death.

The influence of Du Bois and his Negro colleagues in the
program of the N.A.A.C.P. is evident, for that body adopted a
platform essentially that of the Niagara Movement. Broadly,
the aims of the association were — and are — to encourage the
Negro's intellectual development, economic progress, and
social advancement, and to protect his civil rights — a platform declared to be extremely radical at the time. By holding
mass meetings, issuing educational pamphlets, and by frequent
release of articles to the press, the association sought to bring
the Negro's cases before the white public. More practically, it
proposed to discover and by legal action redress individual and
group injustices, and to make systematic studies of conditions
affecting the race.

Much of the early success of the organization was due to Du

Bois's almost fanatical belief in his cause and indefatigable work in advancing it. He became a towering figure in Negro life, reserved, removed, essentially the intellectual esthete. A humorous story is told about Du Bois, concerning his aloofness. After living in New York for some years, he was scheduled to make an address at Harlem's Bethel African Methodist Episcopal Church. On the night of the affair, Du Bois failed to put in an appearance. With hundreds waiting, couriers were sent to find him — only to discover that the *Negro leader* was lost in Harlem, and couldn't find his way to the meeting place!

Besides Du Bois, the association's program was largely carried on by Dean William Pickens, Phi Beta Kappa Yale graduate and orator; Daisy E. Lampkin, co-publisher of the Pittsburgh *Courier*; and James Weldon Johnson, writer and diplomat. When Du Bois retired in 1933, Roy Wilkins, former newspaperman, succeeded him as editor of *The Crisis*, which by then had gained a national circulation; and when Johnson resigned in 1931, Walter White, teacher and writer, took the helm as executive secretary. Today the association has some six hundred branches, in nearly every state, supported by contributions from Negroes and whites.

The organization's first great test was met dramatically. In the midst of the first World War, a two-day race riot broke out in East St. Louis, Illinois — one of the bloodiest in American history. Du Bois in association with Martha Gruening, a white woman, investigated the disorder and reported that white people drove thousands of Negroes from their homes, and put to death two hundred by shooting, burning, and hanging. Black America was aroused. What would the association do? Fifteen thousand Negroes were promptly organized by the N.A.A.C.P. and other Harlem leaders into a mighty demonstration called the 'Silent Protest Parade.' Men, women, and children marched down New York's Fifth Avenue in silence, carrying banners which read, 'Mr. President, Why

Not Make America Safe for Democracy?' Shortly after, the Federal Administration placated the Negro leaders with promises of post-war improvements of a fundamental nature.

About this time a strong radical press emerged, concentrating on injustices to the black man. Even the older and more conservative Negro newspapers spoke more boldly. The streets of Harlem became the scene of nightly outdoor forums. Dozens of orators, challenging the black man's inclination to caution, frankly advanced socialism and revolution as the instruments of complete freedom; some advocated racial self-sufficiency, and others self-government. In later years writers took up the cry of protest. Appalled by the number of lynchings in the South, Claude McKay was moved to write of crowds where men are jostled by steely-eyed women and of 'little lads, lynchers that were to be.' Countee Cullen marveled 'at this curious thing, to make a poet black and bid him sing.' And Langston Hughes noticed Negro porters 'climbin' up a great big mountain of yes, sirs.'

Stimulated by a racial upsurge, the post-war radical movement, and by race idealism, Negroes started to articulate their complaints in writings of protest. What happened in the decade following America's entry into the World War appeared to be a sudden awakening. Actually, it was marked by a renewed, country-wide struggle for the rights of the Negro. A typical development was the formation of the influential National Equal Rights League and the emergence as a national leader of William Monroe Trotter, the zealous editor of the Boston *Guardian*. He was perhaps one of the most fearless and unselfish public figures, with a consuming passion for the rights of his race. Unable to procure a passport, he went abroad as a ship's waiter to place the American Negro's case before the League of Nations. He later went to Paris and filed several petitions with the World Peace Conference. He was the first Negro elected to the Phi Beta Kappa Fraternity at Harvard University. He died a suicide in 1934.

Where a previous generation had all but given up in despair, the war generation found hope in the preachings of new and militant leaders. This was the beginning of a broad political, social, and eventually cultural development — often referred to as the 'Negro Renaissance.' It proved to be a movement that was national in sweep with Harlem as its conspicuous center.

Chapter IV

The United States is one of the few nations that analyzes its international migration on the bases of race.

— IRA DE A. REID

HOW COLORED IS HARLEM?

A VASTLY important but hardly spectacular development was the arrival in Harlem of dark-skinned immigrants. This foreign-born element — today a third of the population — almost immediately lent a cosmopolitan character to the community; their modes of living — eating, dressing, haggling with merchants, among other customs — ran all the way from European and Asiatic through Caribbean peasant to native African. The Bureau of Immigration unimaginatively blanketed all under the easy labels 'African black' or 'Oriental,' when they were in fact of many colors, with caste, class, racially, and national differences.

Somewhat early in its career, Harlem acquired a distinct worldliness. Today nearly every type of person that inhabits the earth is seen on the sidewalks of the Black Metropolis. Here live hundreds of different peoples, subdivided into a bewildering array of clans, tribes, races, cultures, and colors — of red, brown, yellow, white, and black, and unimaginable shades in between. But if one is mystified by the whirl of colors, he is likely to be staggered by the march of diverse types. After three or four decades of intermingling — native with African, Mongolian, European, and Latin American — it would tax the abilities of an anthropologist to pigeonhole the contrasting pigmentations, hair textures, bone structures, varying physiques, and facial characteristics. Loosely, one might say, the Black Metropolis is more heterogeneous than any one section in the United States — except possibly for the west coast cities; and in this sense, its only counterpart in the Western Hemisphere is Port of Spain, Trinidad, garden spot of bizarre mixtures.

Today, in spite of the dissimilar elements in its population, the community is well on its way to homogeneity. Intermixing of the races has become old hat. For the Negro has demonstrated a tremendous capacity (and indeed appetite) for assimilation. In some areas of the United States, the Negro has almost completely absorbed the so-called vanishing American Indian. Even today the young bloods of Harlem scamper out to the Indian reservations on Long Island and return with Shinnecock brides.

The tendency of white people to include every colored element in Negro population is a thing not generally discouraged by Negroes. Not only does it serve to swell the mass, but it gives Harlem great robustness, which in part accounts for much of the community's bumptiousness today. In one sense, the rapid growth of the black population numerically is tied to our national destiny. Today, however, when racial loyalties often transcend national boundaries, the racial make-up of Black America has compelling concern.

At least two thirds of the Negroes in the United States are of mixed ancestry. Full-blooded black men are rare in the Negro Harlem. Perhaps the few in America are mainly the native Africans, who migrated to this country in recent years, mostly from West African tribes in Nigeria, Dahomey, the Gold Coast, the Congo, Liberia, and Sierra Leone. Africans comprise a small, compact group of some two thousand or more, and by occupation are seamen, laborers, and cocoa importers, bearing distinctive tribal markings, or identifications.

Africans in Harlem — regarded with a good deal of awe — expend much of their energies, through organizations like the African Students' Association, in attempting to arouse American Negroes to act in relieving the plight of the African blacks. Sometimes such activity has official design. Emperor Haile Selassie, during Italy's unprovoked aggressions in Ethiopia, sent the native African Malaku E. Bayen, a graduate of Howard University's medical school, and his American-born wife to the United States to stimulate sympathy among American Negroes and to raise funds for war relief. Upon arrival, Doctor Bayen, a slight, intense little brown man, took up residence in Harlem after being barred as a Negro from hotels downtown. He published *The Voice of Ethiopia*, a rabidly pro-African newspaper which urged the 'millions of the sons and daughters of Ethiopia, scattered throughout the world, to join hands with Ethiopians to save Ethiopia from the wolves of Europe.' He finally organized the Ethiopian World Federation, Inc., which still is in existence. After his death, the Emperor dispatched his cousin, Prince Lÿ Araya Abebe, to Black America as his personal envoy. Armed with documents explaining his mission, he launched the Committee to Aid Ethiopia, with the assistance of American sympathizers.

Not every African is a propagandist. Some, indeed, came to this country only for the opportunities it affords the black man. I remember the impatience of Nnamdi Azikiwe, who fifteen years ago was attending Lincoln University, to complete his education and return to Africa. He had a mission. Today, he is the editor-publisher of the sharply outspoken *West African Pilot*, an English-language newspaper circulated among the natives of Lagos, Nigeria. Incidentally, the head ruler of the Nigerians enrolled as a student at Ohio State University in 1940. He is 'Chris' Akeweke Abyssinia Nwafar Oriza, prince of the ruling family of Nigeria — a British protectorate. He is a strapping twenty-two-year-old lad who succeeds his father, His Highness Ezeugbonyamba I.

Then there is Prince Mokete Manoedi, who sought a refuge in the United States. Son of the tribal chief of the Molibeli people in Basutoland, he had left Africa to be educated in London. While there he developed notions about African independence which sorely disappointed the British Foreign Office. Fearful that he might incite the natives, the British authorities barred his return, and he became an embittered exile, later migrating to Harlem.

Several African immigrants have enriched the cultural life of the community. Young American Negroes heard authentic African songs and rhythms for the first time with the Broadway productions of the folk operettas *Kykunkor* and *Bassa Moona*, written, directed, and performed by native Africans. The latter, a Federal Theatre offering, had considerable influence upon the dance locally.

The African's manner is superb. He is rarely belligerent or truculent. Yet he has a disturbing way of making innocent-sounding observations which frequently strike the heart of a situation. It's the sort of thing that embarrassed Negley Farson, who candidly relates an incident of his East African journey which, I believe, illustrates this concretely:

> The last act in leaving [Uganda], as I was getting into my car, was from the old *saza* aristocrat. He clasped my hand and said: 'We were afraid to talk to you, when we heard you were a man from the United States, because of the way you treat Negroes. . . .'
>
> He still held my hand, and looked at me questioningly. The other *saza* and *gambolola* chiefs drew nearer. Obviously, some explanation was demanded. But I couldn't give it. . . .
>
> Then I hastily drove off. Into my eyes came the image of Coffee Bluffs, with its tattered shanties, outside Savannah. My God, what would I have been able to tell them, if they had asked me that question? *We*, who had robbed the African of his dignity!

The largest body of immigrants, a quarter of Harlem's population, roughly a hundred and twenty-five thousand people.

came from the subtropical West Indies — today an area of vital importance to American defense. Numbers of others are found in Boston, and in the Carolinas and Florida. West Indians, as everyone knows, I suppose, are a mixture of African, European, and Carib Indian. Some have Portuguese, *East* Indian, or Chinese blood. Eugene Chen, foreign minister tin he Sun Yat-Sen Government of China, was born in Trinidad of Chinese-Negro parentage. He is the father of the dancer, Sylvia Chen, who was recently acclaimed in New York. Bert Williams, the famous blackface comedian of the Ziegfeld era who so successfully delineated American Negro life, was a Mulatto born in Antigua of Danish-Negro ancestry.

The inclusive name 'West Indians,' therefore, is apt to be misleading. In reality there is as much difference between individuals from each island as between a blond Swede and a swarthy Sicilian — though both white men also are called 'Europeans.' Once scratched, West Indians are of many colors and become Trinidadians, Haitians, Martiniquians, Dominicans, Jamaicans, and so on, and come from islands each having its own tradition, culture, and history. In the Caribbean area there are three independent states: Cuba, Haiti, and the Dominican Republic; two United States dependencies: Puerto Rico and the Virgin Islands; a group of British colonies: Jamaica, Trinidad, Barbardoes and others; smaller islands belonging to France: Guadeloupe and Martinique; and those of the Netherlands; Curaçao and Aruba.

The great mass of immigrants to Harlem came from the British colonies. They immediately found adjustments difficult, both as immigrants and as Negroes. Having left a land where black men were in the vast majority, they found themselves on arrival a minority amidst a hostile white group. They chafed under segregation and discriminations. News of lynchings appalled them. Such things were practically unknown in their homeland. While they often were subject to caste and class divisions in the islands, they nevertheless had access to all skilled trades and professions, and rarely did they suffer discrimination based on color — except perhaps in Jamaica.

An exaggeratedly pro-British attitude on the part of the West Indians followed their clash with the American color line. If there were discriminations or insults by white Americans, the British Consul was visited and a complaint lodged. British protection, in theory at least, meant more freedom and greater equality. Manifestations of loyalty to the Crown sometimes cropped up in curious forms. While many viewed the abdication of King Edward VIII as romantic, and some recog nized its political implications, many British subjects arrayed themselves on either side of the question — solely on the basis of Mrs. Wallis Simpson's social status. Such attitudes apparently have official encouragement. For when five thousand Negroes sumptuously re-enacted the coronation of George VI in a local ballroom, the lodge of honor was occupied by Sir Gerald Campbell, Lady Campbell, and eighteen members of the British consular staff.

Friction arose between native and immigrant, that has faded today only in the face of tremendous issues common to both. The roots of these differences were largely economic and political. Unwitting victims of exploitation, the immigrants were falsely charged with a willingness to work for low wages; also, they were charged with robbing Black America of the use of a potent weapon — *the ballot*. By not becoming naturalized, they obstructed the struggle for equal rights. Only 25 per cent of the British West Indians were citizens in 1930.

These antagonisms found ready expression in appellations like monkey-chaser, ring-tail, and King Mon. The unmistakable accent of the immigrant, described as a sort of hybrid Cockney, became the butt of jokes. Those from Montserrat speak with a pronounced Irish brogue! Sam 'Squashie' Manning, a West Indian-born comedian, achieved considerable popularity on the Harlem stages with his comic distortions of the immigrant Negro. Even the West Indian's white linen suit and cane frequently brought him showers of stones from street urchins. Numerous ditties were sung, some good-naturedly, which ridiculed the foreign-born people:

> When I get on the other side
> I'll buy myself a mango,
> Grab myself a monkey gal
> And do the monkey tango.

> When you eat split peas and rice
> You think you eatin' somethin',
> But man you ain't taste nothin' yet
> Till you eat monkey hips and dumplin'.

> When a monkey-chaser dies,
> Don't need no undertaker;
> Just throw him in de Harlem River,
> He'll float back to Jamaica.

This hostility was met with an aggressive drive for leadership in the community. Compared with the Negro from the rural South, the West Indians were well educated, and although they came from an agrarian society, many of them were skilled workers — carpenters, masons, bricklayers, tailors, printers — in trades which American Negroes lost when the race was excluded from the trade unions in the last century. They entered the professions of medicine, dentistry, and law, eventually to number one third of Harlem's professional group. They also formed a preponderantly large proportion of the business people. Part of their success rested on the West Indian's thrift and frugality. But even more important was the dominant group psychology obtained in a country where the great majority of the people were black, giving them somewhat of a head start in competition.

Much of the West Indians' culture eventually filtered into Harlem life. Besides adding the zombies, jumbies, and obeah men to the gallery of voodoo characters, a number of tropical

items found their way to the tables of American Negroes —
like imported yams, eddoes, mangoes, pawpaws, ginger roots,
avocados, and plantains. So popular did the use of West
Indian pepper sauce — a basic element in tropical seasoning
of food — become that it displaced American-prepared red
peppers on the shelves of the chain stores. A whole thriving
industry was built up to make these staples available.

West Indian music, too, found vogue with American Negroes (and later many whites). As early as 1915 phonographs
throughout Harlem hummed in semi-rhumba tempo to the
whimsical folk tale of the 'Sly Mongoose,' a chicken-stealing
animal of the islands. From Trinidad came the unique
rhythms of the calypso, a rhyming vocal commentary on local
and world events, sung particularly during carnivals in that
island but today a feature of New York's night-club entertainment; and from Martinique came the fashion of the voluptuous
beguine.

Legend has it that the West Indian came to Harlem 'to
teach, open a church, or start trouble.' He has done all these
things. But he has made a fundamental contribution to public
education out of his zeal to improve the lot of black men. He
joined the stepladder brigade, or street-corner meeting, and
in the best traditions of the American Town Meeting nightly
grappled with questions facing the race. The development of
left-wing organizations among Negroes is largely attributed to
him, to the extent that once a Negro radical was described as
'an overeducated West Indian without a job.'

Among the ninety-odd newspapers published in New York
for immigrants, a West Indian press took its place in the
twenties and championed the unity of Negroes — West
Indian, African, and native-born. It finally succumbed for
want of capital and waning interest as the West Indians took
fuller participation in American life. When Harlem's principal newspaper, The *Amsterdam-Star News*, came under the co-
ownership of the West Indian-born Doctor P. M. H. Savory

in 1935, news of interest to Caribbean immigrants began to appear regularly.

Immigrants still keep a wary eye on affairs in the islands. When strikes or natural catastrophes occur, they often band together to aid the stricken. They also concern themselves with matters of a political nature. When President Roosevelt appointed the Anglo-American Caribbean Commission to study the conditions in the British colonies, Harlem West Indians urged the President to name an American citizen of Caribbean birth. (Judge William H. Hastie, an American-born Negro who has been a federal judge in the Virgin Islands, already was a member.) In 1942 a mass meeting was held in Harlem, which several hundred people attended, to hear a report by delegates of the American-West Indian Association on Caribbean Affairs, who had conferred with State Department officials regarding the future of the Caribbean islands.

Hope for national survival is keen among West Indians, but it is no secret that they are eager for the United States to take over the colonies. Frequent mass meetings are held to consider whether 'The United States will take over the West Indies.' Some West Indian leaders have proposed a 'Confederation of the West Indies' under American protection — a status akin to that which Puerto Rico more or less enjoys. Many knotty problems will arise, no doubt, in such an eventuality. One, certainly, will be the 'Negro question' — for Black America would be increased in population by several millions. Then again, there will be the questions of internal political status, low standard of living, and *citizenship!* These may be intensified by volatile native populations. Though the trend of American diplomacy lately has been away from imperialism, the one great fear — both here and in the West Indies — is that American sovereignty may bring the American *color line* to the islands.

Quite a different pattern obtains with the French-speaking

immigrants, several thousands in number, who came from the islands of Guadeloupe and Martinique, and French Guiana, areas which have belonged to France since the buccaneering days of the seventeenth century. These people are augmented by a few French Africans. Though less race-conscious than American and British Negroes, these citizens of France are proud of their racial heritage, even to boasting that Empress Josephine was a Creole born on the island of Martinique. Many of the French colonials are employed as factory workers and are active in trade unions; others are famous French cooks. Their social life revolves around the Mutual Society of French Colonials, a society formed to provide social life, preserve the language, and maintain French culture, but often they belong to the same clubs and organizations as the white Frenchman. They have his reputed taste for good foods and exquisite wines and give an annual dance on Bastille Day — though France's non-intervention policy during the Italo-Ethiopian War dampened their patriotism somewhat. They are distinctly Left in political and trade-union matters to the extent that socialism and communism have attracted many of them. For years they used to receive considerable political stimulus from the radical newspaper *Le Cri des Nègres*, published by Negroes in Paris.

If the French colonials are the most developed politically, then the Haitians, who speak French (and Creole), can be said to be the most cultivated of the immigrants in Harlem. Nearly every educated Haitian has studied abroad, particularly in France. Today they come to the United States in increasing numbers for their education. As a group, they have splendid relationships with American Negroes, mingling freely with them, and resenting equally the prevailing prejudice against colored peoples. Those who have made Harlem their home are engaged in industry and importing (coffee mainly), and have made efforts to interest local Negroes in the commercial possibilities of Haiti.

Increasingly, the problems of Haiti are becoming the concern of Americans, as is evidenced by the formation of such groups as the American Friends of Haiti. Almost two thousand in number — according to the Haitian consul — they are a growing influence in the Negro world. Intrigued by Haiti's revolutionary traditions, Negro writers and artists are more and more traveling to Haiti for material. Many well-to-do Negroes spend vacations there largely because of the absence of color prejudice. Harlem, to put it briefly, is entranced by the Republic of Haiti — the only black republic in the world — with a population that is 90 per cent pure Negro and 10 per cent mulatto, and includes no whites except a few foreigners.

Unless the colored immigrant in New York is decidedly black in complexion, he usually lives in the white neighborhoods of the city. Of necessity he identifies himself as a *white* person, hoping to escape the many discriminations that beset a black person. Knowledge of a foreign tongue is all-important. Yet, only those of the upper-income brackets can 'pass' with any success. This is a problem particularly acute among the Spanish-speaking immigrants from Latin-American countries, who provide a formidable group in Harlem — about fifty thousand in number.

Reliable sources estimate the number of Spanish-speaking people in New York at two hundred and fifty thousand. Any attempt to divide them into white and Negro is extremely difficult. For our purpose, however, we will concentrate upon the colored Puerto Ricans — those who form the largest single Latin group in New York and live in Harlem's Latin Quarter. Residing here, as well, are a number of dark-skinned Mexicans and Cubans and a few South and Central Americans. The Negro press has particularly taken the Cubans to its bosom, largely because Colonel Fulgencio Batista, President of the Republic of Cuba, is of Negro ancestry and hence of interest to the Negro public.

In many ways, the movement of Puerto Ricans to Harlem may be compared to the migration of Negroes from South to North; and in others, to the social effects of Mexican settlement in Southern cities. They have crowded into tenements situated in a tight pocket of lower Harlem. By occupation they are mainly dishwashers, barbers, and seamen, and a large group operate small shops. A professional class is almost non-existent, so Negro and Jewish professional men take up the slack. They maintain places of amusement that have a distinctly Spanish flavor — like El Toreador, a sort of night club featuring rhumba music and dancing; and theaters like Cervantes and Hispano, which offer motion pictures made in South America and Mexico.

Socially, Puerto Ricans in Harlem are clannish; but not to the point where it creates hostility — in fact, it is no bar to easy associations between them and Negroes. Within the Spanish-speaking group color prejudice does not exist as a social handicap. Marriage between Latins and Negroes is taken as a matter of course, and the groups live amicably side by side in the same apartment houses. However, the Latin's many societies and clubs do not attract American Negroes. Limited pretty much to menial employment and low wages, Harlem's Puerto Ricans live in one of the most depressed areas in the city and its people are the most seriously neglected in New York's population, thus perhaps furnishing a reason why prostitution flourishes here even with 'apache overtones.'

Politically, the Puerto Ricans are orphans. They have few articulate leaders. Prominent Puerto Ricans, of very fair complexion, almost invariably live outside of Harlem. They make little effort to provide leadership, nor do they concern themselves with helping to solve the many pressing problems which daily confront the Latin Quarter. Also, the island elects a Resident Commissioner to the United States, who is a member of the House of Representatives, but his interests rarely extend beyond the boundaries of Puerto Rico. Only one Puerto

Rican in the history of New York has held public office, Oscar
Garcia Rivera, who was elected to the State Assembly in 1937
by a Negro-Puerto Rican constituency. Today, Harlem's
Puerto Ricans — United States citizens by right of birth —
are represented in Congress by Vito Marcantonio, a man of
Italian parentage, who is elected not alone by Puerto Ricans
but by an even larger bloc of Negroes and Italians.

By and large Harlem's Puerto Ricans are anti-Fascist —
though some observers find people in certain sections of Puerto
Rico to be openly pro-Fascist. During the Spanish Civil War
many in Harlem turned away from the conservative daily, *La
Prenza*, a Spanish-language newspaper, to a new and strongly
pro-Loyalist tabloid, *La Voz*. Mass demonstrations in the
community were frequent, often emotional. More and more
the Puerto Ricans are reading the Negro newspapers. For the
tendency among Negroes nowadays is to include the Latin
Quarter in all movements for community betterment. It
would be inaccurate to say that Negroes provide leadership
for the colored Puerto Ricans, but it would be correct to say
that Negro leaders are showing uncommon awareness of their
problems and are relating them to those of the Negro population.

A word about Mexicans. Harlem has few. But great numbers are found in Texas, some of the midwestern states, and on
the West Coast. Nowhere in the country is there any real
social intercourse between Mexicans and Negroes, although
the two groups often live in the same neighborhoods in the
very poorest sections of town. Los Angeles, for example, has
thousands who are at the bottom of the heap. They do the
hard and dirty work; are herded into ghettos, and are among
the ill-housed and the underfed. Some 59 per cent of them
live in substandard dwellings, as compared to 25 per cent of
Negroes and 40 per cent of Orientals so housed.

Little hostility exists between Mexicans and Negroes, and a

minimum of friendship, partially because of religious and language differences. However, there is a growing friendship between the younger generation who attend the same schools. There have been abortive attempts to find common grounds for what would be a profitable political alliance. It is said that one difficulty is that when a Mexican raises his head above the crowd, he is apt to discover that he is not a Mexican at all, but a descendant of an old Castilian family. Hence the Mexican goes over to the Caucasian group and has little to do with either Mexicans or Negroes.

Least numerous of the racial elements in Harlem are the Asiatics — mainly Chinese and East Indians, with a few Japanese and Filipinos included. None, however, is in sufficiently large enough numbers to constitute a colony; nor does the social character of the community encourage such exclusiveness. In this connection, a humorous anecdote is told frequently of the Chinese laundryman who, in self-defense on the night of the Harlem riot, hurriedly posted a sign on his store window which read: 'ME COLORED TOO.'

Asiatics in Harlem are mainly Chinese, and number about two thousand or more. Uniformly they make the best adjustment to the Negro community, even to stomping the lindy hop at the Savoy Ballroom. Faced with residential restrictions — if they belong to the low-income group — as formidable as those that face the Negro, many of them have journeyed from the teeming alleys of Chinatown uptown to Harlem. Like their countrymen in other sections of the city, they work as laundrymen, servants, restaurant workers, and shopkeepers. Along a thin strip of Lenox Avenue in lower Harlem, they operate small importing houses and grocery stores, offering a wide variety of goods. Neatly packed in the windows are Chinese vegetables — cabbages, bean sprouts, melons, water chestnuts — and such viands as shark fin, smoked squid, and blubber. Chinese restaurants are very popular with Negroes, though Chinese chefs complain that Negroes pass up Oriental delicacies to eat pork and fried rice.

Chinese merchants, as a rule, maintain their social and family life within the Negro community. Many have Negro wives and children. In Harlem, as elsewhere in the United States, it should be mentioned, the child of a marriage between a Negro and a white or red, yellow or brown person, no matter how little his appearance resembles that of a Negro, is considered *Negro*. And indeed no psychic injury is done the child. Some of the best-adjusted people I know are the progeny of such unions.

In a Harlem bar, Charles Chu, a young man of my acquaintance, the product of a Chinese father and Negro mother, told me with relish of his sister, a dancer. It seems that before the invasion of France, she had assumed the prosaic name 'Ming Toy,' and entered an international beauty contest held in Paris representing China! Holding the clippings before him, this handsome brownskin lad with almond eyes tossed off this story in the flavorous jargon known as Harlem jive talk.

Chinese who reside in Harlem are law-abiding, seldom violently partisan, good businessmen, and devoid of chauvinism of any sort. The extent of their political activity has been to raise funds for China's war against the Japanese invaders. Membership in Negro organizations is more or less confined to lodges of the Elks, whose lusty fellowship, colorful parades, and lavish death benefits Chinese find attractive. Though they are not given to rigid religious stratifications, a small number attend Negro churches, and a handful have been seen living in Father Divine's 'Peace Kingdoms.'

Two pleasant incidents occurred in Harlem which touched the Chinese deeply. When a popular Chinese businessman who had been active in the affairs of the community for more than thirty years died, his funeral was attended by five hundred Negroes. It was reported in the Negro press, with much space devoted to eulogies. On another occasion, a famous quartet eliminated 'Minnie the Moocher' from its repertoire in deference to the Chinese consul, who had been trying for more than a year to get the song banned from the radio networks.

In contrast to this, there is little association between Negroes and Chinese on the West Coast. For one thing, the bulk of the Chinese group is situated in San Francisco, while the bulk of Negro population is five hundred miles away in Los Angeles. Until the beginning of this century, but few Negroes lived in California, and these were fairly well integrated into the population of a very cosmopolitan city — hence little racial feeling was apparent. Racial problems arose with the influx of Orientals, who were mainly Chinese. When racial proscription began to flourish — contrary to the experience of the rest of the United States — it was directed at Orientals and *not* Negroes. If Negroes subsequently felt the ill effects of prejudice based on race, it was because they were lumped with Orientals. Even today old documents prohibiting use and occupancy of land are apt to mention Chinese and not Negroes. Gradually restrictive agreements came to include 'any person not of the Caucasian race.' However, Negroes are protected by a Civil Rights law.

Relations between Negroes and Chinese are very casual. Most Chinese live in a Chinatown — both in San Francisco and Los Angeles. There are, however, a few Negro-Chinese marriages which seem to have been successful and incidentally to have produced some beautiful children. But the real link between Chinese and Negroes has been the Chinese Lottery — the numbers racket of the West Coast. Chinese introduced the game to Negroes by hiring Negro runners and collectors. Beyond this, there was almost no cooperation between the groups until 1941, when Negroes gave a benefit bazaar at which three thousand dollars was raised for China relief. A friend of mine who attended the affair said that the Chinese who were present were rather ill at ease, much as white persons might be. At best, Negroes and Chinese are not hostile to each other, nor are they neighborly — actually, they are strangers.

Harlem's East Indians, who are drawn largely from the intellectual class, may be divided loosely into two groups — Hindus and Moslems. Hindus, a few hundred in number, are mainly students, scholars, and doctors, and a few are seamen. Unobtrusively, they thread their way through the community, here and there dotting social gatherings and political forums and energetically correcting misinformation about India — from the nationalist point of view usually. The degree of integration that has been achieved by these people might be suggested by the exploits of Wilmeth Sidat Singh, a Harlem youth, who received considerable press attention for his athletic feats at Syracuse University — no one in the community even bothered to mention the fact that he was of Hindu-Negro parentage. Aside from those in New York, the only other large group of Hindus found associating intimately with Negroes are those on the West Coast. Here the Hindu population has remained more or less static, because there are few Hindu women in the United States. Hindus have married Negro women in numbers, and they are received in the better homes and mingle fairly freely with whites. Yet when the Hindu poet and savant, Tagore, visited in California some years ago, assurances to hotel-owners that he was 'not a Negro' availed little at all.

Harlem's Moslems run into several thousand. Unlike Hindus, Moslems hold an annual religious festival, I'd-ul-duha (Day of Sacrifice). Since they have no mosque, the faithful worship in private homes and hired halls, where on Saturday mornings their children study the Koran. They live quietly in Harlem, but during their festivals they don rich robes, shawls, turbans, and fezzes of their native land, and the women wear gorgeous brocades and heavy decorative jewelry. Ordinarily Moslems wear American dress, for most of them have lived in the United States more than twenty years. By occupation they are students, bellboys, waiters, garage mechanics, janitors, factory workers, and insurance agents. As a group, they have little of the nationalistic fervor that characterizes the Hindus — at least such is not apparent. But they possess a religious fervor that is expressed in much missionary work among American Negroes. Newark, New Jersey, for example, has a congregation of five thousand Negro Moslems, and there are several other thousands in the Midwest. Whether they are Africans, Arabs, Tartars or American Negroes, Moors, Persians or whites, Moslems intermarry. The racial flow back and forth defies classification.

Filipinos are the reverse side of the same coin. Only very few have contact with Harlem. Rarely do they marry Negroes, nor do they associate with them. Perhaps the sharp competition with Negroes for jobs has dulled the incentive to social relationships. When the Pullman Company sought to smash the Brotherhood of Sleeping Car Porters before it grew powerful, the company announced a wage increase and began to replace Negroes with Filipinos, hoping thereby to raise the race issue.

Almost 98 per cent of the fifty thousand Filipinos on the West Coast are men. They are forbidden by law to marry whites because they belong to the Malay race. Hence these men fall prey to every racketeer who can make a profit out of introducing them to any kind of women. Many have tried to form respectable relationships with Negro women. But here again they are faced with barriers. Yet there have been a number of Filipino-Negro marriages, but Negroes complain that Filipinos tend to isolate the family from Negro life. Some of these marriages have been very successful, albeit the Negro upper crust frown on the whole affair.

Something of this attitude was shown by a Negro legislator, Frederick M. Roberts, who introduced a *repatriation* bill in the

California State Assembly to send the Filipinos back where they came from!

Filipinos are 'nationals,' not citizens, and thus can enter none of the professions. This fact has helped to relegate them to jobs as personal servants and agricultural workers. Some years back they caught the public fancy as houseboys, valets, butlers, and the like. As a result, Negroes in the California area were somewhat antagonistic. Today, however, they have ironed out the difficulties, and relationships between these two peoples are good and intermingling frequent.

Japanese, too, have taken up residence in Harlem. Some came to cushion their contacts with racial prejudice. Not so simple, though, is the explanation for the appearance of Japanese students, scholars, and journalists. But the Nipponese fall into a special category and must wait to be dealt with in a later chapter.

Chapter V

*In some ways it's even an advantage to be colored.
Certainly on the stage it's no handicap. It's almost an asset. And now white editors are beginning to regard Negroes as interesting novelties,
like white elephants or black roses. . . .*

— CARL VAN VECHTEN'S 'NIGGER HEAVEN'

SPRINGTIME IN HARLEM

NEGRO life began to assume new dimensions in the decade following the first World War, which served to give Harlem its unique reputation. For everywhere there seemed to be gaiety, good feeling, and the sound of jazz, ushering in an era of incredible doings. The rhythm of life seemed to beat to the clink of glasses and the thump of drums. From the windows of countless apartments, against a glow of dull red lights, silhouetted figures rocked and rolled to mellow music. Harlem was dancing to the syncopations of Fletcher Henderson's band and listening to the moanin' low of Bessie Smith. Urchins were happily tricking dance steps on the sidewalks. Laughter was easy, loud.

Hundreds of honky-tonks prospered, and money seemed to flow from everyone's pockets as easily as laughter from their lips. Policy kings, hot-stuff vendors, and bootleggers were the peers of any man. Harlem's Imperial Elks Number 127 of the Independent, Benevolent, and Protective Order of Elks of the World erected a sumptuous clubhouse costing three hundred

thousand dollars, and beturbaned A'Leilia Walker, daughter
of a former laundress, startled the community with a 'million-
dollar wedding' — actually costing forty thousand dollars.

Harlem had entered an era of noisy vitality. Much of what
happened was stimulated by jazz, war, and easy money. The
phenomenal boom in property values had made a few enterprising Negroes wealthy. Some real estate operators acquired
large sums by the so-called 'Negro-scare racket' — a scheme
in which Negro tenants, none too prepossessing, were moved
into fashionable neighborhoods where white people lived, with
the result that the alarmed residents bid for the properties of
these racketeers at outrageous prices.

Few Negroes traded in bigotry — most of them earned
money the hard way. There was, for instance, Pig Foot Mary,
huge and deep-voiced, who had trailed her migrant customers
to Harlem. Early in the fall of 1901, she drifted into New York
from the Mississippi Delta penniless, and within a week after
her arrival set up a business in front of a popular San Juan
Hill saloon. Mary, whose real name was Lillian Harris, after
earning five dollars as a domestic, spent three for a dilapidated
baby carriage and a large washboiler, and invested the balance
in pigs' feet. Hot pigs' feet showed an immediate profit.

From early morning until late at night, swathed in starched
checked gingham, she remained at this stand for sixteen years.
Beyond two cotton dresses, her worldly goods was a mounting
bank account. Mary was saving enough money, she often said,
to purchase a place for herself in an old folks' home for respectable colored people. Concern about her old age vanished
when she moved to Harlem, opened her business at 135th
Street on Lenox Avenue, and three weeks later married John
Dean, owner of an adjoining newsstand. He persuaded her to
purchase a forty-four-thousand-dollar apartment-house building, which she sold six years later to a Negro 'underground
specialist' (undertaker) for seventy-two thousand dollars.
Though unable to read or write, Pig Foot Mary became one

of the community's shrewdest business women. Her subsequent dealings in real estate brought her bank account up to three hundred and seventy-five thousand dollars — an ample sum for old-age security.

Substantial incomes were earned as well by prizefighters, who by and large had little concern about tomorrow. Lanky 'Keed' Chocolate, a former Havana bootblack, dazzled Harlem with yellow automobiles, purple suits, and riotous living. Tiger Flowers, a Bible-totin' Baptist deacon, contributed lavishly to the collection plates of Negro churches. Harry Wills, the powerfully built 'Black Panther,' managed to get many lucrative matches by proclaiming the fact that the champion, Jack Dempsey, had drawn the color line. And there was free-spending Battling Siki, the clowning black Senegalese who stunned the boxing fans by beating the adored Georges Carpentier, and later startled blasé Paris by careening along the boulevards in a high-powered automobile with a lion tied to it. He showed up in the Negro capital to continue the revels begun in the cafés of Montmartre, finally meeting a violent death in Hell's Kitchen at the hands of white hoodlums.

Theatrical people, too, were large money-makers. Florence Mills, the graceful and beloved 'Little Blackbird,' delighted downtown audiences in *Dixie to Broadway*. The phonograph recordings of Bert Williams, a Ziegfeld star, still were bestsellers. Charles Gilpin, an intense brown man, once an elevator operator and trainer of pugilists, was acclaimed as the star of *The Emperor Jones;* while big Paul Robeson was appearing in *All God's Chillun Got Wings*, which had a decidedly controversial interracial theme. Roland Hayes, a sensitive and gifted tenor from Fisk University, had triumphantly mounted the concert stage. Bandmaster Lieutenant 'Jim' Europe, a robust, bespectacled figure who had introduced jazz to war-weary Paris, was back and a popular figure at the Winter Garden with his Clef Club orchestra. And hardly had jazz assailed the ears of New York when jovial W. C. Handy arrived with a satchel of music that proved to be a new and popular motif. His 'Yellow Dog Blues' and 'St. Louis Blues' were sung by wailing blues singers in every dive, joint, and basement cabaret — places which, incidentally, did a bouncing business.

The Sugar Cane Club, operated by Edwin Smalls, today owner of Smalls' Paradise, was typical of the era's off-the-beaten-path joints. At the bottom of a steep flight of stairs at 135th Street and Fifth Avenue was a damp, dimly lit cellar, with two-dozen-odd tables surrounding a tiny dance floor. From one side a five-piece band beat out rhythms, while each player in turn would 'take a Boston' — that is, execute some unexpected riffs. (None of the musicians could read music, nor did the lack of knowledge seem important.) To such music, the patrons, mostly Negroes, would stand and shuffle their feet — dancing on a dime, it was called — while others did the aptly titled bump and mess-around.

There also were the entertaining waiters, who, while they sang, threaded their incredible way through packed houses, twirling trays aloft, balancing them precariously on one or two fingers, while they danced skillfully between the tables; the journey ended, they executed a dexterous flourish of the tray, an intricate flurry of taps, and deposited a pitcher of raw gin before the customers. 'Yeah, man!' Nights when business was lively the lights would be extinguished and a spotlight focused on a rotating mirrored chandelier which cast its myriad reflections across the features of Ethel Waters, who sang here before she became known to white audiences. Usually singing a down-to-earth blues, she would in an aloof yet personal manner give a *double-entendre* version in the colorful idiom of Harlem, as she moved from table to table, patting a cheek here, squeezing a hand there:

> Rent man waitin' for his forty dollars.
> Ain't got me but a dime and some bad news.
> Bartender, give me a bracer, double beer chaser,
> 'Cause I got the low-down, mean, rent man blues.

Negroes mostly sought their entertainment at house-rent parties, a distinctly Harlem innovation that became the vogue in other Black Belts of the country. Saturday night was the big night. Thursday night also was a favorite — 'sleep-in' domestic workers usually had time off and were free to pitch and carry-on but found their small salaries inadequate for cabarets. Usually admission to house-rent parties was fifteen cents. What was spent once inside was another matter. A small bare room with a red glow for light served as the 'ball-room,' where the strenuous business of rug-cuttin' was performed. The only furniture was a piano from which a 'box-beater' extracted close harmonies and 'jump rhythms,' or 'gut-bucket,' which is now called boogie-woogie. In the kitchen pots of chitterlings and pigs' feet stood ready for the hungry revelers. A jug of corn was a staple for such affairs, sold at a makeshift bar in the hallway in half-of-a-half-pint portions — called 'shorties.' Then there would be goings-on until day-break, and rent next day for the landlord.

House-rent parties attracted a large transient trade, such as Pullman porters, interstate truck drivers, servants of footloose white folks, and innocent Negro tourists to the Black Metropolis. Additional business was promoted among that army of people who crowded the streets at night, seeking adventure and companionship in preference to remaining in dingy and ill-ventilated rooms. They found their way to these get-to-gethers through little business cards which were distributed by the 'madams' to drum up trade. Only colored people were handed these 'invitations,' for during Prohibition any white face might be that of an enforcement agent; and moreover, the local police appeared more diligent in raiding these places, sometimes called 'Buffet Flats,' than known gin mills, or speakeasies, which flourished on almost every street corner. Here is a typical bit of doggerel sales talk:

> There'll be brownskin mammas,
> High yallers too,
> And if you ain't got nothin' to do
> Come on up to Mary Lou's.

> There'll be plenty of pig feet
> And lots of gin;
> Jus' ring the bell
> An' come on in.

A Barefoot Prophet, so called because winter and summer he strode the streets in bare feet, was a frequent house-rent party visitor. A towering man, with a luxuriant mane of white hair, a flowing beard, and a long heavenly robe, he was an eternal beacon along Harlem's highways. His, whose calling cards identified him as Elder Clayborn Martin, was a beloved figure in the community. This giant carried the 'Word' to gin mill, cabaret, tavern, and poolroom. At the last place he often paused to shoot a game, quote a few passages of the Scriptures, and take up a collection, then disappear in the night.

His origin was obscure. Some said he came from Virginia. For more than fifty years, at any rate, he yearly wended his way from New York to Virginia, walking the entire distance. At an early age — he once told me after marking a cross on my forehead with ointment — he had received a divine message: 'Take off your shoes, for this is Holy Ground. Go Preach My Gospel!' And he literally obeyed, preaching sermons that possessed almost a fable quality:

> Our world is like a fox, brethren, like a fox that catch his foot in the trap of the Devil. Fox knows, brethren, that if he stays long enough in the Devil's trap, the Devil will kill him with a long stick. So the fox gnaws off his foot, and leaves the foot for the Devil and goes home on three legs and praises God he's gittin' home at all. . . . Now, brethren, you see what I mean. We's got sin and we's got sinners, and better than that the sinners should lead us into the Devil's traps, we must cut them off. . . .

As Prophet Martin lay dying in Harlem Hospital, at the age of eighty-six, he sent out his last call, pinned to a candy box and written in his own shaking hand: 'Help Bury the Prophet.' Hundreds heeded his last message.

Life in Harlem seemed to provide easy pickings, so that all the fabulous characters produced in Black America and elsewhere at one time or another descended on this happy hunting ground. The outlanders heard that gravy ran in the gutters — and all one had to do was reach down and sop it up with biscuits. One of the arrivals, for instance, was Casper Holstein, a penniless immigrant, who became a prosperous 'policy banker.' From his income, he established a fund for yearly awards to outstanding Negro artists and writers, and contributed thousands of dollars for social welfare in his native Virgin Islands. His curious career was cut short by white gangsters who kidnapped him and extorted fifty thousand dollars. The impeccable Barron Wilkins, flashy gambler and cabaret host, was another importation. He moved his night club uptown from the Black Bohemia area and became wealthy in catering to the white-quality trade. If his origins were obscure, certainly his end was clear — he was sensationally shot to death by 'Yellow' Carter, a dope addict.

Until the police department, in one of its periodic drives of righteousness, brought to an end the unique entertainment in which black and white cavorted, the annual ball of the Hamilton Lodge of Odd Fellows was perhaps the most bizarre feature of the period. It was the sort of affair in which men dressed as women and women dressed as men and was usually held at Rockland Palace, a dance hall capable of holding eight thousand persons. These people, who packed the place, came from all sections of the country to walk in the fashion parade. Prizes were given to the best dressed. Negro and white men, bewigged, powdered, rouged, and wearing flowing gowns, competed without racial incident.

Harlem loves spectacles. In those days Aubrey Lyles, star of *Shuffle Along* and later *Runnin' Wild*, drove a long red automobile with solid ivory trimmings that made Negroes gasp. It was the first car seen in the community which had the comforts of a Pullman car. The back seat slid down to make a bed.

Behind the driver's seat were a bar and icebox. Somewhat later, Jules Bledsoe, who sang 'Old Man River' in *Show Boat*, broke into the limelight with an expensive, high-powered motor, driven by a white chauffeur in livery. He explained to the complete satisfaction of Harlem, so Langston Hughes relates, that he had a white uniformed chauffeur so that the white public could tell which was the chauffeur and which the owner of the car.

The Black Metropolis was the *Vogue!* Stimulated by the contemporary craze for Negro jazz, Negro musical shows — *Shuffle Along* and *Runnin' Wild* — and Negro dances, Charleston and Black Bottom, many Bohemian whites made nightly sallies to the section. Carl Van Vechten contributed much to the community's reputation as a diverting hot spot with the publication of his novel, *Nigger Heaven*, which had considerable popularity in the twenties. But the section of Harlem that these people came to know was, after all, no more than a brown-skinned edition of life in New York — though perhaps more intense, literal, and noisy. White visitors to Harlem were in fact as much a part of the show as Negroes themselves, and much of the entertainment, at times unorthodox, was seasoned to suit their tastes.

Many night clubs catered to white patrons exclusively — and, curiously enough, drew the color line. For example, Negroes were barred from the Cotton Club, the widely advertised 'Aristocrat of Harlem.' A pair of massive doormen stood at the entrance to reinforce the rule. On one occasion W. C. Handy, accompanied by Gene Buck of A.S.C.A.P., was barred admittance — this in spite of the fact that his music was the feature of the show. While few were wealthy enough to pay the club's exorbitant cover charge, Negroes still resented the restrictions; nor were they taken in by the distribution of Christmas baskets by the Cotton Club owners.

But the theatrical people aspired to appear there. For one thing, the club was famous for its high-yaller chorus; and so lucrative was it as a source of income that white girls often passed as light-complexioned Negroes to procure employment. It was here, too, that Duke Ellington and Cab Calloway made reputations as orchestra leaders.

National attention soon was focused on Harlem, and, to Negroes everywhere, the community became the symbol of opportunity. Wave after wave of migrants teemed into Harlem. The Black Metropolis was indeed coming of age. It had its own schools, newspapers and magazines, labor unions, hotels, hospitals, restaurants, churches, and a multitude of organizations and societies like the Elks and Masons. At first glance, Harlem gave the impression of being self-sufficient, a community unto itself. Actually, it was no more self-sufficient than it is today. Its people were dependent on the financial, commercial, and industrial arteries of the dominant white group for its very life's blood. It was this dependence, as well as economic and social restrictions, that helped to give Negro life its distinct character.

The spectacular Back-to-Africa Movement, which noisily explored the fascinating abstraction of an African utopia and stirred millions of Negroes to wild enthusiasm, was the high note of the period. It was led by the amazing Marcus Garvey, who preached with wonderful zeal of a Black House as opposed to a White House; a Black Congress as opposed to a White Congress; of Black Generals, Black Aristocracy, and a Black God, that swept Negroes along a mighty wave of Black Nationalism. Its mammoth meetings, colorful parades, gorgeous uniforms, and heavy rituals received amazing acclaim and caused Black America to pour its wartime earnings into the stupendous scheme of African redemption. By its operations the mind of the Negro is revealed in many of its subtle shadings and manifestations. If we get a grasp of this movement, a phenomenon that cannot be accounted for by purely intellectual processes, the realities of today are thrown into more searching perspective.

Chapter VI

I asked, where is the black man's government?
Where is his president, his country, and his
ambassadors, his army, his navy, and his men of
big affairs? I could not find them and then I
declared, I will help make them ...

— MARCUS GARVEY

UP, YOU MIGHTY RACE!

MARCUS MANASSEH GARVEY, tempestuous and flamboyant, was unique among Negro leaders. To begin with, he was *black*, an *immigrant*, and without much formal education — decidedly not Du Bois' idea of Talented Tenth material. He was born in Jamaica, British West Indies, in 1887, the grandson of an African slave — a fact that was his proudest boast. Neighbors called him 'Ugly Mug.' He grew up under a color caste system — white, mulatto, and black — which even as a boy aroused his resentment, not only against whites but against mulattoes as well, and it was this resentment that was to be translated into one of the cardinal doctrines of the movement he was to lead. Indeed, it began his odyssey, at the age of twenty-one, in search of a place to escape color prejudice.

His wanderings took him to London, where he lived for several years working at his trade as a printer. Here he soon became acquainted with native Africans to whom he listened attentively while they described the exploitation and squalor of Africa amidst immense riches. It was probably here that Garvey first had dreams of an empire ruled by black men. At any rate he returned to Jamaica and led a printers' strike, but when the men compromised, he was thrown out of work permanently. He then shifted his emphasis to the establishment of a school, and in search of a plan read Booker T. Washington's inspiring autobiography, *Up from Slavery*. He wrote to the American educator and received an encouraging offer to come to the United States, but before he arrived in 1916 the Southern leader died.

A squat, ugly black man with intelligent eyes and big head, Marcus Garvey began to harangue loiterers along Lenox Avenue in the spring of 1917. Harlem ignored him. Worse, he was dismissed as an immigrant carpetbagger. Two years later an insane man dashed into his rooms in a beaten brownstone house on 135th Street near Lenox Avenue and shot him. The bullet grazed his forehead, but with a keen sense of publicity that was to characterize his entire extraordinary career, he rushed into the streets with the blood of the martyr coursing down his cheeks. The next day his assailant, captured and jailed by the police, leaped to his death from a prison window. The affair, involving a woman (later to become his wife), who attempted to shield him from his attacker, was given heroic proportions in the local press. And the name of Harlem's first messiah was on the lips of everyone. . . .

Garvey leaped into the ocean of black unhappiness at a most timely moment for a savior. He had witnessed the Negro's disillusionment mount with the progress of the World War. Negro soldiers had suffered all forms of Jim Crow, humiliation, discrimination, slander, and even violence at the hands of the white civilian population. After the war, there was a resurgence of Ku Klux Klan influence; another decade of racial hatred and open lawlessness had set in, and Negroes again were prominent among the victims. Meantime, administration leaders were quite pointed in trying to persuade Negroes that in spite of their full participation in the war effort they could expect no change in their traditional status in America. Newton D. Baker was particularly vocal on this issue. The liberal white citizens were disturbed by events, but took little action beyond viewing with alarm.

Negroes were more than ready for a Moses — one done in black preferably. Intellectuals of the race tried to rationalize the situation, but not so the broad masses; their acknowledged leader, Du Bois, had gone overboard with the war effort and now found himself estranged from his people. Negroes were faced with a choice between *racialism* and *radicalism*. Marcus Garvey settled the question for thousands by forming the Universal Negro Improvement Association, called U.N.I.A. for brevity, and preaching with great zeal for a pilgrimage of black men 'Back to Africa.' He rallied men to the slogan, 'Africa for Africans!' — for talk was then current about self-determination for subject peoples.

His voice was heard in every corner and crevice of the Black Belts of the country. Leaders like Du Bois who sought to *integrate* Negroes into American life were shocked and dismayed by such heresy, but helpless. Ignoring them, Garvey set up headquarters in Harlem and made his first appeal directly to the foreign-born elements in the community; not only the British West Indians but also the Spanish and French. They flocked to his banner, eventually to form the basic element of his movement. Next, he went on a tour that swept through thirty-eight states. He was acclaimed everywhere, Negroes seeing in him the inspired leader. When the little messiah returned to Harlem, with thousands following in his wake, he built Liberty Hall, a great zinc-roofed shed. Then, he started a weekly newspaper, the *Negro World*, which proved to be his most potent instrument for wielding opinion.

The character of this project deserves a brief word. It had a Spanish and French section and sold for five cents a copy in New York and ten cents elsewhere. Within a few months it had an international circulation. Usually the pages of the *Negro World*, some ten to sixteen, were crowded with 'the philosophy and opinions' of its editor. Edged between his long polemic articles were essays, reports of African and European affairs, patent medicine and beauty preparation advertisements (though skin-whitening ads were excluded), and occasionally a display of Lucky Strike cigarettes. His bombastic editorials referred to the 'glorious' history of the Negro, with particular emphasis on Africa's past regal splendor; recalled the slave struggles for freedom, and recounted stirring tales of the heroism of such Southern leaders of slave revolts as Denmark Vesey, Gabriel (Prosser), and Nat Turner. The exploits of long dead Zulu and Hottentot warriors who had fought against British rule were not forgotten, nor the histories of the Moorish and Ethiopian empires. Toussaint L'Ouverture's leadership of the Haitian Rebellion was stock copy. It was for this reason, perhaps, that the *Negro World* was cited in the report on radicalism made in 1919 by Attorney General A. Mitchell Palmer.

Marcus Garvey sought an economic solution of the Negro's problem through the establishment of Negro business. The Negro, he held, must become independent of white capital and white employers if he wants salvation. This was a page from the philosophy of Booker T. Washington, who had preached individual thrift and enterprise. His disciple, Garvey, envisioned an independent 'Black Economy' within the white capitalistic world, completely ignoring the fact that he himself was dependent on the large finance corporations and banks owned by whites for setting his projects in motion.

Tangible expression was given to his idea when he formed a Negro merchant marine, known as the Black Star Line, to develop trade relations among the darker peoples of the world. Ten million dollars was the announced need to capitalize the Black Star Line. Shares were sold to followers for five dollars each. While the pundits, according to Claude McKay, were proving the scheme a mathematical impossibility, Garvey proudly announced the acquisition of the first boat, the *Yarmouth*. It was purchased from the North American Steamship

Company for one hundred and sixty-five thousand dollars and with proper fuss and feathers rechristened the *Frederick Douglass*. Negroes were thrilled. From every black belt in America they swarmed into Harlem to see (and indeed feel) the wonderful miracle. Thousands journeyed down to the Hudson River, where the boat was moored, and happily paid a half-dollar to go aboard and shake hands with the all-Negro crew.

'Up, you mighty race,' Marcus Garvey thundered in response to hosannas. 'You can accomplish what you will!'

The ship's launching was spectacular. Thousands were on hand, cheering and waving flags and dangerously jamming the pier. There were anxious moments until the ship slid out of port on its maiden voyage under the colors of the Black Star Line. Loaded down with a cargo of liquor to be delivered in Cuba, the boat foundered a few miles outside of Newport News. Five hundred cases of expensive whiskies and champagnes had to be thrown overboard to keep the ship afloat. When the news reached Garvey, he hotly denounced the crew for becoming drunk on the cargo and navigating dice instead of the ship. He charged the Negro captain with being in the pay of enemy white folks, and gained tremendous sympathy which he carefully exploited. Imperceptibly the emphasis of the movement shifted to the nationalistic scheme for the redemption of Africa.

'It is only a question of a few more years,' he solemnly assured his followers, 'when Africa will be completely colonized by Negroes, as Europe is by the white race. No one knows when the hour of Africa's redemption cometh. It is in the wind. It is coming. One day, like a storm, it will be here.'

Anticipating that great day, he formed a social order modeled on a somewhat feudal pattern, and called it the 'Court of Ethiopia.' Trusted aides and large financial contributors were elevated to the ranks of duke, duchess, and lady-in-waiting. He himself modestly assumed the title of Provisional President-General of Africa.' But his boldest stroke was the creation of a Black Religion with a Black God!

He had been a convert to the Roman Catholic faith, and for a time was a devout follower — it was in fact the Saint Mark's Roman Catholic Church which provided him with his first platform in the United States. But he felt that the logic of an all-black world demanded a *Black God*. So his official historians and theologians delved into Biblical writings, reconstructed the nativity of Jesus, properly documented their interpretation, and the African Orthodox Church emerged as the true church of the black man. The Reverend George Alexander McGuire, an imposing man who had kicked over the Episcopalian traces of dogma, was called from his Boston pulpit, and after being consecrated by a white archbishop of the Greek Orthodox Church, he was installed as Primate. The fundamental outlines of the Roman Catholic Church were borrowed, even to much of its ritual and liturgy, and the Holy Trinity acknowledged — in black, of course. An impressive ceremony was held at Liberty Hall, and a 'Special Form of Divine Service' was performed by His Grace, Archbishop McGuire, for the purpose of 'canonization' of the Lord Jesus Christ as 'the Black Man of Sorrow' and the Blessed Virgin Mary as a Black Madonna.

'You must forget the white gods,' Archbishop McGuire was heard to say. 'Erase the white gods from your hearts. We must go back to the native church, to our own true God.'

Since a chosen people must be undefiled, Marcus Garvey naturally pontificated that only those who were 'one hundred per cent Negroid' could hold office in the organization, and thus carried his all-black world to its logical conclusion — *racial purity*. Accordingly, he admonished both whites and blacks that the purity of the races was being endangered. 'It is the duty of the virtuous and morally pure of both the white and black races,' he declared, 'to thoughtfully and actively protect the future of the two peoples, by vigorously opposing the destructive propaganda and vile efforts of the miscegenationists of the white race, and their associates, the hybrids of the Negro race.'

A racial doctrine of this sort brought him the open support of the notorious E. S. Cox, of the Ku Klux Klan, and that of John Powell, of the Anglo-Saxon clubs. Both men spoke several times from the platform of Liberty Hall and extolled the Back-to-Africa Movement, its leader, and its racial-purity program. Negro leaders rained criticism on Garvey, some even saying he had entered into a secret deal with the Klan. A. Philip Randolph, then editor of the radical *Messenger* magazine and today president of the Brotherhood of Sleeping Car Porters, denounced him as an ally of anti-Negro forces, and cited the fact that he was the only Negro who could hold rallies — some mighty boisterous ones too — in Southern cities and not be beaten, driven out, or even lynched. Garvey replied with devastating frankness.

'I regard the Klan,' he countered, 'as a better friend of the race than all the groups of hypocritical whites put together. You may call me a Klansman if you will, but, potentially, every white man is a Klansman, as far as the Negro in competition with whites socially, economically, and politically is concerned, and there is no use lying about it.'

Not alone did he advocate that sharp racial lines be drawn between whites and blacks, but he also insisted upon divisions within the Negro race — between blacks and mulattoes. He formulated this policy under the false assumption that there were three distinct races in the United States — white, black, and mulatto — divisions which existed concretely in his native Jamaica. He began his anti-mulatto campaign with scorching attacks on the 'near-white' leaders of the N.A.A.C.P. In so doing he hoped to create a buffer class which would bear the brunt of race prejudice between whites and blacks. For a time this type of propaganda inflated the darker Negroes, and succeeded in driving a wedge between the blacks and light-complexioned Negroes. But the success of this policy was limited because White Americans, unlike Englishmen, make no distinctions between mulattoes and blacks, nor do American Negroes.

Fanaticism soon took its obvious toll — there were casualties among the wayward. In the year of Garvey's greatest popularity — 1923, to be exact — James W. H. Eason was tried and found guilty of 'acts unbecoming a high officer o the High Executive Council,' and he was promptly removed from his job. Smarting under his disgrace, he attempted to form a rival organization in New Orleans, where he and a disgruntled few set up headquarters. The challenge was met swiftly, inexorably. One evening as Eason made his way to a meeting, he was ambushed and assassinated. His assailants were never apprehended, though it was frankly said at the time that Garvey was in possession of the facts. The incident served to stifle further open revolt and sent his opponents underground for a while.

Garvey's movement had gathered terrific momentum, even to a detail like the manufacture of black baby dolls for children. Negroes swept into Harlem, carried on a tidal wave of race consciousness. The cotton-picker of the South, bending over his basket, the poor ignorant worker of the Delta, crushed beneath a load of prejudice, the domestic of the city, trudging wearily to white folks' kitchens, and even the peasant of the Caribbean islands, dispossessed from the land, lifted his head and cried, 'Let's go to Harlem and follow this Black Moses!' The organization's phenomenal growth was reflected by its reported world-wide membership of more than six million followers. A former official of the organization told me that actually the movement had *two* million 'active dues-paying members' and four million sympathizers scattered throughout the world.

As a youngster I witnessed the movement's first 'Universal Negro Convention' held in Harlem. It was a monster affair, almost approaching medieval splendor in regalia of lush colors. During the whole month of August, 1920, delegates from all the states, the West Indies, South America, and Africa assembled in Liberty Hall, in a demonstration that proved to be a series of rousing 'bravos' and 'hallelujahs' to the black leader. People were fascinated by all the bustle, color, and animation in the streets. There were loud speeches, stock-selling from the curbstones, and indeed fisticuffs as men clashed.

'Is Garvey greater than Jesus Christ?' people asked.

'Give he a chance,' shot back his devout West Indian followers in their quaint English dialect. 'He's a young mon yet!'

Noisy meetings at Liberty Hall were climaxed by a magnificent parade in which more than fifty thousand 'Garveyites' marched through Harlem. His Excellency, Marcus Garvey, Provisional President of Africa, led the demonstration bedecked in a dazzling uniform of purple, green, and black, with gold braid, and a thrilling hat with white plumes 'as long as the leaves of Guinea grass.' He rode in a big, high-mounted black Packard automobile and graciously, but with restraint becoming a sovereign, acknowledged the ovations of the crowds that lined the sidewalks. Behind him rode His Grace, Archbishop McGuire, in silk robes of state, blessing the populace. Then, the Black Nobility and Knight Commanders of the Distinguished Order of the Nile followed, the hierarchy of the state, properly attired in regalia drawn from a bold palette. Arrayed in gorgeous uniforms of black and green, trimmed with much gold braid, came the smartly strutting African Legion; and in white, the stretcher-bearing Black Cross nurses. Then came troops of kilt-clad Boy and Girl Scouts, trailed by a multitude of bumptious black subjects.

Harlem was spellbound. For the first time white New York became aware of the proportions of the movement, its implications, and indeed its divertissements. Marcus Garvey had become a world figure, and his movements and utterances were noted by every European Power with possessions in Africa. He sent a good-will greeting to Abd el Krim, the rebel leader of Spanish Morocco; and advocated unity with all darker peoples — in the Caribbeans, Africa, India, China, and Japan.

On his return from abroad, Claude McKay reported two interesting incidents in connection with the movement. When the African Prince Kogo, darling of smart Parisian circles, embraced the Back-to-Africa Movement, he was driven out of France; and when Garvey elevated Gabriel Johnson, Negro mayor of Monrovia, capital of Liberia, to the rank of 'High Potentate of Monrovia,' the title nearly got the poor man lynched by the black aristocracy.

Incidents like these were only minor swirls on the smooth stream of Garvey's nationalistic course. But he was hardly prepared for the first real surging wave which was eventually to engulf and finally wash away his organization. Early in 1923, after repeated complaints by Negroes, the federal government investigated the Black Star Line. Garvey was indicted soon afterward and put on trial for using the mails to defraud. Yet, with his amazing energy and daring, as James Weldon Johnson observed, he might have carried on longer. He had stirred the imagination of Negroes. But in hypnotizing many credulous people, he had also attracted numerous crafty men who sought to enrich themselves. It was upon the latter group that he laid the blame for his failure. The inescapable fact is that he himself made the fundamental blunder by advancing an amazingly meager design (indeed impossible idea) — not to mention the poor economics of the program — for colonizing the possessions of imperialist nations.

'The whole scheme of a black empire, in the raging sea of imperialism,' Randolph declared, 'would make it impossible to maintain power; nor would it bring liberation to Africa, for Negro exploiters and tyrants are as bad as white ones.'

In reality, the Back-to-Africa Movement was a restatement of colonization schemes advanced on three other occasions in the history of the United States. A plan to colonize Negroes in Africa was vigorously put forth by the American Colonization Society, early in the last century, having such sponsors as Henry Clay, Andrew Johnson, and Thomas Jefferson. Liberia was chosen as the site. Negro opposition was immediate, militant, and widespread. Numerous protest meetings were held. One in Philadelphia in 1817 assumed the proportions of a national demonstration, when three thousand delegates attended and passed resolutions declaring it their right and intention to remain in the United States.

The next plan, ironically enough, was advanced by Lincoln. Before he signed the Emancipation Proclamation, he urged Congress to colonize black men in the West Indies, at an initial cost of twenty million dollars. Six hundred thousand dollars was appropriated and the government signed a contract with Bernard Kock, a promoter who had procured a lease on the island of Vache, off the coast of Haiti. He turned out to be 'an irresponsible and untruthful adventurer,' according to Lincoln, and his contract was canceled. The first boat sailed with a contingent of some five hundred men, women, and children. Kock, despite his reputation, was sent along to govern the colony. The venture proved to be a miserable failure. Two hundred colonists died, and Kock was driven from the island. Lincoln brought back the survivors under a beating shower of abolitionist criticism. The bill for Negro colonization was repealed, not to be heard of again until President Grant's administration; and finally in 1939 when the Mississippi Senator Bilbo, with typical obtuseness, introduced a bill to colonize Negroes in Africa.

Garvey went on trial before Judge Julian Mack in 1923, while Arthur Brisbane, the Hearst columnist, protested that to hold him was equivalent to 'jailing a rainbow.' The trial lasted about a month, during which time Garvey dismissed his Negro attorney and hired a white one. Meanwhile the government's witnesses placed the total deficit of the Black Star Line at seven hundred thousand dollars — though Garvey's wife and secretary, Amy Jacques, estimated that between 1919 and 1921, he took in ten million dollars. The government revealed that there were more than forty thousand

stockholders in this project — and there were several such projects.

Besides the ill-fated *Frederick Douglass*, two ships had been
purchased — the *Kanawha*, a former H. H. Rogers yacht which
was bought for sixty thousand dollars; and the *Shadyside*, a discarded Hudson River steamer, for which thirty-five thousand
dollars was paid. Driven by his critics Garvey had acquired
them when ships were at a premium, many being needed at
the time to bring home the A.E.F. But soon afterward the demand fell off, and they became a drug on the market. The
Black Star Line, such as it was, was worth only the scrap iron
in its contruction.

Plenty of cash had been splashed about, but the government
was unable to find any tangible assets. There were none!
Garvey testified that all the money he had in the world was
some forty dollars and two hundred and eighty-nine shares of
his own worthless stock. In his summation to the jury, the
psychological factors that underscored this wild spending were
touched upon by Henry Lincoln Johnson, a Negro attorney
who represented one of Garvey's co-defendants. 'If every
Negro,' he said, 'could have put every dime, every penny into
the sea, and if he might get in exchange the knowledge that
he was somebody, that he meant something in the world, he
would gladly do it. . . . The Black Star Line was a loss in
money but it was a gain in soul.'

The case against Garvey was admittedly weak, but he succumbed to the temptation to strut before a crowded courtroom
and to see his name on the front pages of the New York newspapers. He brushed aside his lawyer, and handled the case
himself. He cross-examined himself and the witnesses, and
corrected their English; he harangued the judge and jury, and
was finally convicted.

But this was hardly the end of this magnificent dreamer of
empire. Released on bail, pending appeal, he rallied his followers in a terrific demonstration at the old Madison Square

Garden and they quickly subscribed more than a hundred thousand dollars. The next day the Black Cross Navigation Company was formed and a ship, the *General Goethals*, was purchased from the Panama-American Railroad Company. The vessel was in good condition, and the price paid for it was said to be one hundred and seventy thousand dollars. Renamed the *Booker T. Washington*, the ship sailed from New York with passengers and United States mail, but upon arrival at a Caribbean port it was impounded for debt and never seen again.

The Black Moses had a sudden change of heart — but too late. Up to this point, the central idea of his program had meant absolute abdication of the Negro's rights and place in American life. He reversed his stand completely and urged his followers to take immediate interest in American politics and urged his foreign-born members to become naturalized. He formed the Universal Negro Political Union and in 1924 issued a nation-wide list of candidates for whom his followers were to vote. But new lawsuits brought the final financial collapse. Meantime Garvey lost his appeal, was fined a thousand dollars and sentenced to serve five years in prison. He entered Atlanta Penitentiary in 1925. Two years later President Coolidge — whose election he had supported — pardoned him and he was deported as an undesirable alien.

Without its dynamic little leader, the U.N.I.A. fell into quarreling segments. From his island exile in Jamaica, Marcus Garvey made futile efforts to re-form his movement. But without the vast stage of the Black Metropolis and the loud acoustics of Black America — to say nothing of the New York press — his voice failed to carry. He finally gave up and went to London to begin again. He died there in obscurity in 1940, deserted by his followers, but holding tenaciously to his Pan-African dream — though he was never to see the land of his ancestors. Nor were his followers to set eyes on the Promised Land. The truth is, a few may have consented to making an excursion to Africa, but the vast majority had no idea of leaving the United States. The dream of an all-black nation had simply given a sorely driven people a new and abundant dignity, enough to squander.

Concretely, the movement set in motion what was to become the most compelling force in Negro life — race and color consciousness, which is today that ephemeral thing that inspires 'race loyalty'; the banner to which Negroes rally; the chain that binds them together. It has propelled many a political and social movement and stimulated racial internationalism. It is indeed a philosophy, an ethical standard by which most things are measured and interpreted. It accounts for much constructive belligerency today.

'Marcus Garvey opened windows in the minds of Negroes!' one of his followers said.

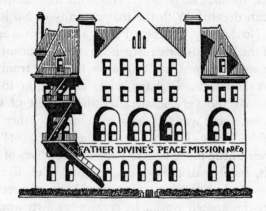

Chapter VII

It is easy for intellectuals who make a fetish of rationality to dismiss him [Father Divine] as a lunatic, which in part he perhaps is, but it is his kind of lunacy, embodied in higher but more sinister form in a person like Hitler, that has so often influenced a considerable part of the world....

— V. F. CALVERTON

I TALKED WITH GOD

UBIQUITOUS Father Divine, the 'Black God,' originator of religion on the chain-store plan, fell heir to the bulk of Marcus Garvey's thousands. For the search of a utopia, among the Garveyites, did not come to an end with the collapse of the Pan-African dream. With the magic trinity of No Race, No Sex, and No Money, Divine's Peace Movement was an extension of the Back-to-Africa scheme in its magnificent attempt to escape realities, and was attractive to many troubled and rudderless thousands. Perhaps it was an antidote to strident racialism. At the very least, after the tumult of Garvey's hectic drives, there was solace to be found in Father Divine's 'Heavens' — 'Peace, I thank you, Father, So Sweet!'

This weird little man, who has affected the lives of so many thousands, is often dismissed as a lunatic. Yet, like Garvey before him, he is a utopian seeker: unable to gain recognition in a white-dominated world, he creates his own world. Dissimilar though the two men are in most respects, they are one in the source of their influence — mass hypnotism. Both believed that they were men of destiny. Both rose to unique places in Negro life in critical periods. Garvey rode in on the wild currents of post-war national and racial hatreds. Divine emerged from the ashes of the Depression. But Garvey, curiously enough, set the stage for the midget messiah with his worship of everything *black*, including that of a 'Black God.' In one sense — to strain the figure a little — the Black Jeremiah was unwittingly Divine's prophet. For today, to many thousands, Father Divine is the 'reincarnated God.'

I talked with 'God.' He seemed quite human. He asked, 'Are you of my expression?' Beyond that he never said a mumblin' word.

Who is this little man that plays 'God'? Much nonsense has been written about him. Actually, he is the good provider in very fundamental down-to-earth terms. The fascinating career of this incredible messiah throws light on the whole curious, often bizarre developments of the Depression period. He rose to influence when hand-to-mouth living was the rule in Harlem. The Depression had driven thousands of Negroes back to the already crowded hovels from which they had emerged during the prosperous twenties. In many of these tenements one toilet served a floor of four apartments; and few had a private bathroom or even the luxury of a common bath. If there was a tub, it usually had been installed in the kitchen. Without exception, the houses were filthy and vermin-infested. Gaping holes in the skylight allowed the winter's cold air to sweep down the staircases, sometimes freezing the toilet flushes for weeks. Coal grates provided the only heat.

Things had come to such a pass that Negroes scoured the neighborhood for fuel, and harassed janitors in the surrounding districts were compelled to stand guard over coal deliveries, until stored safely in cellars. Many of the destitute were reduced to roaming the streets and to foraging in garbage cans. Harlem's increase in population served to sharpen the problem. In twenty years it had increased sixfold, until the average density of population was two hundred and thirty-three persons per acre as compared with one hundred and thirty-three for the rest of Manhattan. The community had become a vast swarming hive in which two and three families occupied apartments meant for a single family.

Ten thousand and more Negroes lived in basement dungeons, cellars that had been converted into makeshift flats. Packed into these damp, rat-ridden holes, they existed in squalor comparable to that of the Arkansas sharecropper. Floors were of cracked concrete, and the walls were whitewashed rock, water-drenched and rust-streaked. In many cases there were only slits for windows and no partitions to separate the space into rooms. In some there was no running water. Packing boxes were used as beds, tables, and chairs. In winter rags and old newspapers were stuffed into the numerous cracks to keep out the wind.

Virtually barred from other sections of the city, Harlem Negroes were forced to pay exorbitant rents, while landlords relaxed supervision and flagrantly violated the city building and sanitary codes. Compared with twenty to twenty-five per cent of their income generally paid by white families for rent, Negro tenants paid from forty to fifty per cent. Frequently whole families slept in one room. Envied was the household that had a night worker as a lodger, as he occupied a bed in the day that could be rented again for the night. This was described as the 'hotbed.' If the family had a bathtub, it too, after being covered with boards, was rented out as a bed.

Discrimination against employment of Negroes had practically closed the doors to many occupations. Generally, the poorer half of the Negro population was living on an annual income that was only fifty per cent of that of the poorer half of the white population. Wage standards had all but disappeared as dispossessed Negro sharecroppers of the South drifted into the Northern cities, swelling the total of destitute persons.

With these destitute people teeming into the Northern

cities, the relief bureaus were deluged with thousands of demands for food, clothing, and employment. There was bitter waiting and more bitter complaining. In New York, meanwhile, twenty-five thousand Negro families — fifty per cent of Harlem's population — were receiving unemployment relief. By 1933 the total of jobless Negroes in the United States had risen to 1,500,000. In such cities as Chicago, Cleveland, and St. Louis, Negroes made up from forty to fifty per cent of the unemployed population.

One block in Harlem was known as the 'lung block,' where more than four thousand persons lived; it had a death rate from pulmonary tuberculosis twice that of white Manhattan. Infant mortality took its toll of one out of ten — twice that of the city as a whole — and twice as many Negro women died in childbirth as white women. Only one hospital was concerned with the health of Negroes — Harlem Hospital, a city institution that had been a sore aggravating the Negro community for many years. Situated in the heart of the Harlem area, it attempted to care for more than three hundred and fifty thousand Negroes, and many thousands of Puerto Ricans, Italians, and Jews who lived on the fringes of Harlem. Harlem Hospital contained only two hundred and seventy-three beds and fifty-two bassinets in 1932. Patients were found sleeping on the floor, on mattresses, and on benches, even in the maternity wards. Those recently operated upon often slept on benches or on chairs. It was no wonder that proportionately twice as many people died at Harlem Hospital as at other city institutions.

Negroes had a great fear of being treated at Harlem Hospital and referred to it as the 'morgue' or 'butcher shop.' Even so, cases were refused admittance because of overcrowding. Sometimes there were as many as fifteen patients waiting for attention in the emergency clinics; and only three ambulances were available for calls. If Negroes turned to other hospitals, they were refused admittance, since many of them practiced segregation. The practice had barbarous results; for instance, in March, 1937, the wife of W. C. Handy, composer of 'St. Louis Blues,' lay critically ill in an ambulance before the doors of Knickerbocker Hospital, while the officials debated for more than an hour whether or not a Negro should be admitted. She died the next day.

These were the conditions. Under the economic stress, hundreds of cultists — fakirs and charlatans of every brand — swept into the Negro communities, set up shop, and began to flourish in a big way. Usually housed in dimly lit, smelly railroad flats in sections where they would not be hounded by the police, these men and women drew their 'clients' and 'members' from that army of bewildered and discouraged Negroes, caught in the economic maelstrom. The cultists were augmented by a number of herb doctors, clairvoyants, and 'jackleg' preachers, who operated in places like the Triumph Church, the Metaphysical Church of the Divine Investigation, Saints of Christ, Pentecostal Pilgrims, and the Sixth Mt. Zion Church. At the last place a sermon was once delivered entitled 'A Big Man Sleeps on a Little Woman's Lap.'

Along the streets, to the accompaniment of much mumbo-jumbo, mystics hawked — as they do today — all manner of products to the credulous, including the 'number' at a charge of twenty-five cents to win at the policy game. High John the Conqueror was Harlem's best known of the love-potion purveyors. The vendors were of many races: American Indians in feathered headdress and buckskin chaps sold snake oil, and roots, herbs, and maize for backyard planting. Native Africans, their faces marked by tribal identifications, offered teak-wood idols, hand-carved ivory bric-a-brac, and good-luck charms. Hindus sold perfume; East Indian Moslems peddled incense, oils, and teas; and gypsies told fortunes. Chinese in mandarin robes offered hand-wrought jade, boxes, and rugs; West Indians vended pamphlets explaining the mysteries of

voodooism. Of the home-grown varieties, there were fire-eat-
ing Rajah Rabo, dream-book author, and the voluptuous
slant-eyed Madame Fu Futtam, a seeress of Negro-Chinese
parentage.

The cultists — those jackals of the city jungles — appeared
to have the right of way. Nearly two hundred places in Harlem were operating as 'spiritualist churches,' where the 'spirits'
needed little inducement to come knocking at the door. The
Holy Star Spiritual Church, housed in the second-floor apartment of a tenement, was a typical outfit. In a small room a
greenish light cast an eerie glow on a picture of Christ, which
hung over a gold-and-white altar. A slick-haired black boy
played rhythmic hymns on an old beaten upright piano, as the
customers filed in to communicate with the spirit world. The
'spiritual adviser,' in this case the Reverend Mme. V. D. S.
Armistead, a skinny woman in a lace-covered black cassock
and jaunty priest's biretta, trailed into the room as sanctuary
bells were tinkled by a black-robed altar boy. 'Before I begin
to transmit messages from the Spirit World,' she would an-
nounce, 'I want to tell you 'bout our Prosperity Oil.' The
product — 'good to awaken slumbering souls' — sold for ten
cents a bottle and proved to be a profitable item. Once that
little matter was concluded, the business of bringing in the
spirits got under way at twenty-five cents a head. Twenty to
thirty persons were usually accommodated at one sitting.

Sometimes closed motion-picture houses, empty stores, and
lodge halls were converted into 'temples,' with announcements
plastered on the buildings that were cheap and alluring, calling
the citizenry to find out what trouble was brewing. The
operators of these places turned neat profits from the sale of
dream books, policy pamphlets, love potions, and incense to
destroy evil spirits. Two questions they unfailingly answered
in the affirmative: 'Am I going to find work?' and 'Am I going
to hit the numbers?' Harlem's *Amsterdam-Star News*, after investigations as late as 1940, estimated the 'take' from these
rackets as approximately a million dollars annually.

These people were small-fry practitioners. None of them had the grandiose sweep and the magnificent scale of operations that characterized Father Divine's Peace Movement; nor had they his intuitive knowledge of the 'underdog' psychology. Undistinguished in appearance from other Negroes though he is, Divine is a middle-aged man, weary with adulation. He lives modestly and dresses stylishly — only his acts are flamboyant. Every costume is decorated with a stickpin made of a shiny five-dollar gold piece. Beyond riding about in the longest automobile in Harlem, and owning a scarlet monoplane in which he makes his rounds of the heavens, he is not considered ostentatious. Though he has an attractive, buxom wife, Mother Divine, he advocates celibacy. There is no record of a son of 'God.' He is opposed to smoking and drinking; but he is very much in favor of dancing and singing, and looks upon these as 'spiritual joys' which give the soul a lift. A Baptist fundamentalist at heart and in precept, he is in his teachings a 'God' in short pants.

So, indeed, is his program quite mortal. In simple terms, it is a sort of communal system of social security: 'One for all and all for one, but not for one who is not for all.' Once the penitents enter the fold, they surrender all their worldly goods — cash, real estate, stocks, bonds, insurance policies, even their furniture and clothes. Those who work for outside employers contribute to the kitty — the purse strings are held by Divine — and all share and share alike. Those who work in the heavens receive no salary, but are entitled to all the earthly benefits of the kingdom. So eminently successful was this venture that Divine became known the length and breadth of the nation, and his influence was felt in every Black Belt in America. In time, the movement became a world-wide affair.

There are no colors or races in heaven. Everyone lives on a basis of equality. 'God' plays no favorites. But this very fact caused the city authorities to frown upon the free mingling of whites and blacks. 'God' sidestepped official action by shrewdly eliminating the sexual element — there is a solemn injunction against sexual intercourse. Asked why she refused to leave heaven and return to her husband, whom she had deserted, one woman said, 'I can't live with my husband, it wouldn't be angelical.' How rigidly this is observed by everyone in heaven is open to much speculation. What is generally known, however, is that the sexes are carefully segregated. Consequently, white women and black women sleep and eat together, as do white men and black men. But everyone, when Father summons the flock, sings, dances, eats, and worships together. By introducing the no-sex taboo, Divine evolved a slick method of discipline which goes a long way in explaining the success of his movement.

Divine started off humbly. He was born, according to the best available sources, about sixty years ago on a rice plantation on Hutchinson's Island in the Savannah River. One follower described his age as 'not last year's calf.' Actually, no one has been able to pin down his age or birthplace exactly, for the obvious reason that only recently did the South begin to keep vital statistics about Negroes.

Sometime in the late eighteen-nineties Divine opened a meeting house in the Negro section of Savannah, Georgia, calling himself 'The Son of Righteousness.' His activities in this community ceased abruptly after trouble with the authorities. He later fled from Savannah to escape white hoodlums who aimed to make him prove himself the reincarnation of Christ by walking on the Savannah River, and turned up in Baltimore in 1906 as George Baker. At first he maintained a miserable existence by mowing lawns, cutting hedges, and doing other odd jobs. But a spark of ambition burned under his dark brown skin, and shortly thereafter he was teaching Sunday School. Inspired one night by a Negro Holy Roller called Father Jehovia, Baker began to think of himself as indeed divine. Then, gathering about him six men and six women, he made an evangelistic tour of the South. When the little preacher arrived in Valdosta, Georgia, he was declared insane and driven out of the South.

The little band set out for the Black Metropolis in 1915. Their leader detoured and instead took a place on Prince Street, Brooklyn, and set up a communal system to keep the wolf away from the door. George Baker, perhaps becoming convinced that he was no ordinary man, adopted the suggestive title, Major Morgan J. Divine. His stay here was relatively brief. Four years later he took his little flock to Sayville, Long Island — a well-upholstered white suburb — where he purchased an eight-room house and turned it into a mission. He obtained a license to conduct an employment agency to supply white residents with domestic help. On Sunday evenings he held prayer meetings, which were followed by a big banquet that lasted way into the morning.

The news spread, and the applicants for food and jobs multiplied. By 1930 his Sayville retreat was well known among Negroes on Long Island for its sumptuous feasts — given free of charge. In between his labors, Divine monkeyed around with giving aid to sick people. One night a white reporter happened into the vicinity and discovered this 'mystic' who healed the sick and performed 'miracles' — Divine became 'good copy' overnight. Bus companies enterprisingly began regular dollar-and-a-half round-trip excursions between Harlem and Sayville, not without advertising the blue-plate dinners that were to be had at the end of the line. The countryside began to reverberate with hallelujahs as a great abundance of delicious foods was devoured, nicely seasoned by preaching, dancing, chanting, and frequent hysterics as the celebrants 'got 'ligion.'

Such doings caused the white townsfolk to become alarmed, especially as Divine's followers began to overrun the area. They complained, too, of the mission's black-and-tan aspect — meaning, the intermingling of whites and blacks. Property-owners feared a sharp decline in real estate values and they

offered to buy Divine's mission place. He politely asked thirty
thousand dollars in cash to sell the dilapidated wooden building which housed his noisy followers. This, incidentally, was a
technique — the Negro-scare racket — he was later to follow
in acquiring large sums of money. Then the incensed Sayville
residents protested to the authorities, saying that a 'Harlem
colony' was rapidly being formed in the neighborhood. Divine
was arrested and tried in Mineola Court for maintaining a
public nuisance. He was convicted and sentenced to serve
one year in jail. Judge Lewis J. Smith, in passing the sentence,
was indiscreet enough to speak of him as 'a menace to society.'
Father Divine intoned: 'Pity the judge, he can't live long. He's
offended Almighty God!' Four days later Judge Smith died
suddenly, a victim of heart disease. The Negro preacher was
heard to say in his cell, 'I hated to do it!'

This was front-page stuff in the white as well as the Negro
newspapers. Divine's followers pointed to the enigma as evidence that he was omnipotent. After all, had he not 'worked a
miracle!' And it was at this point that Divine definitely acquired his reputation as 'God.' He adopted his present name,
and his converts created the maxim, 'Father Divine is God.'
Riding this publicity hard after his conviction was reversed
and he was released, Divine sold his Sayville place for a handsome price and brought his followers to Harlem. Five thousand persons packed into Rockland Palace, a local dance hall,
to see and hear this new messiah. 'God' was made.

Since 'God' has to conduct himself in the grand celestial
manner, he purchased a Turkish bathhouse in which to conduct his 'Get Happy' services. He installed himself in this becoming 'Heaven' and transformed his followers into 'angels.'
They adopted other-worldly names like Heavenly Patience,
Triumphant Virgin, Rose Memory, Immaculate Mary, Holy
Shinelight, Blessed Hope, Pearly Gates, and Beauty Smiles;
and others took names with a yum-yum quality — Happy
Sweets, Truth Delight, Delicious Mary. The fact is, they
registered and voted in New York under such sobriquets.

Before long there were a number of stores in operation —
groceries, barber shops, laundries, restaurants, and pressing
establishments — which on a minute's notice were turned into
halls of worship. And religion on the chain-store plan began
to function. For 'God' is liable to appear at any time of the
day or night and hold services. Every inch the modern messiah, Divine got himself a press agent and business associate, a
white man called Brother Lamb — spoken of as the 'White
Lamb' to distinguish him from a black Brother Lamb. Then,
Father bought a newspaper and named it *The New Day*, which
was printed in seven different languages, and later he established a magazine, *The Spoken Word*, which is edited with
studied incoherence. He resumed his sumptuous banquets,
feeding thousands of hungry people. As the movement
swelled, he bought more and more places in which to feed and
house his followers, and the chain of heavens spread-eagled the
community. They also were fabulously successful as business
ventures. By eliminating salaries, taxes, and even the possibil-
ity of union trouble in their operation, the heavens showed
excellent profits.

The Peace Mission Movement had been launched and
'Peace it's wonderful!' became the salutation. By 1935 Divine
figured he had two million followers. The actual figure was
nearer a half-million. His weekly income — obviously impossible to check — was reputed to be twenty thousand dollars,
derived from his business establishments in all parts of the
country and from large contributions made by a number of
wealthy white people. The latter connections enabled him
to spread the movement into suburban areas in a utopian
dream of a 'Promised Land.' His boldest stroke was the purchase of the Howland Spencer property at Krum Elbow,
opposite President Roosevelt's estate.

What happens when Divine acquires such a property was
illustrated in 1942 when he bought the Brigantine Hotel on
the island just north of Atlantic City, New Jersey, and opened

the first seashore Heaven. Several thousands of his flock were on hand to witness the dedication of the eleven-story structure and to inspect the reconditioned rooms that once rented for twelve dollars a day but under the new order went for two dollars a week. Father Divine presided over the dinner in the banquet hall at an H-shaped table. Only three hundred of the flock were able to crowd into the hall to hear his words, and the rest had to be content with listening via loudspeakers installed in the hotel corridors.

The new Heaven, whose corridors today re-echo to the chant of 'Peace!' was built in 1927 at a cost of one million dollars. Eighty-six followers bought it for a reported seventy-five thousand dollars and then offered it back to protesting Brigantine cottagers for five hundred thousand dollars, 'less furnishings' — the furnishings originally cost two hundred and fifty thousand dollars. Father Divine's own sanctuary is in the choice two suites on the third floor, facing the ocean. Under Divine's operation, all meals cost fifteen cents.

Harlem raised a fuss when he brought his gospel and gravy feasts into brocaded Block Beautiful, the stronghold of Negro society. Much indignation greeted the new Heaven. It was redecorated and hand-made signs were displayed, advertising a menu of hog maws, grits and greens at ten cents a plate — called the 'evangelical rate.' The upper floors of the building were altered for service as dormitories. Whenever 'God' made a personal appearance, the dining-room was converted into a worship hall. Overnight the tranquil atmosphere of the neighborhood was transformed. Odors drifting from Heaven — chitterlings, pork chops, and spareribs — gave additional offense, and above the greasy sizzling was heard 'Peace!' 'Peace!' 'Peace!' Nightly, the shouting, singing, and rhythmic handclapping kept up, exhausting the residents' patience. A Vigilance Committee was formed and an attempt made to oust Heaven — but they never got the cooperation of the authorities, nor had they enough money to buy 'God' out.

Divine is supreme in his Kingdom. But this was not accomplished without a struggle. He had sharp competition from other ambitious cult leaders. On one occasion, Divine threw a picket line of his followers around the headquarters of a rival. His most formidable opponent was Bishop Grace, known as 'Daddy Grace,' who attempted to steal 'God's' thunder by establishing a number of churches throughout the country, known as 'Houses of Prayer.' He began hijacking Divine's followers by vigorous spiritual enticement. The details of the early life of Daddy Grace are clothed in obscurity. His followers say he came from a 'land beyond the sea.' His profession of 'spiritual leader' has proved vastly profitable. It is reported that during a two-week session in Savannah, Georgia, in 1936, almost two thousand candidates were baptized at a charge of one dollar each. In the course of several years he amassed a fortune from what some Negroes call 'the Jesus racket.' His frequent clashes with the law over matters of an extremely worldly nature served only to increase the attendance and the collections, and also to give the Bishop much desired publicity.

Father Divine operates by remote control, but Daddy Grace is an intimate messiah. Walking among the congregation, he addresses his talks, now to one individual, now to another, dropping frequently into a broad Southern dialect. The theme of his movement is, 'Whatsoever a man soweth, that also shall he reap.' But often his sermons turn upon such this-worldly topics as politics, the war, anecdotes of his own journeys about the country, and his persecution by enemies, all of whom 'the Lord struck down dead.' Daddy advises strongly against trusting anyone. 'If the angel from Heaven comes down an' wants an extra pair of wings, don't trust him,' he warns. 'Tell him you ain't got no time to keep books today. He have to pay cash.' He visits each House of Prayer several times each year.

When he takes his leave, there is always much wild sobbing.

Daddy Grace, believed to possess unusual healing powers, was considered a 'bush arbor' preacher until he crashed the urban circuit. His entrance into Harlem was spectacular. He bought Divine's Heaven Number 1 — the Turkish bathhouse — and irreverently bounced the angels into the street. The deal by which he acquired the property was said to have been such as to bring him the disfavor of the authorities. Nevertheless he made a brilliant but brief attempt to win over Divine's angels. The House of Prayer in Harlem was garishly redecorated, the floors sprinkled with sawdust, and the stout posts padded to prevent injury to overzealous worshipers. With colorful garments and paraphernalia the new movement was launched. Revival services were held every night for a month, but the movement never made much impression on Harlem — Daddy Grace only *took* but never *gave!*

Divine is a generous 'God.' 'I thank you, Father!' There was the time, for instance, when he sent five hundred of his disciples to the public night schools to learn to read and write. Perhaps he had his eye on a political career — obviously one must read and write to vote. At any rate, Divine launched an International Righteous Government and auspiciously entered the political arena by supporting Fiorello H. La Guardia for mayor of New York City and Franklin D. Roosevelt for President. He made appeals for the release of Angelo Herndon, a Negro Communist held in Atlanta, Georgia, for inciting Negroes to insurrection, and for the release of the Scottsboro Boys. Then, Divine and his followers participated *en masse* in a 'People's Parade for Peace,' sponsored by the American League Against War and Fascism. Divine's most ambitious effort was to send 'A Bill to Abolish Lynching' to President Roosevelt, requesting that it be enacted. But somewhere along the line, the politicians offended 'God' and he withdrew from the political scene, vowing never to return.

Very early Father learned that being 'God' was no bed of roses. This fact he had impressed upon him by his frequent involvements in the mundane machinations of the law. A convention of the International Righteous Government, for example, was held at which he was proclaimed as 'the One and Only One God.' The lone dissenter in the auditorium was badly mangled by the angels, and Divine was dragged into court to explain why. When, on another occasion, the explosion of a heavenly oil stove caused the deaths of three angels, the city demanded an explanation. The beating and stabbing of a process server by Divine's disciples caused more headaches and more explanations. Litigations — the bane of his existence — produced additional woe. At one point, with no peace in heaven, 'God' became so disgusted that he announced to his flock, 'I may evaporate and disappear for nineteen hundred years!'

I went to see 'God' work a miracle. One day a man dashed into the Harlem office of a newspaper for which I was working, and breathlessly announced that Daddy Gray was dead and Father Divine was going to perform a miracle and bring him back to life. Daddy Gray, whose age was said to be 'near 'bout ninety,' was a beloved figure in Harlem and a devout disciple of Father Divine. Some years back he had acted the father's rôle in King Vidor's all-colored motion picture, *Hallelujah*. He had been unemployed since, which caused some people to say he had died of starvation.

When I came within sight of the brownstone tenement in which he lived, several hundred people were milling about the entrance. It seemed that the whole community had heard about the impending miracle. I pushed my way through the crowd and managed to get into Daddy Gray's grimy room. To my surprise, he was seated in a chair bolt upright and looked as much alive as anyone present. The ambulance doctor assured me, though, that he was very much dead. I, and several other newspapermen, sat down to wait for Divine.

We were anxious to see what hocus-pocus he would attempt, but he never arrived. The body remained in that upright position for two days, open to public view. The Board of Health finally put an end to this nonsense by hauling away the remains on the third day. Later, the Divine judgment was that Daddy Gray had led a sinful life and therefore he let him die. 'I hated to do it!'

Divine has indeed performed miracles, but of a much different kind. He has made honest, upright people out of gamblers, thieves, prostitutes, and felons. He has given some purpose to a lot of hopeless lives. He has done a great deal of good among the poor and neglected, and they, in turn, exhibit tremendous belief and faith in him.

An episode which took place in the office of the Department of Welfare in New Rochelle, New York, I believe, is typical. One of Divine's angels arrived at that office one morning and informed the officials that ten years ago she had received a three-dollar-and-a-half food order when she was in need and now she had come to pay 'her just debts.' 'Father says we must pay our just debts,' she said. 'The government has to do it and we all gotta do it.' Everyone was a little embarrassed, since old records were either stored away or not in existence at all. She was told that the office might not have a record of it; but she said, very decidedly, 'But I know it, and I want to pay it back.'

The woman had traveled all the way from Harlem. She said her name was Victoria Supreme. While the records were being searched, a few people, seeking amusement at her expense, began to question her. Someone asked, 'What kind of a man is Father Divine?' 'Man?' said she in fine scorn. 'He ain't no man. He's God! You ain't never seen no man do what he do!' Her manner was so magnificently sure, so poised, so confident, her enthusiasm so powerful, that smaller souls present began to feel sheepish. 'What he done?' she repeated. 'He taken care of the poor and sick, he git jobs for the people out of work, he give 'em shelter and warmth. I gotta beautiful place to live in and I don't have to ask nothin' of nobody.'

'Where does he get all his money?' another asked.

'He don't *need* no money!' she shouted. 'Where he git all his loving-kindness, he git all the money he needs in the same place. He feeds all those who are hungry. He sometimes has five banquets a day. If you're hungry, he'll feed you, too. And he won't have none of his people on relief. No sir!'

Near the Old Fort, situated in the extreme northeastern section of Savannah, there is a Peace Mission with a membership of about fifty persons who have never seen Father Divine. This little band worships in a small white building, whose wooden floor is thickly sprinkled with sawdust. Except for an old piano, the only furniture consists of several roughly built wooden benches. The walls are hung with placards bearing the inscription, 'PEACE, FATHER DIVINE IS GOD, SALUTATION IS PEACE.' About eight o'clock every evening they conduct services. The ardor of their meetings is not dampened by the fact that the native has never returned in the flesh. They claim that he is always present spiritually and can in this manner accomplish miracles. During these meetings, the converts intone their devotion to Father Divine and recount what he has done for them. Improvised hymns are sung to the accompaniment of the clapping of hands and the stamping of feet. Then, they whirl into a dance. Eyes half-closed, fixed smiles on their faces, every muscle quivering, they stumble on and on, bumping into benches and walls, until they fall exhausted to the floor. Nightly they praise 'God' in this fashion. They say Father Divine was not born, he was 'combusted' one day in Harlem.

One fact is inescapable. Unable to perform cash miracles, 'God' would soon cast bread on stagnant water. For, after all, the remarkable influence of Father Divine is explained in a large measure by the fact that he came along when economic conditions were such that free lodging, cheap meals, human companionship, and spiritual solace met real and fundamental needs. A movement of this character, once described as 'gaudy, metaphysical, and animistic,' also attracts a large element of crackpots and plain psychopathic cases. Indeed, the psychiatrists at Bellevue Hospital in New York City have revealed that numerous persons among Divine's followers have been treated for insanity. The subject has been a point of discussion in such publications as the *Journal of Abnormal and Social Psychology.*

Standing on a street corner in Harlem one day, watching a full-dress parade of Divine's followers, a former high official of the Back-to-Africa Movement pointed out to me many of them whom he knew personally as former Garveyites. I checked this lead by numerous interviews and visits to the Heavens and found this to be a pertinent fact. Essentially, Divine's following is drawn from the very wealthy white people and from the very poor and illiterate, both Negro and white. Though Father has received reams more press attention than any other Negro in America — except Joe Louis — his importance is dwarfed by the fact that his influence will hardly extend beyond the span of his lifetime. For one thing, the movement has no missionaries; and for another, there is no body of dogma to be explained to the multitude. He is chiefly significant as a social manifestation — that is, an acceleration of the search for the better way of life in a period of economic crisis. The fact is, Black America has been visited by several other men who claimed to be the Messiah, but they came in periods when Negroes were in no mood to listen.

Chapter VIII

What is Africa to me ...
Strong bronze men, or regal black
Women from whose loins I sprang.

— COUNTEE CULLEN

THE APOSTLES OF RACE

WITHOUT the fireworks of the Back-to-Africa organization or the gingerbread of the Divine mission, a sober, well-advertised movement fostering pride of race had been under way since early in the twenties. That racial esthete, Doctor Alain Locke, Negro critic and Howard University professor, celebrated the initial transformations in the inner life of Black America in his book, *The New Negro* (1925), by recording the 'dramatic flowering of a new race-spirit.' The movement extended into the thirties with greater power and vitality.

Today, Negro scholars zealously rewrite those chapters of history which ignore or minimize the part Negroes have played in the development of the United States. W. E. B. Du Bois, for example, reinterpreted the events of the Civil War and Reconstruction period in his book, *Black Reconstruction* (1935), to refute aspersions cast on the Negro. Some turned to Africa and sought the historic past of the race, and others concerned themselves with the implications and meanings in the Haitian Rebellion and with re-evaluating British colonial policy as it affected colored peoples. One pundit spoke of the journey of Negroes from the Dark Continent to America as *African Völkerwanderung!* Today solid contributions are being made on the Negro's racial heritage by such serious-minded groups as the American Negro Academy, the Negro Society for Historical Research, and the Association for the Study of Negro Life and History, which sponsors an annual 'Negro History Week.'

'The American Negro must remake his past in order to make his future,' said Arthur A. Schomburg, the Negro bibliophile. '. . . For him [the Negro], a group tradition must supply compensation for persecution, and pride of race the antidote for prejudice. History must restore what slavery took away, for it is the social damage of slavery that the present generation must repair and offset.'

At times, this movement almost took on the aspects of a vogue. Popular writers fictionized and some glamorized Negro figures in history. Formidable assault was made on the concept of the Negro as superstitious, lazy, happy-go-lucky, religious, ostentatious, loud and musical. To combat these stereotypes — sometimes even mouthed by Negroes themselves — intellectuals wrote and preached of Negro inventors, Negro senators, black leaders of slave rebellions, African kings and warriors. To give the canvas sweep and diversity, they included Negro prize-ring champions, Negro Kentucky Derby winners, black cowboys, and even Negro slaveholders and a 'Black Joan of Arc.' Composers, lyricists, and artists, too, had a fling at these racial themes — and more than one painter did a 'Black Christ' in oils. The pamphleteers, who performed much of the early spadework, dug into the past and recounted the contributions that Negroes had made to music, art, and the theater, and to science, medicine, and exploration. They demonstrated to the satisfaction of Negroes, who were hungry for status, that black men had achieved eminence and distinction in competition with white men.

Bespectacled J. A. Rogers, lecturer and traveler and once a member of Garvey's inner crowd, was — and is today — the most widely read pamphleteer in Black America, though rarely heard beyond the Negro world. Back in the heyday of the Back-to-Africa Movement, his writings were required reading — indeed, the injunction appears in the constitution and bylaws of the Universal Negro Improvement Association. Today, he is regarded by certain nationalist elements as something of a 'Black Karl Marx,' or theoretician of the race movement. I have seen black men literally sit at his feet to hear the 'Master' expound his theories of race. His importance in Negro life stems from the influence he exerts on the minds of many Negroes, though orthodox historians frown upon his work.

Tall, light-skinned and erect, Rogers served in the British Army and still walks with the swinging gait of a Coldstream Guard. He was born in Jamaica — the home of Marcus Garvey, whom he still vastly admires. He has spent a good deal of his life tramping across Europe and parts of Africa, searching for material concerning the lives of historical figures of Negro ancestry. While abroad he served as correspondent for several Negro publications here, which gave his work wide circulation among Negroes.

He is no pundit. Today, he is a columnist for the very down-to-earth Pittsburgh *Courier*, the most important and largest-selling Negro newspaper in the United States. He also edits a popular illustrated feature, 'Your History,' a sort of Believe-It-or-Not about Negroes whose achievements 'date back beyond the cotton fields of the South; back thousands of years beyond Christ.' His book, *From Superman to Man* (1924), published privately, was hailed by Marcus Garvey's newspaper, the *Negro World*, as 'The greatest book on the Negro we have ever read. It gives the young Negro the historical authority that his race founded great civilizations, ruled over areas as large as all Europe and was prolific in statesmen, scientists, poets, conquerors, religious and political leaders, arts, crafts, industry, and commerce when the white race was wallowing in barbarity or sunk in savagery and cannibalism.' At a dollar a book, it went into four editions and sold over ten thousand copies, and appeared serially in many Negro newspapers.

A typical work is his pamphlet, *100 Amazing Facts About the Negro*, which now is in its eighteenth edition. It is a small paper-covered copy of fifty pages, which sells for fifty cents, and is written in simple language, each 'fact' being tersely itemized in numerical fashion. It is the 'Bible' of soapbox speakers and lecturers throughout the country, and it is this group which provides his main source of distribution. Here are a few items chosen at random to illustrate:

> Beethoven, the world's greatest musician, was without doubt a dark mulatto. He was called 'The Black Spaniard.' His teacher, the immortal Joseph Haydn, who wrote the music for the former Austrian National Anthem, was colored, too.

> Ethiopians, that is Negroes, gave the world the first idea of right and wrong and thus laid the basis of religion, and of all true culture and civilization.

> There were three African Popes of Rome: Victor (189–199 A.D.); Melchiades (311–312); and St. Gelasius (496 A.D.). It was Melchiades who led Christianity to final triumph against the Roman Empire.

> Jean Baptiste Bernadotte, a colored man, was founder of the present royal family of Sweden. Enlisting as a private in Napoleon's army he rose to be field-marshal. In 1818 he ascended the throne of Sweden as Charles XIV.

Black nationalism, torn from its circus aspects, and made more palatable to a wider section of the Negro population, permeated every phase of Negro life. A group solidarity began to form, as Negroes developed new racial sentiments and loyalties, which cut sharply across the class lines of the community. How deep these roots had penetrated is reflected in the Negro's growing confidence in the ability of the race (and his leaders) to cope with whatever the future brings; and by a growing *world* consciousness, expressed in feelings of racial kinship with colored peoples elsewhere in the world. This development has brought about a unique racial morale, which today is being restimulated by the insecurity of the times.

These were the attitudes. But what actually remained of black nationalism as an organized movement, without the dynamic Garvey, fell into quarreling remnants. In time, though, a number of loud-mouthed charlatans, styling themselves 'race missionaries' and 'race apostles,' who preached according to the gospel of Marcus Garvey, leaped on the racial bandwagon and reorganized a section of the dispersed nationalist ranks. Their noisy activities served to keep black nationalism alive as a *movement*, and stimulate a recent expression of anti-Semitism.

Before discussing this complex feature of Negro life, we must examine the curious course of the nationalist organizations, those groups which evolved from them, and the factors which kept them in motion, for today they are the main sources of much anti-Jewish and pro-Japanese sentiment.

Perhaps the whole business of a *race* movement might have been forgotten under the impact of the Depression, or at least ceased to be an active force, and a *group* movement taken its place, had not Isaiah Morter, a wealthy Negro resident of Belize, British Honduras, left a will that cried for litigation. Back in the exciting days of the Back-to-Africa Movement, Marcus Garvey had elevated Mr. Morter to knighthood in the 'Court of Ethiopia.' When Sir Morter died in 1924, he left his entire estate, valued at three hundred thousand dollars in American money, to the U.N.I.A. expressly for the 'redemption of Africa.' It later developed that Sir Morter had lived somewhat in primitive luxury, and taken unto himself a number of concubines. The children of these women lost no time in contesting the will, and after four or five years of litigation, the case was taken to the courts in London, where it was decided that the estate belonged to the original U.N.I.A.

By this time Marcus Garvey had been deported from the United States, and had set up a new organization in the West Indies, which he called the parent body of the U.N.I.A. When he sought to obtain the money — as the London courts had directed — he found that Doctor Lionel Francis, who had seized the leadership of the movement in the United States, had already brought legal action to prevent his control of the estate. Once again the worldly goods of Sir Morter were wheeled into litigation. In time, the claimants became legion. With mushroom fecundity, new organizations sprang into lusty life, and traveling under some variation of the U.N.I.A. label, they all sought to share in the lush estate. Each insistently claimed to have *the* program for the 'Redemption of Africa.' Not until late in 1940 was the legal bickering brought to an end, when the courts handed the estate to Doctor Francis, who went off and disappeared in the tropics.

With the Italian assault on Ethiopia in the winter of 1935, a tailor-made issue arose for the racialists, one cut in nice precise proportions. Here, at long last, was some sort of tangible idealism — certainly a legitimate issue — around which the black nationalist could rally, and indeed rally a great section of the black population. They zestfully went into action on the issue that an independent black nation of Africa was being threatened with extinction. Almost immediately it put the nationalist organizations on sound agitational footing, and increased their memberships considerably. When white liberals and radicals took up the cry of Fascist aggression, the prestige of the nationalist groups was given a decided boost — which, as we shall see, proved to be a stinging boomerang.

White people wondered at the phenomenon of Negroes' being fiercely stirred by an affair abroad! Yet this was no new thing in Negro life. Once before Negroes had been aroused by struggles beyond the borders of the United States when black men in Haiti struck for freedom in 1791, and the distant but heroic figure of Toussaint l'Ouverture, black leader of the revolt, fired the imagination of the sore-beset American Negroes. In those days only Jefferson among the white leaders seemed to understand what was happening. 'The West Indies,' he remarked, 'appears to have given considerable impulse to the minds of the slaves in the United States.' Later, some thirteen thousand Negroes migrated to Haiti, whose constitution, while providing for exclusion of former slaveholding whites, had virtually invited 'every African, Indian, or their descendants, born in the [American] colonies,' to become citizens.

While the white population in the United States stood aloof from the Haitian revolt, it nevertheless had important effects on American affairs. Among other things, it directly forced Napoleon to sell the vast territory of Louisiana to the United States, beginning a new era of American development. So, too, did the Ethiopian struggle have profound effect upon the American scene — we know now that the Fascist attack on Ethiopia was one of the first shots fired in World War II!

Ethiopia, sometimes called 'The Switzerland of Africa,' covers an area larger than Italy and France combined. Its population, however, is slightly less than the total Negro population of the United States. A mountainous country, Ethiopia is one of the richest in natural resources, and was on the threshold of a modern development when the war began. Negroes first became aware of the black nation back in 1919, when Ethiopian dignitaries arrived in the United States on a diplomatic mission. The group included Dedjazmatch Nadou, who later was to be one of the signatories for Ethiopia when it was admitted to the League of Nations, and Belanghetta Herouy, the Mayor of Addis-Ababa and later Minister of Foreign Affairs. While staying in New York at the old Hotel Waldorf-Astoria, they received a delegation of Harlem citizens. From the Waldorf the group journeyed to the Metropolitan Baptist Church in Harlem, where addresses of welcome were made, not only in the name of Harlem but in the name of Black America. At the close of the ceremonies, the

audience was assembled in front of the church, where pictures
were taken with the Ethiopian delegation in a nice show of
racial unity.

In his parting message to Black America, Mayor Herouy,
through an attaché of the Persian Legation, had this to say:

> On the part of the Ethiopian Empire we desire to express the
> satisfaction we have felt on hearing of the wonderful progress
> Africans have made in this country. It gives us great confidence
> in the Government of the United States to know that through
> the independence given you by America, you have increased
> in numbers and developed in education and prosperity. We
> want you to remember us after we have returned to our native
> country.

Some eight years later, Doctor Azaz Wahrnek Martin, later
Ethiopian Envoy Extraordinary and Minister Plenipotentiary
to the Court of St. James's in London, came to the United
States on a special mission. While in New York he invited
American Negroes to come to Ethiopia as settlers. Also to encourage the migration of farmers, mechanics, engineers, physicians, dentists, and scientists, in an attempt to modernize the
ancient empire, Emperor Haile Selassie offered them free land
and high wages. Several hundred went to Ethiopia and in
1930 the Emperor appointed an American Negro, Doctor
John West, of Washington, D.C., as his personal physician;
made another American Negro, John Robinson, a Chicagoan,
his personal aviator; and a number of World War veterans
were given commissions in the Ethiopian Army. Even Negro
missionaries were welcomed. As the United States tumbled
further into the Depression, it is very likely that numbers of
other Negroes would have migrated to Africa, had not the
war interrupted.

Tall, tan, terrific Hubert Fauntleroy Julian, Harlem's
romancer extraordinary, fashion plate and daredevil of the
air, was one of those who popped up in Ethiopia. For the
dapper amateur flier's profitable love of his race encompassed

the whole world of black folk, and explains why he appeared wherever Negroes were troubled — a race missionary of individual persuasion. He first splashed across the front pages of the Negro press, when he showed up at a Back-to-Africa convention, with the tantalizing announcement that he would fly the Atlantic — the first man to attempt it, white or black. Next day the *Negro World* carried a banner headline: 'NEGRO AVIATOR ELECTRIFIES CONVENTION.' Somehow that flight never materialized. On another occasion, he attempted a transatlantic flight that ended in the mud-flats of Flushing Bay, Long Island. Before going to Ethiopia, however, he added to his fame by doing a parachute jump while garbed in the red tights of Mephistopheles and tooting a saxophone as he descended.

Burning with ambition to serve Ethiopia, he cabled the Emperor Selassie that he was coming to save the country. He arrived in Addis-Ababa clad in a gorgeous general's uniform — handiwork of a Fifth Avenue tailor and pranced about the capital in full regalia until the Ethiopian authorities made him take it off. Irrepressible, his other antics were equally fabulous. Once he made a touch on the Ethiopian treasurer of a few thousand francs, ostensibly to buy military supplies, and hurried off to Paris, where he splashed up the money in the fleshpots of Montmartre.

The straw that finally broke the back of the patient Ethiopians was Julian's bald announcement of his engagement to the Princess Tashi, the Emperor's daughter — though he himself was much married to a Harlemite. In despair, the Emperor finally decided to send him to the front, but Julian fell desperately ill. A friend who was on the scene tells me that when last seen in Ethiopia, Harlem's playboy had a pack of creditors howling at his heels as he ran for the train out and away from Addis-Ababa. He returned to the United States calling himself Huberto Fauntleroyana Juliano. To-day the reconstructed Julian is a sergeant in the United State:

Army Air Corps. The Negro press, which he had so often bilked, celebrated the occasion of his enlistment with a spread of pictures detailing his life in the Army — perhaps as proof for the army of unbelievers.

From the beginning the Ethiopian crisis became a fundamental question in Negro life. It was all but impossible for Negro leaders to remain neutral, and the position they took toward the conflict became a fundamental test. The survival of the black nation became the topic of angry debate in poolrooms, barber shops, and taverns. Emperor Haile Selassie I was hailed by some Negroes as the new 'messiah' — one writer described him as 'a black edition of the pictured Christ.'

The Ethiopians had asked, in a public letter to American Negroes, that 'an independent Red Cross of colored peoples act with other groups for us.' In Harlem the response took the form of the United Aid for Ethiopia, a group organized to collect funds for war relief. A mass meeting was held at Madison Square Garden which attracted more than twenty thousand people. Later the International Council of Friends of Ethiopia was organized with the historian Doctor Willis N. Huggins as executive secretary. In 1933 Ras Desta Demtou, Haile Selassie's son-in-law, while visiting New York, placed a golden ring on Huggins's finger and bade him 'Keep Ethiopia alive in the hearts of the American blacks.' Afterward Huggins took a leading part in all Ethiopian affairs in the United States.

No figures are available as to the council's actual following, but Doctor Huggins went abroad in 1935, representing it at the League of Nations in behalf of Ethiopia. The four points raised by the council are of contemporary interest. It held that Fascist destruction of Ethiopia would (1) put the peace of the world in peril, (2) provide strong arguments for the spread of subversive political theories, (3) increase the hollow mockery of the professions of Christianity, thus bringing more and deeper disgrace to Christian principles, and (4) increase the guilt of modern Christian nations 'who, yesterday, raped Africa and carried away millions of her children to be enslaved in the Americas.'

When Doctor Maluku Bayen, a native Ethiopian, arrived in the United States in 1936 as the Emperor's official representative, the United Aid to Ethiopia was dissolved, other similar groups coordinated, and a new and more substantial organization was formed, the Ethiopian World Federation, Inc. With broader political objectives, it became a national organization. The Emperor's gesture to racial brotherhood was not lost on Negroes! Its New York membership, drawn largely from the nationalist ranks, formed the basic element of the movement. Subsequently, a weekly organ was established, the *Voice of Ethiopia*, which was rabidly pro-Negro as well as pro-Ethiopia.

The organization conducted vigorous propaganda meetings in nearly every city where Negroes resided in any numbers, and race missionaries were dispatched to the small cities to set up locals. The membership was kept abreast of developments through the organization's newspaper, and, in turn, the locals kept the home office informed of their activities. The Wichita, Kansas, Local No. 16, for example, reported in the *Voice* 'enthusiastic attendance' at its meetings. At one of its affairs, the guest speaker was a man 'who taught Black History in the l'Ouverture Opportunity School.' The correspondent was optimistic. 'We feel that ours is a unit that will stand.' Today, the Ethiopian World Federation is in existence as a healthy national entity, with Finley Wilson, Grand Exalted Ruler of the Negro Elks, at its head — which perhaps suggests the drift of Negro thinking these days.

There is no doubt that wild currents of racialism, whipped up by the race apostles of the U.N.I.A. groups, among other things, spotlighted white exploitation of darker peoples. Colored peoples everywhere began grumbling loudly about white imperialism and oppression. Haile Selassie is quoted as saying, 'We cannot cut up Ethiopia like a cake, handing sugared parts to this and that country just to win their smiles and satisfy their sweet tooth.' And querulous editorials of this same character appeared in the *Voice of Ethiopia:* 'What are we, the Sons of Freedom, going to do about the modern slavery? Will we suffer quietly this economic slavery? Will we suffer quietly the robbing and enslavement of Africa? Will we let Mussolini get away with his brigandage? Black men are to decide. Shall the words "Shame and Cowardice" be branded on our foreheads, or will we take up arms for liberty?'

I know of no event in recent times that stirred the rank-and-file of Negroes more than the Italo-Ethiopian War. Doctor Huggins once said it marked Ethiopia's return to the black race. Finding insufficient material in the white dailies, Negroes were eager for information about Ethiopia, its people, and the progress of the war. The *Courier* enterprisingly dispatched J. A. Rogers to the Ethiopian war front, and in a matter of months doubled its circulation. When Rogers returned to the United States, he published a provocative illustrated brochure, *The Real Facts About Ethiopia*, shrewdly devoting a whole section to the subject, 'Of What Race Are the Ethiopians?' It was an immediate best-seller. As a war correspondent, he was in great demand on the lecture platform in Negro communities, and went on an extensive and profitable tour throughout the states in the South and Midwest.

Rumors that the Ethiopians were *not* Negroes nearly ended the unity of black men in this country with those in Africa. Doctor Bayen, himself a distinctly Negroid type, attempted to counteract such propaganda with the explanation that the Ethiopians reject the term 'Negro' because of its connotation of slavery. But this, he added, did not prevent the Ethiopians from aligning themselves with American Negroes in blood brotherhood because of common ancestry. This statement — coming straight from the horse's mouth, so to speak — was wholly reassuring to the nationalist elements in this country. The fact is, Ethiopians think of themselves as a *nation*, and not as a *race*.

Even Doctor Huggins had gone abroad, prior to the outbreak of war, and visited the chief Ethiopian legations to check the 'racial classification' of the Ethiopians. He was told, he reported, that 'The Emperor is very conscious of the fact that he is today the only Black Sovereign in the world, and he considers himself as the natural leader of the (black) Negro race. He is fond of repeating the phrase that "Ethiopia is the trustee for the future of the black races." '

Clearly, Negroes in America had cast their lot with colored peoples elsewhere in the world!

Chapter IX

*Those of us who are active in this work are at
a loss for a reason why the police andother agencies are so opposed to this campaign . . . the In-
spector of Police has warned some of our members that he will break up these meetings, even
if he has to bring 5000 more police to Harlem
and shoot down every speaker . . .*

— FROM OPEN LETTER DISTRIBUTED
BY HARLEM LABOR UNION, INC.

THE JOBS-FOR-NEGROES
CAMPAIGN

WHILE the Negro's eyes were lifted toward a racial utopia of
some sort, the Depression had picked his pocket of its final
shekel. Along with the heat about Ethiopia, mass-action organizations sprang up to grapple with the stern realities of
every day living. This movement, an aspect of the Negro's new
racialism, was not confined to any one city but was in fact
national in sweep — though actions were localized — and
came to be known as the Jobs-for-Negroes Campaign. The
gains made were not momentous but they were significant of
a trend. Actually, and more important, the campaign served
to dramatize the unemployment problems of Negroes and
served as well further to stimulate racial unity.

The movement had its first expression in the Midwest, and
as it swept east gathered momentum. In St. Louis, for example, when a white-owned chain store which did business almost
exclusively with Negroes refused to employ Negro help, the
local Urban League organized a boycott. Later, this campaign extended to the employment of Negroes in trucking

companies and bakeries, and as motion-picture operators in houses that catered to Negroes. A Negro Housewives' League was formed by the Pittsburgh *Courier* to demonstrate the buying power of Negro customers to white advertisers. When one large dairy company, which served Negroes, refused to hire them, the Housewives' League launched a boycott that caused the company's sales to drop alarmingly.

The Jobs-for-Negroes movement reached terrific, often bloody proportions in Chicago, where it was led by the Illinois Civic Association. The campaign had the support of the entire Negro community, and particularly of the aggressive Chicago *Whip*, a Negro weekly, and of the powerful Pilgrim Baptist Church, of which the Reverend J. C. Austin is pastor. Chicago's South Side seethed with resentment against the chain and department stores, whose absentee ownership often frustrated the Negro's demands. Picket lines became a noisy feature of life in Chicago's Black Belt, and served to keep feeling pitched at fever heat. Eventually, Negroes were given jobs in these stores and the movement was broadened to include bread, beer, whiskey, and milk companies. It spread to Cleveland, where the Future Outlook League had set a similar campaign in motion. Down in Baltimore, meanwhile, a job campaign was in full swing and finally a boycott of the public utilities took place. Here the Prophet Costonie, university-educated part-time clairvoyant, was the moving spirit. In nearly every Negro community of any considerable size there was an economic drive of some character.

Biggest of these mass-action drives was the one launched in Harlem, and it had a profound effect upon affairs in Black America. In the summer of 1933, the Citizens' League for Fair Play was organized by the Reverend John H. Johnson, former Columbia University basketball star and rector of Saint Martin's Protestant Episcopal Church, and Fred R. Moore, editor and publisher of the New York *Age*, a Harlem weekly. It attempted to persuade white merchants doing busi-

ness in the community to employ Negroes, and argued — as
other groups had argued elsewhere in the country — that
white businessmen in the Negro neighborhood received the
bulk of their trade from Negroes and therefore should employ
them.

To strengthen its argument, the league started a campaign
to collect the sales receipts of purchases made at stores that
were the targets of this drive. A typical case occurred at
Blumstein's, the largest department store in Harlem. One
morning a neatly tied bundle was thrown on the desk of William Blumstein, the store's owner. He remained adamant to
requests or persuasion to employ Negroes as clerical workers
and salesgirls. As a sponsor of Negro charitable institutions,
and as the employer of Negro elevator operators, porters, and
maids, he explained that he had done his share for Negroes, and
refused to budge an inch in response to the demand for more
jobs.

Months of similar negotiations with other shopkeepers led
nowhere. Finally the league began to picket the stores on
125th Street, Harlem's main shopping district, and a vigorous
boycott was carried on with the slogan, 'Don't Buy Where You
Can't Work!' A store that did not employ Negro help in any
capacity was labeled 'lily-white.' Some hotheads charged
the white merchants with committing 'a crime' against the
community in not employing Negroes. Street meetings were
held and the soapbox agitators — race missionaries whom the
league had attracted — swung into action. Needless to say,
they warmed to the task at hand. Harlem supported the
drive, loudly and wholeheartedly. Everyone in the community, it seemed, participated in the boycott, even to giving
social affairs to raise funds.

Business dropped to the vanishing point — with a good
deal of strong feeling on both sides. The white merchants
changed their attitude somewhat, and a handful of young
Negroes were placed in jobs as salesclerks. But as soon as the

league relaxed its vigilance, they lost their jobs. The A. S. Beck Shoe Corporation added fuel to the fire by seeking a court injunction to restrain picketing by the league.

Indignation soared, with two main currents feeding the mounting discontent: the war in Ethiopia and the Jobs-for-Negroes Campaign. Both were going badly for black men. In nightly harangues along Harlem's highways, the nationalist elements who were a large factor in the movement charged the league's leaders with not having conducted the fight aggressively. They pointed to the undeniable fact that the white merchants still had shown little intention (or faith) to cooperate with the community. The leaders of the league — all responsible men — began to lose prestige with the rank-and-file.

Yet they were powerless to meet the situation, for the organization they led was not a trade union, nor was it prepared for the strong-arm tactics of industrial strife. The league was merely the outgrowth of a spontaneous movement, loosely formed, and supported financially by popular contributions. It thus was hardly equipped — physically or psychologically — to meet the problems inherent in employer-employee relations, which were further confused by the dark specter of race. What remained of the league's influence with Negroes rested on the tricky quicksand of goodwill — but the white merchants unwisely did little to give it support.

About this time, the movement brought forward a number of dangerous men. One of these was a crude racketeering giant who entered the confused, defeated ranks, posing as an evangelist of black labor. He was Sufi Abdul Hamid, who drew heavily on the Koran for authority but who made his appeals in the streamlined terms of modern Harlem. He was propelled by a slick Negro press agent named Ace Parker. In short order Sufi brought about a stormy revival of the jobs campaign.

By now, one would think that Harlem was satiated with

bizarre characters. But when the huge statuesque figure of Sufi, with his brown bearded face and searching eyes, resplendently dressed in turban, green velvet blouse, Sam Browne belt, riding habit, patent leather boots, and wearing a black crimson-lined cape carelessly around his shoulders, strode out on Lenox Avenue, he was an immediate sensation. He set up offices in a loft at 135th Street, which served as a combination meeting hall, butcher-shop, and grocery store. There he established the Negro Industrial Clerical Alliance, and — as Harlem would say — the panic was on!

From a stepladder platform on Lenox Avenue, an area where people were suffering most acutely the pangs of the Depression, he harangued crowds with some truth and much steam about the millions of dollars Negroes poured into the coffers of white retail merchants. He pointed to the stores and charged their white proprietors with 'taking the Negroes' money!' He impressed hundreds with such preachings, always of course interspersing them with high-sounding platitudes. Dramatically he would point to the doorways of the stores, and in his deep, rumbling voice, cry, 'Share the jobs!'

A motley crowd joined his organization, at one dollar a head per month for the promise of a job — if and when. The bulk of his followers were hoodlums, idlers, relief recipients, and a discouraged fringe of high-school and college graduates, not to mention the numbers who ordinarily lived by their wits and hoped to enrich themselves at the expense of the gullible. All these people were dispatched to street corners to carry on the leg work of agitation.

Harlem reeled dizzily under the rain of propaganda. No business owned by a white man was too small, or too big, for them to tackle. They swept through the community and put the heat under grocers, druggists, butchers, and owners of other small establishments, bludgeoning them into signing up with the Sufi organization — which, in fact, meant paying tribute for 'protection' against violence. The 'take' was sev-

eral hundred dollars a week. These roughhouse tactics drove
the white merchants into the lap of the conservative Citizens'
League, which once more was able to place a few young people
in jobs. But Sufi's roughnecks kicked up a fuss because 'only
light-colored Negroes were employed.'

The boycott grew, but broke out in bitter racial discord,
with, curiously enough, the Jew bearing the brunt of the
attack — though quite a few Greeks, Italians, and Irishmen
also had establishments in the community. But since the large
majority of Harlem storekeepers are Jewish, the campaign for
jobs soon assumed the ominous proportions of a crusade
against Jews. Thoroughly alarmed, the Jews branded Sufi as
a 'Black Hitler' or 'Harlem Hitler' — which, as Stanley High
observed correctly, displeased neither Sufi nor his followers —
indeed, eyewitnesses reported seeing Nazi agents make direct
contact with him. His chief lieutenant, Francis Minor, a vivid,
intense young man, was labeled a 'Goering.'

Soon after, Sufi was haled into court on charges of fomenting racial strife between Negroes and Jews — for Negroes
now were less cheerful when they shopped on 125th Street.
Edgar H. Burman, commander of the Jewish Anti-Nazi Minute Men, appeared as a witness against him and accused the
Harlem agitator of anti-Semitic acts of violence. Sufi was
freed after a three-day trial. 'From this point,' he told me
wearily, 'I stepped out of public life.'

Actually, Sufi only stepped beyond the reaches of the law.
His troubles began anew when he wooed and married in a
'ninety-nine-year' pact the rich Madame Stephanie St. Clair,
a policy queen with a French accent. A temperamental lady
from the West Indies, she ended the whirlwind romance
abruptly — at the point of a gun. And Sufi returned to the
hocus-pocus of cultdom, as the safest of occupations.

Before his arrival in Harlem, Sufi had been known to Chicago's South Side as Bishop Conshankin, a Buddhist missionary and a devotee of Oriental magic. But in the Black Me-

tropolis he passed simply as an itinerant prophet and Egyptian scholar who spoke Arabic and Greek. With some suddenly acquired money — some said he had been bought off by the white merchants — he purchased an airplane, hired a white female secretary, indulged himself in the luxury of a mistress of Oriental extraction, and erected a gaudy temple of worship. He became His Holiness Bishop Amiru Al-Mu-Minin Sufi A. Hamid, head of the Universal Holy Temple of Tranquillity. But this glamorous life was cut short when he was killed in an airplane accident. The none-too-glamorous police records revealed his true identity: he was plain Eugene Brown, born on Lombard Street in Philadelphia.

Anti-Semitic propaganda, which began with the street fulminations of Sufi, did not end with his demise. Even before his death, two accomplished street agitators, dark and lanky Ira Kemp and black, stockily built Arthur Reed, had formed the Harlem Labor Union, Inc., to obtain jobs for Negroes. The crusade against Jews now took on a fierce character. From soapboxes, they echoed every Hitleresque charge against the Jewish community, merely giving their utterances a local twist to fit the propaganda needs at hand. They flirted with the Christian Front movement, even to sending emissaries with feelers for funds. How successful they were in these missions is open to speculation. But the fact is, the attack broadened in time to include not alone Harlem merchants but Jewish labor leaders and Bronx housewives who employed Negro help. In attempting to mobilize Negroes on a trade-union, dues-paying basis, they became a thorn in the side of organized labor.

Both Kemp and Reed were self-styled race missionaries, who leaned heavily on Garvey's teachings and sought to form Negroes into a black phalanx against the white community. Arthur Reed, the general organizer, a former youth leader in the Back-to-Africa Movement, was — and still is — a master of inflammatory invective, and was perhaps the more effective of the two. A brilliant street speaker, with a sure knowledge of idiomatic phrasing, he had an unfailing talent for arousing Negroes to action.

He began his career as a race missionary heading a firm which manufactured black baby dolls, and did a thriving business until the Pan-African Movement collapsed, leaving him stranded. Eventually he turned up as president of the African Patriotic League, and later as head of the African Business League. His influence rested on the fact that he was a member of that section of nationalists who advocated the development of Negro business — that is, whenever the white merchants refused to employ Negro help. He was able to reach a respectable section of the community, and even to gain the tacit support of at least one important Negro newspaper.

His preachings, in fact, dovetailed nicely with the programs that had already been started. As early as 1930, Albon Holsey, secretary of the National Negro Business League, organized more than one hundred Negro-owned stores into the Colored Merchants' Association, a group known as the C.M.A. Stores. By buying merchandise cooperatively, the group hoped to undersell the white merchants and eventually to eliminate them as competitors. An attempt also was made to harness Harlem's buying power by organizing the Housewives' League and directing its purchasing to Negro establishments. But two years later both the league and the C.M.A. Stores, which had developed into a national organization, were wiped out by the Depression — and the white merchants kept rollin' along. The remaining Negro-owned stores then attempted to capture Negro trade by an appeal to 'race loyalty.' As a lure to Negroes, during the job campaign, they hung out such signs as 'This Place Owned and Operated by Negroes,' and some managed to turn an aroused racial feeling into cash — but they still enjoy no discernible degree of trade monopoly.

Meanwhile, the jobs campaign had gathered new momentum and was moving along at a terrific pace, highlighted by its attendant anti-Jewish propaganda, which, by now, had reached the point where anti-Semitic handbills, bearing bogus union labels, were openly distributed in the community. Those who had the temerity to cross the Harlem Labor Union's picket lines were roughly handled by thugs. The group was successful in obtaining only a few jobs. Beyond this, the impression that the Harlem Labor Union made is indicated by the fact that its president, Ira Kemp, was chosen by the Republican politicians — those solid realists — as the party's candidate for the State Assembly. What is more important, however, is that he lost by only the barest margin — which perhaps suggests Harlem's turn of mind. At any rate, he died before he could cash in on his unrealized popularity.

Kemp's associate, Arthur Reed, is today a free-lance agitator. The Harlem Labor Union, after many clashes with the law, has gone into the hands of new leaders who today keep the jobs campaign very much alive.

Chapter X

It would be a mistake to conclude that there is a Negro-Jewish problem in the nation. There is not. The Jews are simply the victims of an overdose of the anti-white psychology unfortunately gripping the large mass of Negroes. . . .
— CHANDLER OWEN

JEWS IN NEGRO LIFE

ANTI-SEMITISM among Negroes is complex and curious, and essentially an *artificial* issue, revolving around *manufactured* enemies. Yet it is a very real problem, and as such should be given the widest airing.

Anti-Jewish sentiment among Negroes — to throw the whole question into proper perspective — is a very recent manifestation, perhaps about ten years old. At first it was hardly more than faint gossip, uneasy rumor, an almost imperceptible feeler radiating from the Back-to-Africa Movement. Its effect upon Negroes was negligible. Yet a steady trickle of propaganda continued which emanated from the splinters of the movement after its collapse. The fact is, Marcus Garvey was the first Negro leader to raise the 'Jewish question' in Negro life. He disclaimed being anti-Semitic, but he spoke of 'Jewish control' of the Negro's economic life.

The rise of Hitler in Germany threw blazing focus on the Jews, giving momentum to propaganda against Jewry in the United States. Its overtones were heard in the Negro community. Against this background was the Depression, with thousands of Negroes facing actual starvation. With the ar-

rival of Jewish refugees, few though they were, stories circulated that they would eventually take the jobs of Negroes, and
the concern of Negroes was doubled by the fact that tradition-
ally they are the last hired and first fired. A few refugees did
replace Negroes, but the number was infinitesimal. Nevertheless the rumor persisted that wholesale dismissals would follow.
Finally, when Negroes sought to obtain employment within
the limited orbit of the Negro community — as we have seen
— they eventually were brought into headlong clash with the
small shopkeepers, who were mostly Jews. Together, these
developments made the 'issue.'

Actually, the whole business of anti-Jewish sentiment among
Negroes is largely an urban manifestation, and stems directly
from the Negro's own depressed condition socially and economically, and is essentially an *anti-white* manifestation. To
begin with, the Northern Negro comes into contact with the
white race, and thus *white* discrimination and *white* antipathy,
at four vital points: fellow worker, landlord, merchant, and
employer. It is within these areas that the friction between
whites and blacks exists. By some unique accident, it is the
Jew who is today the Negro's main point of contact with the
white race — landlord, merchant, employer, and, to a small
degree, the professional people. Thus the treatment which
the Negro experiences from the white group is mainly at the
hands of Jews.

Back in the last century, when Negroes were in daily competition with the Irish, conflicts arose between them. Most
of the early race riots in New York City involved the Negroes
and the Irish. Much of the bitter feeling that existed between the two groups was caused by external factors, beyond
the control of both. The Irishman had two strikes against
him when he stepped off the boat as an immigrant: he joined
the most depressed elements in the country and, in addition,
he was mainly of the Roman Catholic faith in a country predominantly and aggressively Protestant. Much of the Eng-

lishman's prejudice toward the Irish people had leaped across the ocean and entered the cultural stream of American life, eventually becoming a very real issue. The opportunities of the Irish were sharply restricted until Tammany Hall championed their cause. Yet, at the same time, they quickly absorbed American attitudes toward the Negro.

Negroes, naturally enough, adopted the prevalent prejudice against the Irish. Antipathy between the groups lasted for almost a century; that is, until the Irish were able to lift themselves up by their bootstraps. The bitter feeling which once existed has pretty much passed. Beyond longshoreman and seaman work, Negroes are no longer in sharp competition with the Irish. Thus the Irish people have ceased to be the Negro's immediate contact with the white race. The progressive leadership of the trade unions in these occupations, as well as the pointed educational programs launched by the Roman Catholic Church in the last ten years, has played a large part in eliminating overt racial conflict.

Despite the important merchandising services rendered the Negro communities by Jews, who have shown keen knowledge of the small consumer's needs and psychology, the merchant-consumer relation is nevertheless a chief source of anti-Jewish feeling.

I asked a Negro businessman in Harlem his opinion about this. He began by saying that the Negro's limited buying power was really the source of friction. He illustrated this point by citing the practice of buying merchandise on the installment plan, which the Jews introduced into Negro life. Back in the days when the average Negro was earning eight to ten dollars a week, and a suit of clothes cost twenty dollars, only by the most rigid saving was he able to amass the entire amount to make the purchase, and this often took more than a year. Now, by installment buying, even with the very smallest alary, a Negro is able to lift his standard of living considerably. One of the big furniture outfits maintains a large Harlem store with a haberdashery department, where a man's shirt costing the customer two dollars is sold on the installment plan — fifty cents as an initial payment and twenty-five cents a week plus interest and charges until the balance is paid. But the Negro's inability to meet regularly any kind of payments creates irritability; and, if pressed for payment, he is stirred to anger, which is expressed in hostility to the merchant.

Yet, to flip the other side of the coin, it is a fact that the retail stores in Negro neighborhoods overcharge outrageously. For a number of years the Negro press has campaigned against what it calls 'fleecing.' Investigations conducted by responsible agencies have revealed the fact that the merchandise sold in Negro communities is usually second-grade stuff — stale bread, tainted meats, defective furniture, and damaged garments — and the prices excessive. Furthermore, the Negro housewife loudly complains of dishonest weighing and short-changing. Because the merchants in Negro neighborhoods are mainly Jewish, these charges are placed at the Jews' doorstep. Obviously, sharp business practices are common to all merchants, gentiles as well as Jews.

The pattern is somewhat the same in housing. Not Jews alone, but the entire white Christian community herd Negroes into Black Belts by refusing to rent them dwellings outside of a rigidly circumscribed area. This Jim Crow policy has been reinforced by public opinion, residential covenants, 'lily-white' agreements among the property-owners, and indeed by actual violence. This situation is not of the Jew's making, nor is it of his inspiration, but he receives much of the abuse intended for all whites.

No statistics exist to determine how many Jews actually own the properties in which Negroes live. More often it is a bank or large real estate interest which owns the property, and institutes a form of absentee landlordship. Housing authorities regard the number of properties owned by Jews as extremely small. Thus it is impossible to prove anything about Jewish landlords on a basis of records. Actually, it is either the renting agents or rent collectors with whom Negroes have contact, and since many of these are Jewish, the popular belief prevails in Negro neighborhoods that the large majority of the landlords are Jewish. So prevalent is the belief that agitators can easily charge the Jews with responsibility for the Negro's housing plight. When a Negro tenant complains of exorbitant rents, much-needed repairs, inadequate service, and indeed the unfairness of it all, and no way to improve his condition, his resentments are directed at the white persons nearest at hand — and thus he charges the rent collector with 'gouging' and 'rent-hogging.'

But the most inflammatory point of friction is the employer-employee relation. The so-called Bronx Slave Markets in New York once were the symbols of this conflict. Unable to find positions through regular employment agencies or daily newspapers during the Depression, Negro women journeyed to the Bronx in search of a day's work as domestics. After frequent complaints of exploitation Ella Baker and Marvel Cooke, both experienced Negro newspaper reporters, visited the areas, and describe their experiences in a magazine article. They found the women seeking work, posed wearily against buildings and lampposts, or scuttling about in attempts to retrieve discarded boxes upon which to rest while they waited for bidders. 'Not only is human labor bartered and sold for slave wages,' the reporters said, 'but human love is also a marketable commodity. Whether it is labor or love, the women arrive as early as eight A.M. and remain as late as one P.M. or until they are hired. In rain or shine, hot or cold, they wait to work for ten, fifteen, and twenty cents per hour.'

The tales told by the domestic workers themselves followed a fairly uniform pattern. They complained of being overworked for low pay, under rigid supervision, and finally of having to haggle over the money due them. The employers had complaints, too. Together, they served to sharpen the friction. Harlem agitators, meanwhile, pointed to the Bronx Slave Markets as 'Exhibit A' of Jewish exploitation.

These street-corner markets became a public scandal, after attention was focused on them by the Negro and white press, and attempts were made to combat the conditions by Jews as well as non-Jews. The Bronx Citizens' Committee for the Improvement of Domestic Employees was organized specifically to tackle this problem. A semi-official group, the Committee on Street-Corner Markets, made a careful investigation which was productive of some changes. It found, among other things, that such free labor 'markets' existed in every large city in the country (with or without Jewish populations) and were known to the nation as early as 1834. The committee held — correctly ignoring the Jewish element — that the street-corner markets were an economic phenomenon, arising out of the urgent necessity of workers for jobs and the need or desire for cheap labor of employers of low-income groups, who perhaps could not employ help otherwise. 'The markets,' it observed, 'are a part of the whole economic picture of employment, and cannot be considered apart from it.'

This problem was eased somewhat when Mayor La Guardia, responding to public clamor, opened employment offices in convenient areas of the Bronx. The Harlem agitators still fumed. The mayor, they complained, had merely 'put a shed over the markets,' for conditions remained the same. Actually, there was improvement. Civic and social organizations began educational programs designed to reorientate the attitudes and habits among the Bronx housewives of hiring domestic help. A fundamental contribution was made by the Domestic Workers' Union, a section of the Building Service Employees' Union, which made considerable headway in organizing the Negro workers and in establishing standard rates of pay.

The pawnshops, owned almost entirely by Jews in the Negro neighborhoods, constitute another phase of the problem. Using a suit of clothes as collateral, to borrow two dollars for a month, for example, one must pay a dollar for 'storage' plus the usual interest rate. Negroes complain that the pawnbroker, aware that Negroes are unable to borrow money elsewhere because they have little valuable collateral or steady employment, drives a hard and unfair bargain by taking advantage of the situation.

Contrary to the popular assumption among Negroes, there are among the Jews individuals who have dared, at the risk of economic and social injury to themselves, to extend to Negroes counsel, fellowship, money, and overt support. Many Negro doctors are indebted to the Jewish medical men for opportunities to practice in some of the country's largest hospitals. It is generally accepted by Negroes in Washington that Nathan Straus, former Administrator of the United States Housing Authority, who was attacked as a Jew on the floor of Congress, was forced to resign his post in 1942 because of his liberalism toward Negroes (as well as toward other underprivileged groups). W. M. Kiplinger, Washington editor, finds that the 'Jewish question' is closely related to the 'Negro question' in the minds of many Southern members of Congress.

Being of very recent vintage, anti-Semitism has hardly penetrated the surface of the Negro's thinking, and thus has little or no roots; though, as observed by Doctor L. D. Reddick, Negro curator of the Schomburg Collection of Negro Literature, 'There is, to be sure, a small body of rhymes in the folklore which stems from the anti-Jewish elements in the Christian tradition.' If these have been translated into active opinions, it certainly is not apparent in Negro life, he says.

Negroes have never been associated with any overt forms of anti-Semitism, such as the 'Buy from Christians' movement, though attempts have been made to enlist their support, even to plastering stickers and posters on the buildings and subway stations in Negro neighborhoods. Actually, a good deal of the anti-Jewish feeling is stimulated by unscrupulous Negroes, and Axis agents — both white and Negro — who seek to exploit the Negro community's legitimate grievances. For example, a street meeting is held ostensibly as a 'rent protest,' presumably sponsored by responsible people, but somehow the affair quickly turns into an anti-Semitic demonstration, with certain speakers vilifying the 'Jewish landlords' and indeed lauding Hitler. 'Captain' Carlos Cook, a Harlem race missionary picked up by the F.B.I. in 1942 while addressing such a gathering, was heard to say in referring to Hitler that 'What he's trying to do, we're trying to do!' Vicious sheets like *Dynamite*, which had a brief life in Chicago some years back, and the *Negro Youth*, a recent product of extreme nationalist elements in Harlem, also contribute a very large share to the anti-Jewish feeling. Yet, there are no organized movements supported even tacitly by any large section of the Negro community.

A point which race agitators dwell on, and with much effect, is that Jews — a persecuted people — support the existing prejudice of the white community against black men. While it is true that as a group Jewish people in America have *not* adopted the Jim Crow attitudes of non-Jewish whites, there are among the Jews those who have followed the pattern in their thinking and daily lives and in the conduct of their business.

In the minds of most Negroes, the Jews are a separate and distinct unit from the white community and, as a 'Jewish community,' expected to take unified and liberal action. Yet the irony in this is the fact that actually no 'Jewish community' exists — that is, not in the sense that there is a Negro community. Jews are, in fact, as diverse in their thinking as non-Jews. (I have been told that in New York State alone there are well over two hundred and fifty different Jewish organizations, each with its own particular program, concerned with solving the 'Jewish problem.') Nor is there any such thing as a Jewish cell, unit, or cabal; and neither is it true that *all* Jews 'stick together' — there are, to cite an obvious example, Jewish Communists as well as Jewish capitalists.

What most Negroes do not clearly understand — and many whites too — is that the Jews in the United States have never had an all-inclusive organization that spoke for all Jews; nor is there one today. Their sharply different backgrounds and economic, social, and cultural levels have made unity of all the Jewish people impossible. Moreover, the opportunities for education, access to varied careers, equal treatment before the law, and the ability to maintain social relations of equality outside a Jewish community have adjusted them to existing American patterns. This of course implies, among other things, prejudice against blacks. Thus the Jews find themselves in an anomalous position. They are, as a group of people, generally among the most liberal elements in the white community. Yet to give full expression to liberal convictions is to bring down the wrath of the white reactionaries. Not to be liberal is to be damned by Negroes and all other underprivileged groups.

Negroes contend, however, that anti-Negro sentiments among Jews are indefensible. Yet the Jews have never been enemies of the Negro people; nor, on the other hand, have they ever presented a solid front with Negroes against the failure of American society to grant equal rights to the Negro. They have indeed tended to identify themselves with the non-Jewish whites, and to adopt attitudes of white superiority. Essentially, according to Louis Harap, Jews have perhaps erred by omission rather than by commission.

In canvassing organizations, both Jewish and non-Jewish, which were interested in democratic rights, and concerned, too, with actively combatting anti-Semitism among Negroes, I asked the officials what programs had they set in motion to combat anti-Negro sentiment among Jews. At first, they were surprised, for apparently no one in the organizations had thought much about the anti-Negro problem. Finally, they admitted that nothing was being done. Beyond a few articles which appeared in the Jewish *Daily Forward*, I found that very little had been written on the subject in Jewish newspapers until recently, nor had any articles appeared in Anglo-Jewish periodicals.

Today forthright action is being taken by pulpit, press, and civic groups as the danger signals of Hitlerism at home flicker ominously. One organization, in a straightforward statement to the Jews, urged the end of anti-Negroism as a means of counteracting anti-Semitism among Negroes. As an initial step, it recommended that Jews doing business in Negro communities should be persuaded to end their 'shortsighted relationships' and that, if necessary, a survey should be made of their business methods and attitudes. It urged that more Jewish leaders become interested in the Negro's problems. 'For the Jews to link themselves with the Jim Crow psychology,' it wisely concluded, 'and battle to keep the Negro "in his place," would ultimately hurt all minority groups.'

The fact is, thousands of Jews — but not necessarily as Jews — are members of every liberal organization which has as its objective the extension of democracy to Negroes as well as to other groups. Jews were among the founders of the National Association for the Advancement of Colored People and the National Urban League, and are today among the heaviest contributors to these largest of the organizations championing the cause of the Negro. It is a well-known fact that Jews and foundations established by Jews have given liberally to the education of Negroes in the South, and to the cultural advancement of the whole race. The Julius Rosenwald Fund, to name one, specifically offers fellowships to Negro scholars and scientists to enable them to do further study.

In spite of the critical comment from Negroes, they still have a great admiration for the Jewish people — so much so that they often seek to emulate them. Negroes see an example in the fact that the Jews are not the *servants* of the community, but in many instances its *leaders*. And the fact that the Jews have risen to the governor's mansion and to the United States Supreme Court bench gives the Negro hope. The expression is frequently heard in Negro life, 'Look at the Jew!' meaning, 'Look at what the Jew has accomplished, in spite of being dispossessed, broken, scattered and harried everywhere and in every century!' Negroes frankly envy the ability of the Jew to survive and even to prosper in hostile communities. Today many Negro intellectuals boldly advocate that the Negroes adopt the Jew's techniques of survival.

Until 1938 agitators held the floor. That year a full discussion of Negro-Jewish relations began among Negroes, and Black America's vision was sharpened thereby. Writing in the *Amsterdam-Star News*, Claude McKay, Negro poet and novelist, held that 'American Jewry is a very important part of the oppressing white majority,' and 'more than any other whites, the Jewish group touched the vital life of the colored minority,' through their 'control' of houses in which Negroes live and shops in which they buy and seek jobs. 'But this is a labor and social issue,' he concluded, 'that should not involve anti-Semitism.' Langston Hughes, Negro poet and playwright, asked, 'How can the average public-school Negro be expected to understand the exigencies of the capitalist system as it applies to both Jew and gentile in America ... since both groups act strangely like Hitlerian Aryans ... when it comes to colored folks?' Yet, he observed, Negroes often share space with Jews on anti-Semitic, anti-Catholic, and anti-Negro leaflets.

With the erection of racial barriers and quotas to limit the number of Jews entering the professional schools throughout the country, a number of Jews turned to the Negro institutions for their professional education. Howard University's medical school, one of the leading Negro institutions in America, had twice as many Jewish applicants in 1935 as Negro applicants. Of a student body of one hundred and ninety-five that year, sixteen were Jews, two white gentiles, and the rest Negroes. The number of Jewish applicants has increased every year since, and though the number is small, Jewish refugee professors have also found a place teaching in Negro schools.

Recently pulpit and press have united in aggressively opposing anti-Semitism among Negroes. A characteristic statement came from Elmer A. Carter, editor of *Opportunity* magazine, organ of the National Urban League, who called upon Negroes to stop anti-Semitism from taking root. A tangible expression of the trend was evidenced when the congregation of a large Harlem church contributed a substantial sum of money to the Joint Distribution Committee to help aid the Jewish refugees. In the campaign to combat anti-Semitism among Negroes, *The Crisis*, magazine of the N.A.A.C.P., brought the prestige of its pages to the movement. It published, among other articles, a series entitled 'Jewish Friends of Negro Emancipation,' by Rabbi Harry Essig and Leonard Greenberg, which recounted the rôle of the Jewish abolitionists in the fight to emancipate the slaves.

Early in 1942, the *Amsterdam-Star News* commented editorially that the racial persecutions by Hitler should make every Jew 'seek an immediate alliance with colored Americans.' This statement sounded a note that has risen to a clamor in the Negro press. So today, relations between Jews and Negroes have entered a totally new phase. Some Negro intellectuals seek not only to end discord between Negroes and Jews, but to weld the two peoples into a united and aggressive unit to struggle against Hitlerism at home and abroad. Indeed, a section of the Negro community has started a campaign to establish what is described as 'racial *rapprochement*.' Negro advocates of such a movement say that the two peoples, aligned with other liberal forces, would be a formidable unit for progressive action.

This line of thinking has emerged out of certain gains that Negroes have made as a race, which they feel have also been beneficial to the Jews. They cite as an example the President's Committe on Fair Employment Practices, outlawing discrimination because of race, creed, color, or national origin in war industries and government services, which was established by President Roosevelt as a result of agitation by Negroes. The Pittsburgh *Courier* stated rather petulantly late in 1942, when the life of F.E.P.C. was threatened, that the 'Jews should *fight* with us if they hope to share the benefits of our fighting.' The same day this comment appeared, the *Amsterdam-Star News* was saying editorially that Negroes and Jews 'could both well afford to rid themselves of adopted prejudices and band together on a common front.'

The trouble with this kind of reasoning, as Doctor Reddick, a chief proponent of the racial *rapprochement* idea, himself observes, is that the Jews in the United States are fighting to *maintain* their rights, whereas Negroes are fighting to *win* theirs. The two struggles, many Jews feel, are on entirely different levels. An analogous situation arose before the Civil War, when Negro abolitionists sought somewhat unsuccessfully to enlist the suffragist movement in support of the anti-slavery movement on the ground that both movements were essentially fighting the same battle.

The need for some such unity is beginning to be felt by some Jews. Louis Harap reported in *The Negro Quarterly* that the Committee on Justice and Peace of the Central Conference of American Rabbis in 1942 demanded 'Justice for Negroes.' The statement was widely reprinted in the Anglo-Jewish press. A more aggressive statement, according to Harap, appeared in *The National Jewish Monthly*, organ of B'nai B'rith, the largest Jewish fraternal order in the United States, which held that 'Jews should be foremost in the practice of justice in dealing with the Negro and always vocal in protest whenever the Negro's rights are abridged.' *The Jewish Survey*, a monthly magazine founded recently, has opened its columns to discussion of mutual problems by both Negroes and Jews. Individual Jews, however, have gone much farther than Jewish institutions with the racial unity idea, and this is evidenced by a growing understanding between the groups.

A pleasant incident occurred in the spring of 1942 which deeply touched Negroes in Pittsfield, Massachusetts — perhaps illustrative of this new understanding. Members of a little Negro Baptist church in that city — so the story goes — could not pay a twenty-four-hundred-dollar mortgage when it fell due. The deacons reported the church's plight to the holder of the mortgage, the Beth Israel Synagogue of Springfield, Massachusetts. The situation was explained to the synagogue's congregation, and the members promptly voted to burn the mortgage, so that the Negro church would not have to close.

The inability of Negroes to achieve this racial *rapprochement*, however, may very well serve to restimulate anti-Jewish sentiment, for they most likely will conclude that the Jews are opposed to their aspirations. Without something approaching racial unity, the only other way to end anti-Jewish feeling among Negroes, it appears, is to get at the root of the Negro's social and economic problems. For the condition of chronic unemployment and inadequately paying jobs, which a few charlatans capitalize upon for their own gain, is essentially what ails Black America. Obviously, this is a problem that cannot be solved overnight. For the present, then, anti-Semitic agitators must be silenced, and greater momentum given the movement to end anti-Negroism among the Jews.

The large mass of Negroes, it is well known, have long been wedded to American ideals and therefore are basically not anti-Jewish. What traces of anti-Semitism exist among Negroes are not based on (or even inspired by) religious differences. For if this were true, certainly the Black Jews would be the *first* victims of anti-Semitism among Negroes.

Chapter XI

In keeping with the sacred custom and rites of centuries, Harlem's Black Jews joined with their [white] co-religionists throughout the world in celebrating the 5702d anniversary of Jewish liberation from Egyptian bondage. Their observances started with the sounding of the Ram's Horn at sunset. . . .

— NEWS ITEM, 'AMSTERDAM-STAR NEWS'

FOUND: THE LOST TRIBE OF BLACK JEWS

SOME twenty years ago, when a slight, black, almost effeminate African Jew, who spoke Hebrew, Arabic, and German as well as English, gathered together eleven of his black *landsmen* to worship in a Harlem basement, the first Negro synagogue came into being in the Black Metropolis — and, more important, people suddenly became aware of the existence of thousands of Negro Jews scattered throughout the country.

In those days, I remember distinctly, sections of Harlem were essentially Jewish in character, abounding in kosher butcher shops, Yiddish theaters, Hebrew schools, and Jewish delicatessen stores. Lilly Daché was operating a popular hat shop on Lenox Avenue; Nettie Rosenstein was turning out dress creations off on a side street; and crowds gathered nightly for tasty snacks at The Pomerantz Delicatessen. Along the sidewalks, people stumbled over fat housewives who sat on chairs in an almost endless row, their amiable chatting punctuated occasionally by the shrill cry of a neglected baby. In the background hovered Stars of Zion, standing squat and sturdy above countless temples.

Yet the Black Jews were without adequate quarters for worship; nor were they lucky enough to inherit one of the deserted houses of prayer when the white Jews made a pell-mell exodus to the Bronx and Brooklyn as Negroes by the thousand surged into Harlem. Unable to raise the necessary sum to purchase one of the vacant temples, the Black Jews were forced to remain in their makeshift place of worship and watch the black Baptists take over the temples.

These were indeed the 'Jews without money!'

Today that hardy little band of Black Jews has expanded to a determined congregation of more than five thousand souls, known as the Commandment Keepers, and is living a rigid, self-sufficient communal life according to the solemn dictates of the Talmud. Independent of white Jews, they maintain a second-floor *schul*, Beth Hatphala Number 1, in the loft of a red-brick tenement on Lenox Avenue. Here a Talmud Torah, or Hebrew school for Jewish children, is conducted in conjunction with the synagogue; and here, too, there is a Yeshiva, or college for adults and advanced students. The group supports a Beth Zekanim, a home for Jewish aged; maintains its own burial grounds, and controls a number of small businesses. From Friday sundown to Saturday sunset, men, women, and children abstain from all manner of work and assemble in their synagogue, passing the time in prayer.

Truckloads of nonsense have been written about Harlem cults. At first glance the congregation of Black Jews is often dismissed as yet another religious freak. Even Negroes ask, 'Why does a black man want to be a Jew, and pile more trouble on his head?' It may indeed seem a strange phenomenon to white people, if not downright fraud. But white Jewish circles acknowledge the existence of Black Jews and their kinship to the Jewish community. Rabbi Levinger, in his authoritative *The Story of the Jew*, describes them as a tribe 'who have almost forgotten their Judaism, and in every way but a few religious rites resemble the dark-skinned, thick-lipped [African] natives among whom they have lived so long.' Harlem's Black Jews, in the view of Jewish scholars, are the descendants of the Falashas, whose form of worship is distinct from white Jewry, influenced as it is by African culture. As far as I can learn, white and black Jews are branches of the same tree, with striking similarities as well as curious dissimilarities.

As to be expected, the history of the Black Jews goes back a long way. The legend — according to Jewish authorities — is that about twenty-six hundred years ago a band of Jews, fleeing from Palestine, which was then under the oppressive rule of the Babylonians, sought refuge in Egypt and along the cataracts of the Nile. They pushed on into the deserts of Africa and ultimately penetrated the highlands of Ethiopia, where they became known as Falashas, or outsiders. They designated themselves as Beth-Israel — the House of Israel.

The wanderings of this tribe are still clouded in obscurity. But it appears that from time to time the group was augmented by refugees whose lands had been conquered by the Romans, and toward the end of the fifth century, by others escaping the wars of the Ethiopians. These people gathered in the same province, almost the same centers, and fused finally into a single community. Protected by the mountains and supported by natives converted to Judaism (and assimilated), they evolved a small independent state, and this independence they maintained for hundreds of years. The Falashas played a prominent rôle in raising the material and intellectual stand ards of their adopted country by strict adherence to the faith of their forefathers. A self-reliant and self-supporting people they earned their livelihood as farmers, blacksmiths, masons potters, weavers, tanners, saddlers, and basket-makers; an others, curiously enough, as mercenaries. Until modern time the Falashas were virtually the only skilled workers in Ethiopi

When Christianity was adopted by Ethiopia in 333 A.D., the lot of the Black Jews changed radically. Thousands of them were ruthlessly slaughtered and many compelled to embrace the new religion. Others were driven from their lands and scattered in search of new abodes in more hospitable — and indeed more inaccessible — sections of Ethiopia. Century after century they persevered as Jews. Eventually the number of Falashas, estimated originally at several hundred thousand, dwindled to a mere remnant. Many Jewish centers were completely dissolved, imperiling the continued existence of the entire Falasha community. Today only sixty thousand live in Ethiopia — a country in which every fourth person belongs to the priesthood. Traits that these long-isolated people have exhibited are those that their white co-religionists have come to accept as inherent characteristics of Judaism: cohesion, unity, industry, thirst for knowledge, long-suffering fortitude under persecution.

For centuries the Black Jews regarded themselves as the only surviving Jews, living in entire ignorance of the existence of any other Jews — white or black. Nor had world Jewry at large any inkling of the Falashas' existence in the hills of Ethiopia. They were first discovered by James Bruce, a Scotch traveler who brought the story back to London in 1790. Not until the early part of this century, when Doctor Jacques Faitlovitch, a European Jew, organized an expedition and penetrated the interior of that country, was the first actual contact made with them by European Jews. He reported to white Jewry when he returned that though their skins were 'black,' they 'possessed the characteristics of our [Jewish] race.' Family life, he said, was patriarchal; great respect for parents was shown by children; there were no bachelors, nor was concubinage or polygamy tolerated; and all professed the same faith, practiced the same customs, and everyone lived on a basis of equality. Soon after this journey, Faitlovitch founded a movement, according to his own words 'to further the efforts for the spiritual redemption of the Abyssinian Jews.' The movement was transferred to the United States in 1922, and the American Pro-Falasha Committee was organized and sponsored by prominent white Jews.

Besides the Falashas, there are three distinct tribes of Black Jews in existence — the Sudanese Jews, the Black Jews of Cochin, and the Beni Israel of India, apparently descendants of the Jews who migrated to Asia and Africa after the final destruction of Jerusalem. The Jews of Soudan are mainly a scattering of small tribes who resemble the Arabs. Moslems once called them Yahoodee, meaning Jews. A unique group are the Beni Israel — the Black Jews of India, who know very little of their own history. They are said to be the descendants of the Jews who were sent to India by King Solomon to capture elephants and to work in the gold mines. Today they are indistinguishable from the natives. Perhaps the most famous are the Black Jews of Cochin, with a strong Chinese strain, who live in Bombay, maintain a thriving temple and number about eight thousand. Unmistakable traces of Hebraic influence among the various African tribes are found to survive even to this day — evidenced by the groups called 'Judaized tribes' and 'Judeo-Negroes,' whose existence helps to document certain survivals of Hebrewism among African Negroes.

Arrival of the first Black Jews in America probably coincides with the early days of colonization, when they might have been shipped here among other African captives to work the plantations. Only a rare handful was ever seen in this country. Yet as early as the turn of the last century, according to the records of the Common Council, Black Abyssinian Jews immigrated to the United States as free men to escape anti-Semitism abroad and opened a synagogue in lower Manhattan, where they observed freely all the traditions and customs of Judaism. There is no record of their ever having disbanded, nor is there any trace of their descendants. Whether they left this city to join a Zionist movement then active that sought to establish a Promised Land outside of Buffalo, or eventually were absorbed by the black population (or the white), is a moot question. But considerable speculation surrounds the fact that in 1808, in a wooden shack on Waverly Place, eighteen black men from Abyssinia started the Abyssinian Baptist Church, a Negro institution that is in lusty existence today.

It is obviously impossible to check the numbers of Black Jews that have entered the country. But a census taken in 1938 quoted by the *Jewish Family Journal*, and so far as I know the only one ever taken, estimates the Black Jewish population in New York City at ten thousand, and another hundred thousand scattered throughout the United States, in such principal centers as Salt Lake City, Cincinnati, Youngstown, Philadelphia, Newark, and St. Louis. There are perhaps a quarter-million living in the Western Hemisphere. Some authorities say that there are more than three million black adherents of the Jewish faith living in Africa today.

Until Hitler began to persecute the Jews in Germany, and American newspapers dramatized the atrocities, Harlem's Black Jews were denounced as imposters, fakers, and fools; their bearded rabbi was excluded from *Who's Who in Colored America*, and local wits irreverently called him Rasputin. The majority of white Jews hardly knew of their existence, nor was there any manifest concern when the fact was mentioned. The one Jewish organization aware of Black Jews had its eyes turned toward Addis Ababa, Ethiopia, where it was supporting a Hebrew school. Today, however, the Black Jews have gained status, a status born of the persecution of their white co-religionists. Their dignified rabbi, Wentworth Arthur Matthew, is frequently invited to conduct services in the white synagogues about the city, and he has been a candidate at the yearly elections for delegates to the American Jewish Congress. A few Negro Jews have been admitted to the Cantors' Association of America. The United Yeshivos

Foundation, when raising funds for white Jewish colleges in recent years, has shown sympathetic interest in the educational work of the Harlem tribe. They also receive favorable attention from the Negro newspapers, which devote considerable space to reporting the events of the holy days. The Jewish press is no less interested nowadays. Before the holy days in 1941, one publication carried a full-page picture of the black rabbi on its Yiddish title page.

The organizer and spiritual head of Harlem's congregation, Rabbi Matthew, is a picturesque and attractive character. He is a grave, intelligent black man who appears to be about fifty years of age with the vigor of a man of thirty. He dresses in severe black — definitely unusual in Harlem — and wears the traditional yarmelke, or skullcap. He looks like one of the Negro figures in Rubens's *Bacchanale*.

His origins are humble. He was born of poor laboring parents in Lagos, British West Africa, center of a large colony of Black Jews, and was given the Hebrew name, Yoseh Ben Moshea Benyehuda. His father was a Falasha, or African Negro Jew, and his mother a Christian whose father had been a slave in Nevis, B.W.I., and had returned to Africa with his family when the British Emancipation Act freed him. The mother of Harlem's rabbi met and married the cobbler Benyehuda in Lagos. How Harlem's rabbi comes to have the name 'Wentworth Arthur Matthew' is plausible: English traders, finding the elder Benyehuda's name difficult to pronounce, called him simply 'Matthew's man,' after his white employer. His mother adopted the name after the death of her husband and her return to the West Indies with her son. Later, young Matthew tacked on the 'Wentworth Arthur' to give it an 'English sound.'

He is eminently prepared to lead his flock. Shortly after going to the West Indies, he left and came to New York, where he entered the Hayden Theological Seminary and later the Bishop Ecclesiastical School, both Christian institutions. But when he suddenly heard the 'call' to Judaism — a period he recalls as the most thrilling of his life — he enrolled at the Rose of Sharon Theological Seminary in Cincinnati, an institution once conducted by Falashas. He returned to Harlem in 1919 and organized the congregation of Commandment Keepers, of which he is now chief rabbi. Five years later he went abroad to study theology at the University of Berlin, on a scholarship obtained for him by an influential white rabbi. In his absence, Rabbi Arnold Josiah Ford, a Negro immigrant from Barbadoes, a Garvey follower who later migrated to Ethiopia to join his African co-religionists, carried on his work until 1927, when Rabbi Matthew returned to his flock and his rabbinical chores.

Harlem's Black Jews do not practice conversion, and in this they follow strictly the dictates of their faith — yet many of the followers are former 'Garveyites.' The chief factor in swelling the congregation — though Rabbi Matthew did not mention it — was the phenomenal growth in Harlem's Negro population. The law of averages alone would have brought a few Black Jews to the community, but hundreds seemed to have arrived to make their fortunes in the Black Metropolis. They came largely from the West Indies, where it is said more than a hundred thousand live, and from faraway Africa. To build the Commandment Keepers, I was told, only 'enlightening' was necessary, a fine distinction that Rabbi Matthew explained in an interview with the Pittsburgh *Courier*.

'The black man is a Jew,' he said, 'because he is a direct lineal descendant of Abraham. Isaac, son of Abraham, was father of Esau (whose skin was hairy, like the white man's) and of Jacob (whose skin was smooth, like the black man's).

'Jacob, also known as Israel, was the father of the Twelve Tribes, and King Solomon, son of David, was a great-grandson in the Tribe of Judah. King Solomon mated with the Queen of Sheba, who returned to Africa, where she bore him a son, known in Biblical history as Menelik I.

'When Menelik was thirteen years of age,' Rabbi Matthew continued, 'he was sent to Palestine to be confirmed. And at the age of twenty-four his father sent him to Ethiopia to colonize that country as part of the great King Solomon empire. That household has ruled continuously in Ethiopia for three-thousand-odd years. There has been an unbroken succession of six hundred and thirteen kings from Menelik I to the present Haile Selassie ("King of the Tribe of Judah"). Hence, all genuine Jews are black men.'

That the kings of Ethiopia have sworn allegiance to the Coptic Christian Church is a fact that Rabbi Matthew dismisses as the result of a diplomatic appeasement policy. This interpretation of their history settles the ancestry and racial loyalties of the Black Jews, and condition their outlook upon the contemporary scene. For example, the Black Jews do not acknowledge themselves to be 'Negroes.'

'Don't submit meekly to being called a Negro,' Rabbi Matthew has been heard to admonish his flock. 'The Negro, so-called, has no history prior to the fourteenth century. And when that history began, it began in bondage, poverty, humiliation, and degradation. Insist on being called an *Ethiopian*, an *African*, or even an *Afro-American*. As such, yours is the most glorious history in the world. You are descended from kings, and the white man knows it. It is his purpose to keep you ignorant of your past so that he can exploit you. That is why he has falsified the history of the world.'

In practices of Judaism, however, there is little difference from white Jews. The rite of B'rith or circumcision is performed on the eighth day after the birth of a child. The ritual is done by white rabbis or mohelim only. It is in this one respect that Harlem's rabbi confesses to a lack of recognition. This rite, however, is the only one delegated to a white rabbi. Otherwise, Rabbi Matthew officiates at all religious services, appoints functionaries, and has the power of ordaining new rabbis. Besides himself, there are nine ordained Negro rabbis and two elders who assist in ministering to the Commandment Keepers.

At their *schul*, during the holy days, strict orthodox services are conducted by Rabbi Matthew, who recites much of the Hebrew Holy Scriptures from memory. He is assisted by a seventeen-year-old Negro cantor who sings the litany. To accommodate the entire membership of 5702, it is necessary to hold services from six o'clock in the morning until nine at night. Those who live in New Jersey, Brooklyn, Bronx, Long Island, or other outlying sections, and would have to travel to Harlem in violation of certain Jewish tenets, are provided with rooms above the synagogue so that they may stay overnight. A sprinkling of white Jewish merchants, who live in the neighborhood, often join their colored co-religionists in worship. (The white Rabbi Philip Goodman, of the Harlem Institutional Synagogue, at 37 West 116th Street — which serves white Jews primarily — reports that a number of unaffiliated Negro Jews attend his services, Hebrew school, and institutional activities.)

During the observance of Yom Kippur, the Day of Atonement and most sacred day in the Jewish religious calendar, the women attend services wearing white trailing veils; the men dress in ordinary business suits and wear their hats. When I attended the services, a soft light flickered from the ornamental Menorah, or seven-candle candelabra, and gave the low-ceilinged synagogue a quiet, subdued air — decidedly rare for Negro worship. But this loftiness was quickly dispelled when the whole congregation lifted its voice in the plaintive chant of the hallowed hymn, *Kol Nidre*. Suddenly, they flung their hands up in supplication — throwing startling shadows against the isinglass-covered windows. If you have seen the Reuben Mamoulian-directed 'Wake Scene' from *Porgy and Bess*, then you have a fair idea of what that temple was like.

Harlem's Black Jews, like their more successful white

brethren, seek to be self-sufficient. They have built up fifty-odd business establishments that include cigar and stationery stores, tailor shops, laundries, a gas-range repair shop, and restaurants serving kosher dishes. They patronize almost exclusively stores owned by Jews, whether white or Negro; and wherever possible, Black Jewish merchants employ Jews. There is also a similarity of employments: the Negro Jews are garment workers, painters, plumbers, and carpenters; Rabbi Matthew himself once earned his living as a carpenter. A few are Yiddish-speaking dairy salesmen.

But from here sharply vivid differences enter: not one Black Jew is a night-club entertainer, musician, or actor — traditional occupations of the Negro that attract many white Jews. The bulk of them, unlike white Jews but like most Negroes, are employed as domestics — not as ordinary domestics, however; they are 'certified kosher cooks'(!) and carefully observe all the Jewish dietary laws, even to the use of separate dishes, towels, and soaps. But they work for orthodox Jews only. Few will accept employment with Reformed Jews because they do not maintain 'kosher homes.' Although the killing and preparation of meats is an all-important rite of Jewish life, there are no butchers in the congregation of the Commandant Keepers, so they must depend on the white kosher markets, which of course is little hardship.

'Not more than three or four Black Jews have ever received public relief,' Rabbi Matthew says in his proud comment on his congregation's self-sufficiency. 'And,' he adds, 'no member of our connection has ever been arrested for a felony or misdemeanor.'

These people are rational and law-abiding. They do not drink, fight, or quarrel among themselves. Nor will they quarrel with anyone else, particularly about their faith — in this respect, they follow their rabbi's solemn admonition not to argue religion. Nowadays there is, of course, general recognition and respect for their beliefs in the community. Negro

Jewish children who attend the public schools of Harlem are excused from classes during the holy days like other children of the Jewish faith — the Board of Education makes no distinction between Black and white Jews. The Jewish youth move normally in the stream of community life, even to stomping at the Savoy Ballroom.

Negro characteristics curiously enough thread through their practice of Judaism (as witness 'certified kosher cooks'). During the Jewish holidays, bearded rabbis attired in orthodox ceremonial robes proudly lead the faithful in processions through the community, on their way to the Lenox Avenue temple. Through membership in Masonic lodges, affiliated with the Royal Order of Ethiopian Hebrews, they also march in colorful parades that provide the community with highlights during its marching season (from April to October). Through these lodges also they are in constant touch with other Black Jews throughout the country.

White and Black Jews draw their culture, religion, and philosophy from the same sources, yet they have little contact with each other, beyond perfunctory business and employer-employee relationships. There is of course an occasional social meeting. When the Educational Alliance staged a Yiddish show, *A Night in Harlem*, the Black Jews were invited. Certainly, no antagonism exists between the groups. Rabbi Matthew is frank to say, 'The white Jews regard us very, very sympathetically.' However, sheer principle makes the Black Jews prefer not to have social relationships with white Jews, an attitude that once caused their rabbi to be roundly criticized by the *Daily Forward*, a Jewish newspaper.

The Black Jews are particularly against 'crossing tribal traits.' This was the case when a white Jew approached Rabbi Matthew about his plans to marry a Negro woman of the Jewish faith. The marriage was opposed, as the amiable little rabbi put it, on the ground that 'Each of the Twelve Tribes of Israel should strive to preserve its own traits.' But when a Black Jewish woman sought to marry a white Jew, after assuring her rabbi that the prospective bridegroom earned sufficient money to support her in style, he sagely gave his approval and indeed performed the ceremony. 'Since she was outside the breeding age, I could give my consent without violating the unwritten law,' he explained blandly.

The Black Jews oppose intermarriage for a deeper and more significant reason, a reason they share in common with other Negroes of whatever faith. The exigencies of American life, they believe, make the conditions of such a relationship prohibitive. Yet, to be sure, they feel a genuine kinship to the white Jews — especially in the broad question of anti-Semitism, although they themselves have felt its lash in a minor way only. They are alarmed, too, by the anti-Jewish disclosures in recent years, because they feel that if anti-Semitism takes solid root in the United States, they will suffer doubly — 'Not only as Jews,' Rabbi Matthew says candidly, 'but even as so-called Negroes.'

In their efforts to stamp out anti-Semitism, the Black Jews have actively taken up the cudgels of white Jewry by holding anti-Nazi meetings in Harlem to bring the menace of Naziism and Fascism before the Negro public, and many have contributed to and participated in anti-Fascist organizations. Rabbi Matthew is quick to defend white Jews against the charge that they are exploiters of the Negro, and attributes the appearance of anti-Jewish feeling in Harlem to the careless expressions of street speakers, both white and Negro, who seek to capitalize upon the desperate condition of the Negro people.

'We are determined,' he says, 'to put our shoulders to the wheel and cooperate with white Jews in driving out anti-Semitism wherever it may be found in America; for in doing so we shall be protecting ourselves.'

Yet — to illustrate further the complex character of anti-Semitism in Negro life — the Black Jews have aligned themselves with organizations like the U.N.I.A., a principal source of anti-Semitic propaganda. They have participated in demonstrations held by this group, and seem not to be feazed by its anti-Semitic character nor by the frequent anti-Jewish utterances of its leaders. The reason for this apparent contradiction is that the Black Jews — like many of their co-religionists — seek a homeland. They await the Messiah who will re-establish a Negro nation — not a Jewish nation — through the redemption of Africa. The U.N.I.A. still dangles before the Negro, Marcus Garvey's dream of an African utopia as a homeland for the black man; many Black Jews were formerly members of the Back-to-Africa Movement, and to them Africa, not Palestine, is the homeland of the Jew. So, captivated by the 'Black Zionist' character of the U.N.I.A., they regard its anti-Semitic features as merely incident to the larger, more compelling dream of Africa's redemption. And since the anti-Semitism of the U.N.I.A. does not by any means include *black* Jews, the Black Jews are apathetic to the broader implications of the movement's anti-Jewish propaganda.

The Black Jews, it appears, are more intensely Negro than Jew. Actually, the movement of the Black Jews in the United States largely has the form of the Jewish *Landsmannshaften* organizations in its spirit of self-help and concern for the weak, needy, and oppressed. Whatever its true character and ultimate aims, the future of the Black Jews — inescapably identified as they are with the Negro people — is bound to the future of the black man. They apparently know this well!

Chapter XII

. . . a Harlem tenement is a hundred delta cabins, plus tuberculosis.

— THOMAS SANCTON

THE SLUM-SHOCKED

ON THE morning of March 20, 1935, the people of New York awoke to learn that in the heart of the city, the citadel of advancing Black America, a riot had occurred the night before involving upwards of ten thousand Negroes. Overnight, in the home of happy feet, 'crowds went crazy like the remnants of a defeated, abandoned, hungry army.' The outburst — a sequel to resentments nurtured by agitation — was called the 'Black Ides of March.' So formidable a demonstration did it become that the alarmed Harlem Merchants' Association, a group of white shopkeepers, appealed to Governor Lehman to send troops to patrol the district.

An absurdly trivial incident furnished the spark which awakened the Negro's deep-seated sense of wrong and denial and even memory of injustices in the South, and set ablaze smoldering resentments against racial discrimination and poverty. A Puerto Rican lad caught stealing a ten-cent penknife from the counter of a five-and-ten-cent store on West 125th Street — Harlem's main shopping thoroughfare — desperately sank his teeth into the hands of one of his captors. In the excitement, Negroes attacked the store's white employees, trampling a few in the mêlée. Meantime the boy was whisked away to the cellar of the store, and the rumor spread that he had been beaten to death. Negroes tumbled out of taverns, barber shops, basements, beauty parlors, and pool-rooms, and rushed to the scene intent upon revenge. Street speakers mounted stepladders and harangued the crowds, charging the police with brutality and the white merchants with racial discrimination in employment. They were pulled down by the police and arrested. But this act served only to inflame the crowds, and large detachments of uniformed police, plain-clothes men, and mounted police had to be summoned from other parts of the city.

Later in the night, I saw patrol cars driven onto the side-walks to disperse the rioters. But the crowds grew in numbers and hostility, stirred to anger by their hatred of the police. Negroes surged through the streets smashing store windows, hurling bricks, stones, and other missiles at the police. The huge mob broke into bands which plundered and looted stores owned by white merchants only — the discrimination was almost studied. On Lenox Avenue, scene of much of the dis-order, rioters ducked into shattered shop windows, while women stood on the fringes of the crowds shouting their choice of articles. I heard one ragged youth who outfitted himself with a new coat from a wrecked tailor shop wryly re-mark that he would be unable to return for alterations.

Sporadic outbursts continued until the rioters dispersed from sheer exhaustion in the early hours of the morning. At least two hundred stores had been smashed, gutted, and their goods carried away. The total damage in property was estimated at more than two million dollars. Three deaths — all Negroes — were reported by the police department, thirty-odd people were hospitalized for bullet wounds, with more than two hun-dred others receiving treatment for minor injuries, cuts, and abrasions. Some one hundred persons, the majority of them Negroes, were arrested on charges of inciting to violence, un-lawful assemblage, and looting.

A few days later the metropolitan newspapers reported with

relieved satisfaction that the number of policemen had been doubled in Harlem and a roundup of suspicious characters and subversive elements started. Mounted police were — and are today — stationed at all the danger points in the community. The police searched for the answer to the outburst in taverns, basements, barber shops, and poolrooms! Mayor La Guardia named a bi-racial group, known as the Mayor's Commission on Conditions in Harlem, to investigate. Its report, prepared by E. Franklin Frazier, a professor of sociology at Howard University, gave as the riot's cause the '... resentments against racial discrimination and poverty in the midst of plenty.'

What at first was thought to be the natural ebullience of a volatile population was in fact a manifestation of profound social unrest. A number of factors, emerging out of the American pattern for black men, had converged to crush Negroes. Harlem's population, for one thing, was pushing hard toward a half-million as Negroes from the rural South poured in and flooded the community's two square miles. The Depression, rather than retarding the drift North, actually served to accelerate the movement. For in the South — where widespread unemployment had driven Negroes as well as white people to the relief stations — there were differentials even in poverty! And Southern Negroes were rejecting, with increasing frequency, a life of want and oppression to come North where there was some promise — or at least some hope of a job, or even W.P.A. work.

The tidal wave of migration which washed up on the shores of Northern cities during the Depression was a most significant shift in population. There were three main streams: one came through the tobacco fields, rice swamps, and sugar farms of the eastern seaboard and headed pell-mell for New York; another came from Mississippi, Alabama, and Georgia and ended up in Chicago and Detroit; and a third came out of Texas, passed through Arkansas and Oklahoma, and over-

flowed into St. Louis and Chicago. Before 1930 there was but
one Northern city in the entire country with a Negro population of more than a hundred thousand. By 1935 there were
eleven. Recently, the migration North has been quickened
by the added incentive of jobs in the war industries.

The backdrop against which these racial émigrés began
their new life was composed of greasy and rundown tenements
in filthy and evil-smelling, littered, crowded streets. Whether
they went to St. Louis, Chicago, Detroit, or Cleveland, or to
Pittsburgh, Philadelphia, Washington, Buffalo, or New York,
they eventually became the bulk of destitute slum dwellers.
Their situation in one city varied only in degree from another.
Those who came to Harlem lived in unheated railroad flats,
typical of thousands in the Negro communities of the nation,
with dank, rat-infested toilets, footworn nondescript linoleum,
dirty walls ripped and unpainted, and roaches creeping about
the floors and woodwork. From dark unlit hallways came
musty odors mingling with the smell of cooking. Ever present
was the cacophony of grinding jukeboxes, squalling infants,
and angry argument. For all this, white landlords had the
effrontery to hang signs on the buildings specifying, 'FOR
SELECT COLORED TENANTS ONLY.'

Drying clothes dangled from the fire-escapes, already clut-
tered with scrawny plants, mops, pails, and discarded tin cans.
Everywhere signs ballyhooed the dismal poverty: fifteen-cent
fish-and-chips dinners, cut-rate drugs, second-hand laundry,
and the inevitable three gold balls of the pawnshops, called
'Shylock Castles.' Elongated wooden boxes stood upright at
the entrance to basements, marking the location of fuel-
sellers, who dispensed bundles of wood and bagfuls of coke.
Leantos — squat unpainted shacks of wood and tin built
against larger structures housed hopeful little enterprises —
fish frys, moving-van concerns, news-stands, and shoe-shine
parlors. Posters and handbills covered the walls, and incidentally helped to keep the occupants warm in winter. An

ancient oil stove usually served as the only heater — and doubled as the cook stove.

Slum shock was brought on by years of living in such houses — plus chronic unemployment, dependency, discrimination, delinquency, disease, and death. Chronic unemployment was the major factor that set off the Harlem riot. Long periods of enforced idleness had deteriorated morale. The men had lost their self-respect, pride, dignity, and independence, and with this came loss of authority in the family — which eventually brought about desertion and broken homes. Even today many of these men can be seen loitering on the street corners or in poolrooms and gin mills. The crowded streets, a marked characteristic of slum neighborhoods, are largely made up of unemployed people. Able-bodied men, unable to support their families by their own toil, turn to petty crime and vice, but mainly to playing the numbers — hoping to gain through luck what has been denied them through labor.

The policy racket is the most widespread form of lawbreaking in Harlem, as elsewhere in Negro communities. In every street either a candy store, barber shop, beauty parlor, or tavern is a collection headquarters — called a 'drop.' Many Negroes, who otherwise would be on the relief rolls, earn a living by collecting the numbers. The annual 'take' is estimated at ten million dollars. I know from personal knowledge one Negro policy king who made a bank deposit of eighteen thousand dollars a day! In the early thirties the smooth running of the policy game was halted for a while when Thomas E. Dewey, as New York City's district attorney, conducted a drive against the numbers racketeers. Incidentally, before Dewey became a candidate for re-election his campaign managers conducted a poll in Harlem to determine what reaction Negroes had to his campaign against the number barons. The results showed that they were overwhelmingly in support of him.

Today, the policy racket is flourishing as openly and prosperously in Harlem as before Dewey smashed the numbers empire of Dutch Schultz. By actual count, one day in the spring of 1942, a *World-Telegram* reporter saw seventy women and seventy-one men go into a drop within a period of forty-five minutes. The traffic included, significantly enough, boys and girls of 'teen ages. One boy about ten, tightly clutching the hand of his sister, was seen to give slips of paper to a lookout who stood guard outside the door.

What excites people about the policy game are the gaudy returns — one cent played on a number brings five dollars, but the chances of winning are one to nine hundred and ninety-nine. Yet not a day passes in the Negro neighborhood but somebody wins, and naturally shows his winnings to the neighbors. The despondent players are thus given new incentive — and so it goes. Obviously, few people can make a living playing the numbers, so the bulk of the population, unable to secure work, apply to the city for relief.

A tremendously large proportion of Harlem's population exists by some form of public hand-out. Until the war, Negroes constituted more than twenty-five per cent of the relief rolls although they were only five per cent of New York City's total population. And life as a reliefer was no bed of roses. Cold statistics ignore certain very human elements, which are all the more important because of the enormous number of persons who receive public assistance. Procedures, conceived by streamlined pundits, do not often take into consideration the peculiar needs, or problems, of Negroes.

Southern states — to cite one example — are not concerned with the registry of births and deaths of Negroes. The relationships of Negroes are not always clear because there is no official recognition of their status. The majority of Negro relief recipients are recent migrants from the rural South. They are mostly illiterate and ignorant and are placed in bewildering dilemmas by official red tape. They often fail to understand fully the requirements, and are in constant fear of having their relief stopped because they are unable to answer questions satisfactorily. Besides food and rent, other simple needs are not adequately met. For example, money is not allotted or carfare to those seeking work or for students to attend school. Not until recently was a regular or anything approaching an adequate clothing allowance granted.

There certainly is little recognition of the rising cost of living since the war began. In Harlem food prices are considerably higher than in other parts of the city. For every dollar spent on food the Negro housewife has to spend at least six cents in excess of what the housewife in any other comparable section is required to pay. For a woman with a family of four, even though she feeds them on the moderate amount of five dollars per person per week, it means that she spends literally one dollar and fifty cents per week extra. There is only one place in Harlem where meats of the finer quality are sold, and few stores sell Grade A eggs.

The products of poverty, overcrowding, ignorance, and lack of adequate health facilities are illness and crime. The figures for the past ten years, with little variation, show that the death rate from tuberculosis in Harlem has been four times higher than that for the city as a whole. Twice as many cases of cancer are treated at Harlem Hospital as at other hospitals in the city, and almost twice as many deaths result from accidents. Tougher still is the problem of syphilis, a subject about which a boatload of nonsense is current. As a social disease, it ravages the lives of city and rural slum dwellers. In New York City the Negro rate in 1940 was seven times higher than that of whites; and the first million draft registrants examined — from all sections of the country — showed a syphilis rate for whites of 18.5 per thousand; and for Negroes it was 241.2. The lack of adequate facilities and treatment, and general neglect of the Negro's condition, both North and South, are factors not to be overlooked.

Because of the inability even to maintain themselves simply, many women have turned to stealing and others to prostitution. Today, in Harlem's most notorious red-light district — 'The Market Place' — streetwalkers brazenly accost men in broad daylight as well as at night. They are a shabby, hunted, exploited group living on the threadbare edge of poverty, victimized by pimps, dope-peddlers, and other low elements of the community. A few of them — called 'roundheels' — are a pretty vicious lot, and it was they who introduced that violent crime called 'mugging,' a form of assault with intent to rob. The woman's rôle is to lure a man into a tenement hallway, where he is set upon by three, four, or five accomplices — called 'muggers' — usually armed with switch-blades. One grabs the victim around the throat and strangles him, while the others strip him of his clothes and money. If the man resists, he is pummeled brutally or stabbed. Often independent bands of youths — without these women — dart in the shadows of darkened streets, stalk intoxicated men and rob them in this manner.

One aspect of prostitution in Negro communities — which differs radically from that in white areas — is that it affects the Negro home directly, and serves as well in reducing the moral standards of the respectable community. Thus even respectable families are forced to have elbow acquaintance with such traffic. I don't believe it would be an exaggeration to say that on nearly every other street in Negro neighborhoods there is at least one brothel or house of assignation maintained for the almost-exclusive patronage of white men. In many Negro communities, there is no such thing as a *strictly residential* area, largely because of relaxed supervision and total indifference of absentee landlords.

Negroes become irritable, touchy, and frequently belligerent. All this of course is true of white slum dwellers. But there is this vast difference: Negroes bear the double cross of indigence and discrimination, whereas white people have greater job opportunities, freedom of movement, and the hope that there might be some release from the situation. Today every white man and woman who wants work can get a job because of the war's increased demand for labor — but thousands of Negroes still are knocking at the door of industry.

One of the tragic but vivid reflections of these conditions is juvenile delinquency. There are roughly seventy-five thousand Negro children in New York City and the bulk of them are crammed into Harlem. Deprived of home supervision, places for wholesome fun, and facing a blind alley of opportunity, they naturally congregate on street corners, where they witness the most sordid forms of crime. They seek the society of vicious gangs and try to emulate the overdressed underworld figures seen parading the streets — who, to all appearances, are among the few prosperous people in the community. Many youngsters are truants from school. It is not unusual for some of them to come to classes intoxicated or under the influence of marihuana, a narcotic often used by muggers. They steal fruits from the stands of vendors, drink whiskey in basement dives, and at night frequent dance halls, gin mills, and poolrooms.

Unrest in the adult population is often reflected by the children. Some are hypersensitive to the bitterness and rebellion of their parents, who they feel have received unfair treatment at the hands of white people. In one sense, then, juvenile crime is an inarticulate protest of the most depressed elements. This seems to have been the case when fifteen-year-old James O'Connell, a white boy, was stabbed to death by three Negro boys — ages twelve, fifteen, and nineteen. This was front-page stuff in most of the daily newspapers. What did not appear in the accounts was the fact that white people had been breaking windows and terrorizing Negroes in nightly forays into the Negro neighborhood because Negroes had moved into a near-by 'white' section on the fringe of Harlem. Perhaps the violence of these boys was retaliatory, or at least defensive aggression. For no doubt they were reflecting, albeit crudely, the resentful attitudes of their parents.

That juvenile delinquency is not 'racial' — as some observers would have us believe — is demonstrated by the fact that throughout the country there has been a marked increase in delinquency and crime among white children since the war began. This fact has been brought home forcibly to white mothers, who have been working in factories either on the day or night shifts, and therefore are unable to give their children the proper care and supervision. England has had an increase of forty-one per cent in juvenile delinquency (those under fourteen years of age).

Penny-pinching by the city administration, which abolished or handicapped departments concerned with children and adolescents, is among the main reasons offered by social workers for the increase; besides, of course, there is the excitement of the times and the dislocation of families incident to the war. The situation among the whites should throw the Negro's juvenile problems into proper perspective. These are obviously abnormal times. But Negroes have known long years of poverty, appalling in extent and intensity, which have caused widespread disorganization of families. Nearly every Negro mother must seek work outside the home in the hope of supplementing the family income. Meantime children are left to roam the streets, frequently far into the night. To make ends meet, Negroes also are forced to take in boarders and lodgers. The Negro newspapers devote three and four pages to advertising rooms for rent, which is indicative of the extent of renting and indeed its impersonal nature. In this way, total strangers enter the home, many of them questionable characters who sometimes corrupt members of the family.

The schools in Harlem further complicate the juvenile problem. Curtailment of funds has been a crusher to the morale of teachers and students. Until very recently white teachers were frequently assigned to the Negro neighborhood

as a punitive measure, a fact which hardly served to improve
their morale. Because of overcrowding, many of the schools
operate on a three-shift system, and the irregular schedule
throws the pupils on the streets for a greater portion of the day
than is the case in schools that function on a regular plan.
After classes the schools have few recreational facilities for the
students — and practically none in the evenings.

The vocational-guidance program in New York as elsewhere also operates to the disadvantage of Negro pupils.
The public-school teachers spend much time in attempting to
determine the interest, aptitudes, and fitness of Negro boys for
certain types of employment, and in encouraging them to prepare themselves for the future. However, once Negro students
enter the vocational high schools, because 'industry will find
no place for [Negro] applicants,' they are frequently barred
from specialized vocational and technical lines — particularly
gas and Diesel engines and aircraft. Thus, one branch of the
school system fills Negro pupils with dreams of democracy and
opportunity, while the other half spends its time in tearing
down those dreams.

Even more acute is the plight of the homeless and neglected
boys. During the five-year period 1930–35, the Children's
Court in New York City declared six thousand Negro youngsters to be delinquent and three thousand neglected. Yet no
provision existed for Negro juvenile delinquents in New York
until 1937, when the Wiltwyck School was opened for them at
West Park by the Protestant Episcopal City Mission Society —
it accommodates about eighty boys. Today, with the sharp
increase in juvenile delinquency, wayward boys are a sore in
the hearts of Negroes who are helpless to correct the situation
without official assistance.

The case of Lee Edward Wilkes will illustrate this point:
One night late in 1941, this homeless Harlem boy was met by
two acquaintances he had picked up three weeks earlier who
asked him to come out on a mugging job. Cold, neglected,

and hungry, he agreed. After sizing up a few prospects, they waylaid Joseph Keelan, a white man, mugged him, rifled his pockets of seventeen cents, stole his suit, and left him dying of a fractured larynx in Morningside Park. The suit was pawned the next morning for one dollar and was the clue that led to their apprehension.

The case history of a mugger — in this instance, Lee Edward Wilkes — which Albert Deutsch and Tom O'Connor, both competent *PM* reporters, took pains to run down, throws light on a problem common to every large city where a Negro population lives in considerable numbers. The facts were almost prosaically typical.

When arrested for murder Lee was eighteen years of age — his companions were seventeen and twenty. He was born in Memphis, Tennessee, and as an infant was left in the care of an aged grandmother. She died in 1939; the boy came North to his mother, who was working in a beauty parlor, and the two shared a little room in a tenement. A few months later, Mrs. Wilkes died of tuberculosis, and the sixteen-year-old boy was now alone, without relatives or funds. With but a few months more to finish a printing course at the New York Vocational High School, he left and unsuccessfully sought work. A kindly woman, Mrs. Olivia Hicks, a friend of the boy's mother, took him into her home for a time, and tried to obtain assistance from the welfare agencies.

Then began a period in which his mother's friends took turns in keeping him as long as their own meager funds permitted. Finally he was sent to a home for indigent boys. In the spring of 1941, he obtained a job paying twelve dollars a week as a delivery boy and moved to a rooming-house. He lost this job, but got another at twelve dollars a week as a truck-driver's helper, often working fifteen hours a day, which job he lost in the autumn of 1941. Dreary weeks of unemployment followed, and finally the events that involved him in a murder.

'He was like a child just throwed away when his mother died,' Mrs. Hicks told the *PM* reporters. 'I tried to get help for him, but it was no use. Nobody wanted to watch out for him. He was like a child just throwed away.'

Within the community's restricted area, housing, educational, cultural, spiritual, and recreational facilities have never expanded sufficiently to meet the phenomenal growth of the population. Lack of adequate correctional facilities for Negro delinquents is an important factor. A shocking aspect of this problem is the anti-Negro discrimination and segregation practiced by many charitable agencies in liberal New York. What makes Negroes in Harlem especially indignant is that a large number of the private institutions — openly barring Negro juvenile delinquents and neglected children — are supported mainly by city taxes.

Encouraging efforts by many sincere white people have helped to combat these conditions. Since few of these people are yet ready to go to the root of the problem, Negroes will have to string along with palliatives. The Children's Aid Society, in particular, has done much preventative work in its large modern Harlem plant. George Gregory, a former Columbia University basketball captain, directs its program of planned recreation in the community's worst slum area. In 1942 the anti-Negro policy of other private agencies was met in a fundamental way by the City-Wide Citizens' Committee on Harlem, a bi-racial group of which Algernon D. Black and the Reverend A. Clayton Powell, Sr., are co-chairmen. It sponsored an amendment to the city budget, which the Board of Estimate adopted, barring payments by the city to private child-caring agencies refusing to accept Negro children. This appears to be the trend today.

Negroes often blame the police for crime in Harlem. Some look upon them as oppressors and even exploiters. The fact is, there have been repeated complaints of police brutality by whites as well as Negroes, so much so that when Fiorello La

Guardia became mayor of New York City, one of his first official acts was to abolish the use of clubs by the police. Said Harlem's *People's Voice* editorially: 'Harlem is damned sick and tired of brutal police who strike first and make prisoners after. We recognize that some police cases require violence, but [we] also insist that too many peaceable persons are vilely maltreated by officers who are unfitted for their jobs and who are stationed in Harlem as the "Siberia" of the city police department for misconduct elsewhere.'

The bitter feeling which exists between the citizenry and police bars full cooperation and hinders law enforcement. But many Negroes are afraid to aid the police in reporting or solving crimes, for fear of themselves becoming involved — especially if a white person is mixed up in the affair. I witnessed an incident that somewhat illustrates this. From the window of a Seventh Avenue apartment one afternoon, I saw an open roadster, driven by a white woman, stop for a red light. Two boys, who couldn't have been more than twelve years of age, ran to the car and in a flash had snatched the woman's pocketbook, which had lain on the seat beside her, and ran off. Since no policeman was about, the woman appealed to a handful of idle men who stood on the corner watching. They shuffled uneasily, but did not move. Later, when I asked them why they had not assisted her, they chorused, 'You ain't gonna get us in no trouble with the police!'

Much of this feeling is engendered by the police themselves. White policemen in Harlem, Negroes say, are inclined to react with racial bias to crime. If a Negro is robbed or murdered by a Negro (or a white man), to illustrate, the case is given routine attention and soon forgotten; whereas if a white man is murdered or robbed by a Negro, the whole machinery of the Police Department is set in motion — with no uncertain urging from the white press — and usually the criminal is tracked down. Such double standards of law enforcement exist in many cities throughout the country — it certainly is the rule in the South. George S. Schuyler, a responsible Negro observer, reports that the police raid any place where Negroes and whites are associating as equals, scrutinize every suspiciously light-colored woman with a dark escort, beat up and shoot 'bad niggers' in 'self-defense,' and raid homes without warrant. He says that one Middle-West chief of police threatened to cancel the license of any Negro taxicab driver seen transporting a white passenger, particularly a white woman.

In Harlem Negroes are daily plagued by sneak thieves of every variety. There are few apartments that do not have every window facing a fire-escape barred with iron grilling to prevent robberies. Few doors are without sturdy locks, iron bars, and chains, but robberies take place daily. One is considered naïve to appeal to the police and expect something to be done about it.

Myth or reality, it is an open secret in Harlem that some policemen receive various forms of gratuities from the underworld. It is also said, with a trace of bitterness, that whenever police headquarters plans a raid in Harlem, the underworld is tipped off in advance so that they can quickly take to cover and remain there until things blow over. To operate unmolested, according to the stories current, pimps, prostitutes, dope-peddlers, brothel-keepers, and owners of gambling places pay weekly tribute to certain members of the police force and to high-placed political figures. Police association with the underworld has its nickel-and-dime aspect, too: there are policemen who — on their off time — act as 'bouncers' in 'gyp joints' at a salary of ten dollars a night.

From a Lenox Avenue tavern window one night, I saw a prostitute accost a white man and steer him into a near-by hallway. Five minutes had hardly elapsed before he ran into the street shouting that he had been robbed. Negroes walking along the street ignored him. Two white detectives — I later learned their identity — who had been cruising along the avenue in an automobile heard his cries and stopped. After a moment or so of discussion, they took him away. But pretty soon they returned, and one of them went into the house where the white man had been robbed, and dragged the woman out into the street. They wrangled with her for a few minutes, threatened to arrest her, and finally drove off. She came across the street and into the tavern and ordered a 'double gin shorty.' Then I overheard her tell the bartender that she had been given 'the shakedown,' and remark, 'It's tough on the turf, being robbed every day!'

A sharp editorial appeared in the *Amsterdam-Star News* in the summer of 1942 which seems indicative: 'We in Harlem do not condone candy stores that are headquarters for gambling where our children go in and out, see and hear things that cannot but help catch on in their minds. Neither do we condone police protection of prostitution where street women openly solicit on our main avenue, turn our most respectable areas into redlight districts. . . . What we expect, demand, and intend to get is complete separation of police activity in Harlem from the underworld.'

Chapter XIII

Probe the tissue of Negro social life and the Negro reacts to the same illusions that feed the vanity of white men.

— E. FRANKLIN FRAZIER

THE CAFÉ-AU-LAIT SOCIETY

THE upper crust of Negro society was shaken to its foundation with the onset of the Depression, and hasn't recovered as yet. The once sharp lines between the upper and lower reaches were nearly wiped out under a succession of economic shocks, a barrage of liberal ideas, and the passing of the old-guard politicians as important social figures. Today, the flow back and forth defies clear distinctions. Roughly, though, Black America is divided into three classes: the upper class, which is in fact a *petite bourgeoisie*, made up of relatively small business-men, physicians, lawyers, dentists, druggists, ministers, profes-sors, school teachers, and a few well-to-do Southern farmers; a middle class, which is formed by the skilled workers and those who have regular low-paying employment; and at the bottom of the social ladder a black proletariat composed of the un-skilled laborers, domestics, and agricultural workers. There is no leisure class.

Lately, and indeed for the first time in the history of Black America, a fourth and rather well-defined group has emerged to which anyone may aspire — a colorful café society, com-posed of intellectuals, with Harlem as its capital and principal social centers in Chicago and Pittsburgh. Back in the days when Frederick Douglass was the outstanding Negro political leader, and the church formed the cornerstone of Negro life, St. Louis was the social capital of the North, and the social élite were the Mordecais, the Wilkinsons, the Helms, and the Russells. The Victorian Age came alive when they gathered at the decorous surroundings of Old Stolle's Hall, observed the social amenities, and danced the cakewalk. In the South the social center was Atlanta, where the Negro's first 'Blue Vein' Society came into being. The older generation of politicians, largely descendants of old free families, constituted the colored aristocracy. Together with a small group of dignified domestics who had been long employed by the white aristocracy, the Bruces, the Langstons, the Thomases, and the Elliots formed the top layer. Meantime, Washington had come into prominence as a social center, where full sway was exerted by the descendants of such Civil War personages as the well-known mulatto caterer, Wormley.

Social distinctions developed among Negroes as early as slavery. At first, house-servants drew the line against field hands; later the mark of distinction was the amount of aristocratic 'white' blood one possessed, and finally the length of time one was freed. When freedom came, the Negroes who in culture and refinement approximated the master-class comprised a sort of natural aristocracy and provided the race with leaders. Of the twenty congressmen and two senators who represented the race during the Reconstruction Period, all but three were mulattoes. Ten had a college education — some at the expense of their white fathers. Under the old order many of the Negro leaders had been house-servants, artisans, and blood-relations of the dominant class, which inclined them toward an affectation of aristocratic graces, traditions, and manners. Not only did these distinctions give many of them a feeling of superiority over other Negroes, but it even made them feel superior to poor and lower-middle-class whites.

A Negro society did not jell until the closing years of the last century. Thousands of free Negroes of light complexion disappeared into the white race, but the descendants of those who remained in the Negro group — with roots in the white upper class — constituted the basic element in the emerging society. For example, one family prominent in Washington's Negro society today loftily traces its family tree straight back to George Washington through one of his various mistresses. To document the institutional character of these old Negro families, E. Franklin Frazier, a Negro sociologist, traced the sources of a typical family — the Varicks of New York. He found that James Varick, one of the founders and later the first bishop of the African Methodist Episcopal Church, who married in 1798, was succeeded by five generations of descendants to the present day: four children, sixteen grandchildren, thirteen great-grandchildren, five great-great-grandchildren, and one great-great-great-grandchild. This family is said to be related to a distinguished white family sired by Richard Varick, a banker.

In New York — to illustrate — a Negro society came into being in the eighteen-eighties with the formation of the Society of Sons of New York, a group described as 'the cream of Afro-American society.' An anonymous 'Black Ward McAllister' handed down the dictum that only those were admitted who satisfied 'the most delicate taste of gentlemanlike tone and behavior.' Recent Southern migrants were among those barred. The group was made up of the most prosperous merchants, real estate speculators, doctors, druggists, politicians, head waiters, and the descendants of New York's oldest free families.

The *Sun* was somewhat curious about these people. Two long articles appeared almost twenty years apart. The second, perhaps a check to see how they were doing in the interim, was an illustrated feature entitled, 'NEW YORK'S RICH NEGROES.' It estimated that there were more than three hundred Negro families, mostly living in Brooklyn, who could afford to buy houses ranging in value from forty to one hundred thousand dollars, and who spent from ten to twenty-five thousand dollars a year. Rogers Peet, a fashionable clothier, enterprisingly attempted to capture the male trade by employing a Negro salesman, a Mr. Fred P. Hayes. This gentleman wrote a number of 'letters — on the firm's nicely engraved stationery — to prominent Negroes soliciting business, but not without carefully observing that Rogers Peet 'is the first and only prominent house that has employed a colored salesman.'

The members of Negro society were accused by Negroes outside the halo of being only 'lampblack whites,' or bad copies of white people. And they did indeed adopt the prevailing patterns. The well-to-do Negroes filled their homes with oak and mahogany furniture and drew their servants from the Scandinavian and German immigrant groups. Here and there an English butler was seen. They drove their own carriages, and later automobiles, and imported costly clothes from Paris — in order that 'the beauty of wives and daughters may shine resplendent at the balls of the gay season.' The sons of such families attended schools abroad, or went to Howard, Harvard, or liberal Oberlin. The girls enrolled at the few fashionable Northern colleges for women which admitted Negroes. They studiously kept their family and social affairs out of the sight of the rest of the community, especially as far as white people were concerned, for they were deeply sensitive to reminders that they were despised because of their color. Barred from popular restaurants of the day like Delmonico's and Sherry's, they spent their money on fine homes, expensive foods, lavish parties, and travel. Rarely did they visit the saloons, the restaurants, and the night clubs frequented by the Negro sporting element.

Just before the first World War a simple, hard-working Negro woman bought two old brownstone buildings on West

136th Street in Harlem, tore them down, and built a ninety-thousand-dollar dwelling of Indiana limestone. At its formal opening Booker T. Washington was a guest. This was the auspicious entrance of Madame C. J. Walker, inventor of a hair-dekinking process, who was to become the first acknowledged social dictator of the Black Metropolis. Before her arrival in New York, she had been a St. Louis laundress without distinguished heredity who liked to recall the day she wearily stole a nap on a rude wooden bench and 'dreamed a dream' which showed her a new method for transforming the stubborn lusterless crinkle of the Negro's hair into shining smoothness. With 'two dollars and a dream' she built a prosperous manufacturing concern which has touched the lives of nearly every woman in Black America.

Before Madame Walker's day, Negro women had tried many ways of straightening their hair in order to dress it in the current fashions. It had long been their practice to spread the freshly washed hair against a flat surface and press out the kinks with a heated flatiron. But irons were unwieldly for such a purpose, and the process was awkward and hazardous. Madame's long experience as an expert laundress proved of great value. After applying a softening pomade, she carefully flattened out each snugly curled strand with a small iron comb she had invented. Thereafter, whenever a white employer inquisitively asked her radiant slick-haired Negro maid what she had done to yesterday's thatch of kinky locks to make it so gleaming and straight, the maid nonchalantly and a bit mysteriously answered that she had 'used Madame Walker's.'

In a short time Madame Walker had more customers than she could accommodate. She set up a shop, trained other women to assist her, and soon founded a school from which graduates received diplomas permitting them to operate shops of their own, using the 'Walker System'; always, however, with the solemn admonition not to call themselves 'hair straighteners.' They were crisply told to use the title 'hair culturist' or

'scalp specialist.' All necessary metal implements and oint-
ments were purchased from Madame Walker, and so profitable
was the sale of equipment and the return from tuitions that her
yearly payroll mounted to more than two hundred thousand
dollars. The dekinking process developed into a sizable industry, soon found vogue with crinkly-haired white women,
and Madame Walker became a millionaire — one of the
first women, white or black, to achieve this goal by her own
efforts in business.

Married at fourteen and widowed at nineteen, with a small
daughter to support, she had had little opportunity for schooling; but with the acquisition of wealth, and her dazzling entrance into Negro society, she engaged a tutor and learned to
speak correctly. Once ensconced in her town house, she attempted to purchase a property in a middle-class residential
section of Long Island. When the white people objected, she
abandoned the plan, reasoning that if moving into a white
neighborhood would create a stir, she might as well choose
the snootiest locality and make it a sensation. She secured a
strip of land at swanky Irvington-on-the-Hudson, where in
1917 she built an elaborate, cream-colored Georgian mansion,
designed by a Negro architect, Vertner W. Tandy. It was
erected at a cost of $250,000, and invested with $400,000 worth
of furnishings, and was called the Villa Lewaro. The name
was suggested by Enrico Caruso, the famous opera singer.
For years afterward sight-seeing busses carried the Negro *hoi
polloi* up to the estate to stare and marvel.

In this fabulous palace Madame Walker drew social lines
closely. She gave dinners, musicales, balls, and entertainments which at one time or another were attended by nearly
every influential Negro in Black America. Marcus Garvey,
one of her closest friends, was a frequent visitor. Those who
thronged the place fairly gasped at the splendor of a twenty-
four-carat-gold-plated piano and a phonograph to match; at
the wide marble stairway which swept gracefully to the second

floor; and at the landscaped gardens, with two prayer trees imported from Japan at a cost of more than ten thousand dollars. There also were rich tapestries, French Renaissance furniture, enormous oil paintings, a sixty-thousand-dollar pipe organ, and an occasional piece of Hepplewhite; as well as beautiful linen, costly bric-a-brac, fine glassware and china, handsome silver services, and magnificent Persian rugs.

Madame Walker died at the age of fifty, leaving large sums to Negro charities and educational institutions; among these was an academy for African girls, founded by her in West Africa, to which she left one hundred thousand dollars. The bulk of her two-million-dollar estate was bequeathed to an only daughter, Mrs. A'Leilia Walker Robinson, a statuesque, cocoa-colored woman, addicted to extravagant gowns and exotic turbans, who subsequently astounded Black America with a 'million-dollar' wedding for her daughter. The rites were performed at Harlem's Saint Philip's Protestant Episcopal Church. More than fifteen hundred guests were invited, taxing the edifice to its capacity. During the ceremony nine thousand persons milled about the entrance, while traffic was snarled for hours with crowds eagerly awaiting a glimpse of the bride — granddaughter of the woman who, having pulled herself up by the roots of other people's hair, founded America's first black plutocratic dynasty. Following the ceremony an elaborate wedding breakfast and reception, served by a leading Fifth Avenue caterer, was given at Villa Lewaro.

The Mahogany Millionairess, as some called A'Leilia Walker, spent money recklessly as she carried on at a tumultuous pace. This, and her outlandish clothes, caused the securely familied folks to frown. Eventually she turned to those liberal elements who were active in the cultural world. She redecorated her town house, established a salon known as the Dark Tower, and presided as a patron of the arts. Assisted by Sari Price-Patton, a Harlem Elsa Maxwell, she entertained the black literati, many influential white people, and visiting royalty, and in the process evolved a new and more daring society.

At Dark Tower one met James Weldon Johnson, Zora Neale Hurston, Langston Hughes, Countee Cullen, Florence Mills, Charles Gilpin, Bruce Nugent, or Aaron Douglas. Here as Gurdjieff's disciple Jean Toomer, after a sojourn at Fontainebleau, introduced inner observation and silent concentration to Harlem. Here, too, one heard the racy anecdotes of Rudolph Fisher, the novelist. Hughes quotes Geraldyn Dismond, a Harlemese stylist, reporting a typical party of the period in the old *Inter-State Tattler*:

> 'What a crowd!' she exulted. 'All classes and colors met face to face, ultra-aristocrats, bourgeoisie, Communists, Park Avenuers galore, bookers, publishers, Broadway celebs, and Harlemites giving each other the once-over. The social revolution was on. And yes, Lady Nancy Cunard was there all in black (she would) with twelve of her grand bracelets. . . . And the entertainment on the up and up! Into swell dance music was injected African drums that played havoc with blood pressure. Jimmy Daniels sang his gigolo hits. Gus Simons, the Harlem crooner, made the River Stay Away from His Door and Taylor (Gordon) brought out everything from "Hot Dog" to "Bravo!" when he made high C.'

One of this crowd, Wallace Thurman, wrote a delightful satire of his colored colleagues, whom he called the 'niggerati.' His book was aptly titled *Infants of the Spring!*

Following a rash of temperament in 1930, A'Leilia closed the town house, disposed of her mansion overlooking the Hudson River, and the next year died suddenly — ending a colorful era in Negro life.

Today, that loosely formed group known as colored café society, a serious group like many of the intellectuals who frequented Dark Tower, is composed mainly of people of congenial tastes and somewhat the same progressive social outlook. They are drawn from among the artists, writers, com-

posers, musicians, actors, labor leaders, and the higher brackets of civil employees. Personal achievement, educational
attainment, and a measure of economic success are the chief
requirements for admission. Thus, at the top of this world sit
the Ellingtons, Burleighs, Carters, Robesons, Dunhams, and
Simms Campbells. Not infrequently is this group augmented
by a sprinkling of Haitians, Africans, Chinese, and white intellectuals active in the cultural and liberal movements.

This is the glamour set of Black America. Flourishing in
social esteem among the masses, the Negro newspapers zealously report their sayings and doings, and their comings and
goings. They meet frequently at each others' homes, or at the
popular cocktail lounges of the Hotel Theresa, Jimmy Dan-
iels', Dick Wheaton's, or Ed Smalls', where they drink expensive whiskies and fine wines, and discuss the arts, social movements, and the color problem. By and large they are New
Dealers, though all shades of political thinking are given ample
expression without rancor.

While in New York, Cecil Beaton, an English artist, attended a café-society gathering in the Harlem apartment of
a Negro city employee. His reporting was superior in tone,
but accurate in detail. Imitation ivy, he said, climbed around
the hot pipes; vases of dyed pampas decorated the drawing-
room; and the walls were painted in bright colors. A cocktail bar in the kitchen was the focal point of activity. His
hostess, 'in black satin, with a Duchess of Windsor coiffure,'
had little time for the guests as she busied herself tipping cigarette ash trays into a fancy tin.

Left to his own devices among fifty-odd guests, he met
the brother of a famous Irish poet, a Negro pianist who
played well but recited mediocre verse in a tragic voice, a
'distinguished' taxidermist, and an elderly Negro who eulo-
gized Russia. Two girls particularly intrigued him. One was
'a lovely young girl' from Haiti, a student of rural education, who spoke proudly of her country and Christophe; the

other was 'beautiful and almost white.' By midnight he was involved in discussions of Pareto and Spengler.

But by no means are café-society gatherings always quite so stuffy. As a matter of fact, they often sparkle with humor expressed in Negro idioms, and those who would save the world are frequently shunted to one side to allow talk of swing music — the relative merits of Count Basie and Benny Goodman, or the possible musical importance of Duke Ellington's 'Concerto for Cootie.' There also is much chit-chat and gossip, and discussions occasioned by sports events. Today, conversations mostly hinge on the war and its meanings to colored peoples.

The colored café society is without social aspirations. Yet the old Negro families, foundation of the upper class, look upon this new group with a good deal of suspicion because of its upstart nature, espousal of liberal doctrines, and associations with white people. While there is considerable overlapping of the groups among the younger members, the die-hard old families still maintain a semblance of rigid social lines. This small exclusive unit is known as 'respectable' Negro society, and has its capital in Washington, with important centers at Atlanta, Durham, Philadelphia, and Boston. Rarely are its members seen in public places of amusement. Wedded to middle-class standards, they have all the conservatism inherent in this class, and struggle to realize the values which give status within their group. Thus, they are usually college-trained — Howard, Fisk, or Atlanta Universities; generally vote the Republican ticket; attend the Episcopalian or Presbyterian church; and are among the local community leaders. They represent the most stable element in Black America.

While the café group earns a livelihood by competing in the white world, the Negro upper class moves smoothly and complacently within its own segregated orbit, content to live upon the Negro market as doctors, lawyers, dentists, and merchants. To such Negroes, establishing a business or procuring a profession means more than economic salvation. It is indeed a way to escape the white man's kitchen and to become a member of the Negro upper class, and they often maintain their upper-class standing by exploiting the Negro who remains in the kitchen. They may have an inferior economic status to whites, but in the world in which they live they are certainly not down-trodden or despised, but enjoy a sheltered and relatively secure position, and enjoy as well various forms of distinction. Many of them look with alarm upon a world where they must com-pete with whites and thus lose their unique status. 'They pre-fer,' one Negro observer remarked, 'the overvaluation of their achievements and position behind the walls of segregation to a democratic order that would result in economic and social devaluation for themselves.' Nevertheless, they provide the vanguard of the race's economic and cultural progress, and constitute a leavening group in the Negro population.

To reinforce their upper-class position in some areas — particularly in the South — they make attempts to maintain a caste based on color. There are a scattering of organizations whose memberships consist entirely of fair-skinned or mulatto types, and where the blackball is rigorously employed against any crasher whose coloring is deeper than high yaller. Yet, even within the mulatto clique, class distinctions exist which are based chiefly on property, education, blood, or family. The church in Charleston, South Carolina, which reputedly did not admit blacks certainly did not welcome nameless mulatto nobodies. However, these distinctions do not extend with equal force to men — that is, if they have education and good incomes. From these developments have evolved today's *café-au-lait* society, which somewhat resembles the upper classes of Latin America.

To white people these distinctions may seem trivial and in-consequential, but in the Negro world they are social realities. Perhaps the light-complexioned women, the props of Negro society, seek to reduce the amount of competition. At any rate, since they meet more nearly Caucasian standards of beauty, they possess enviable positions in the Negro community, and are much sought after as wives. W. M. Kiplinger, a Washington editor, heard one Negro leader say, 'If the whites could see some of our beautiful Negro girls at Howard University, they would understand why we Negroes are perfectly happy to forget about intermarriage.' The entrance lately of white women into the Northern Negro group has produced new and perplexing problems for the Negro social leaders. The mulatto women, often enjoying a position in the Negro group far beyond their social and personal worth, view with the fiercest antagonism the competition of white women. To combat the situation, they effectively raise the slogan of race pride.

No small ripple was caused in Harlem when the *Amsterdam-Star News* appeared in the winter of 1936 with the headline, 'MIXED COUPLES CHARGE BAN BY BOTH RACES; FORM CLUB,' and later with 'INTERMARRIED COUPLES OPEN FIGHT TO END ALL BARRIERS.' The new group called itself the Penguin Club — a body similar to the Midwestern Manasseh Societies — and was composed of more than one hundred interracial couples who had banded together to fight social ostracism. Its members were selected after a character investigation. Prospective candidates had to have at least one child to attest to the stability of the relationship. Declaring itself to be without sectarianism or political aims, in a formal statement to the press it demanded that 'all barriers in both races which now ban interracial couples' should end and that 'whites in Harlem should be accepted into civic and community organizations on the same basis as Negroes.'

The Negro upper class has an annual income averaging between three and seven thousand dollars. Usually husband and wife work, since there are few if any children. If there happen to be sons or daughters, they attend the large Northern colleges and belong to the Negro Greek-letter fraternities and sororities. The girls make formal débuts into society and make conventional marriages as well. Such families usually own one or more automobiles. Home furnishings show taste, orderliness, and, in some cases, more than a hint of luxury. There are few books about the home, and many untuned pianos. Household routines are conducted much in the manner of white people of middle-class incomes, though servants are not equally prevalent. The women's clothes bear the labels of fashionable specialty shops owned by white stylists. The men lean toward tweeds and slack suits of modest colors. The *Ladies' Home Journal* published a splendid article in 1942 on one of these typical Negro families — the Hinksons of Philadelphia. The husband was a doctor and army officer, the wife managed a well-ordered, tastefully furnished home which they owned, maintained a country place, and their two daughters attended school. They were found to be prosperous, educated, of very light complexion and, well rooted in a community out of the reach of the special pressures of the color line.

Home ownership is basic among those of recognized social importance, though this is a fact chiefly among the Southerners. They have been heard to scoff that city Negroes are 'po' niggers livin' in rented houses.' In Virginia, for example, twice as many rural Negroes own their homes as Negro city dwellers. This is fairly typical. The urban upper class, many of them property-owners, live sedately in the better-kept areas of the Black Belts, where there are broad shaded avenues and modern buildings.

Prim tree-dotted Strivers' Row, so named because of the efforts its residents made to maintain upper-class status, is Harlem's exclusive residential area. The spacious three-story dwellings, designed by Stanford White, cover the two blocks of 138th and 139th Streets, between Seventh and Eighth Avenues. They are similar in status to Washington's smart Le

Droit Park section, St. Louis's Enright Street, or the swankier
Negro area of West Philadelphia, or the few select blocks on
Chicago's Westchester. Beyond these, and similar neighborhoods, apartment dwelling is characteristic of urban life
among the Northern upper-class Negroes.

Harlem's Sugar Hill, sweeping north from the blue steeple
of Saint James's Presbyterian Church to the Polo Grounds, is
perhaps the most modern and beautiful residential area for
Negroes in Black America. Its row of brick and granite apartment houses, with colorful canopies stretching from doorways
to sidewalks, are the homes of the upper class and café society.
The most imposing of these buildings are the twelve-storied
Colonial Parkway Apartments and the Roger Morris Apartments, with smartly uniformed elevator operators and doormen, and penthouses overlooking the Harlem River. Rents
are high, and only the more prosperous can afford to live in
them without lodgers. Here, too, are found the ultra-modern
bars, restaurants, and cocktail lounges. But the odor of barbe-
cue, pork chops, greens, and chitterlings is as familiar here as
in the poorer sections. The decaying grandeur of Sugar Hill,
which is nicely bordered by Bradhurst Park, has only one
counterpart — that section at the southernmost tip of Harlem
known as Cathedral Down Under, separated by Morningside
Park from the Cathedral of Saint John the Divine.

Housing — the need exists at every income level — is particularly acute among Negroes in the higher-income brackets,
since they cannot escape the Black Belts despite their ability to
pay for better quarters. Formidable arguments are generally
used to oppose Negroes' entering the better sections where
white people live. It is said that they cause deterioration of
property, decline in neighborhood standards, and depreciate
property values; and that the two races cannot live together in
the same areas harmoniously. Others say that Negroes are
loud, destructive, unclean tenants and therefore undesirable
neighbors. These allegations form tangible bars against the

Negro. They have been repeated so widely and so insistently that they have found general acceptance among the American people.

Yet such talk is mouthed chiefly by banks and real estate operators who seek to cash in on segregated housing — obviously, if the Negro cannot move out of the Black Belt, the landlord can ask any amount of rent. By skillful appeals to racial and religious prejudice, reinforced by custom and residential covenants among landlords, the Negro is banished to slum corrals. Yet the methods are not always so involved; often they are baldly and openly direct. Faced with the problem of where to direct Harlem's rapidly expanding Negro population, a prominent member of the New York City Real Estate Board proposed an area which poor whites were already attempting to escape. 'A logical section for Negro expansion,' he said, 'is East Harlem. At present this district has reached such a point of deterioration that its ultimate residential pattern is most puzzling. Many blocks have a substantial section of their buildings boarded up or demolished and a good percentage of those remaining are in disrepair and in violation of the law. . . . An influx of Negroes would not work a hardship on the present [white] population.'

Several years ago two Negro professional men, Doctor Errold D. Collymore, a dentist, and Doctor Arthur M. Williams, a physician, moved into a white neighborhood of White Plains, a Westchester, New York, community occupied by middle-class people, and started a train of events that reveal a typical pattern. Doctor Collymore, who had won the respect of the community, was a strong character. Doctor Williams, a man of culture, was quiet, courteous, and attractive in manner. Three days after they moved in the press carried scare headlines, and that night agitators burned a Ku Klux Klan cross on Doctor Collymore's lawn. The next day bankers and real estate men formed a Highland Property-Owners' Association to force them out of the community, loudly saying they would use 'extra-legal' methods if necessary. A meeting was held at which Hebert J. Seligmann, white public director of the National Association for the Advancement of Colored People, appeared unexpectedly. After several speeches were made, designed to inflame anger, he secured the floor and was successful in averting violent action.

A banker tried to use his personal friendship to persuade the two Negroes to move, and when this failed, he threatened economic boycott. The official board of the Y.M.C.A. removed the two men from the board of management of which they were members. But pressure failed to frighten them or to force them to return to the Negro neighborhood. Finally twelve white religious leaders denounced the lynch spirit. Two of them, Doctor James I. Fairley and Rabbi V. Goldman, preached effective sermons. Within a few weeks, it was apparent that the doctors would remain with the support of many whites. The affair closed with a statement by Mrs. Mary Palmer, a prominent white leader, who asked, 'Can't we at least try to find out how agreeable decent colored folk may be as neighbors?'

How this problem should be met is no longer in the realm of abstractions. The greatest changes have already begun. Public housing projects have of course reduced slums, and residential segregation itself is being attacked by the government's enlightened policy which has brought Negroes and whites under the same roofs. Actually, though, only the Negro small wage-earner has been affected — the high-income group is not eligible and the lowest elements do not have regular incomes. However, more than twenty-odd projects in cities like Chicago, Pittsburgh, Philadelphia, Newark, Los Angeles, and New York are occupied by Negro and white tenants. Prophecies of race riots have failed to materialize. There is manifest pride in the upkeep and appearance of grounds and buildings, and there is easy association between the races. A Southern white family on one occasion accepted an apartment in a New York housing project with some misgivings because of the presence of Negroes. Nine months later they gave as their reason for remaining the happiness they found in the project's small-town atmosphere of friendliness and neighborly cooperativeness. These developments point the way.

Before the war, the Negro's top income group frequently went abroad summers to escape the restrictions of the American color line which bars Negroes from every public and private resort. George S. Schuyler, a well-known author, wrote to a hundred advertised hotels and resorts on the eastern seaboard to secure summer reservations for his family, and of thirty-five replies, only one place said it would welcome a Negro family. Such is the problem Negroes face if they seek to escape the cities during the summer months.

Negro society has managed to circumvent this problem by establishing its own summer colonies. Today, for example, Southerners may spend their vacations at exclusive Highland Beach, Maryland; Midwesterners can go to fashionable Idlewild, Michigan; and the Easterners, with a fairly wide selection, may live in several sections of New England, upstate New York, Long Island, and along the coast of New Jersey. They enjoy a gracious rural community life and live in spacious and attractive country homes in Asbury Park, Greenwood Lake, West Hampton, and Martha's Vineyard. Motoring is difficult because the tourist cottages do not accommodate Negroes. But the summer town calendar includes tennis and golf matches, yachting parties, moonlight sails, and an occasional horse show. Harlem has a horsy set which rides regularly on Central Park's bridle paths.

The Black Metropolis is the scene of the most active, varied, and glamorous social life in Black America — though visiting Southerners complain that many hosts are none too choosey about the guest lists. The extent of that life is indicated by the presence of seven hundred social clubs which sponsor affairs

ranging from noisy chitterlin' suppers and barrel-house parties
to formal balls, soirées, symposiums, musicales, and art exhibits. In these, Negroes strive earnestly for correctness. This
apparently was the case at a housewarming party held in the
spring of 1942, as reported by Billie Chase, the society editor
of Harlem's *Amsterdam-Star News*. Obviously impressed, he
described the affair as 'a new high that will be extremely difficult to top.' The house, it seems, was conceived by a California architect, who 'combined all the charm of the Golden
State, including rough-hewn beams, stucco and paneled walls,
terraces with gay awnings, arch-doorways and such.' The
guests strolled about 'the beautifully kept backyard where a
waiter dispensed beer and frankfurters, while a three-piece
band gave out with music from a second-story terrace.' Below, a downstairs terrace contained a cocktail bar where still
another waiter served champagne, 'which flowed like Niagara
Falls, just cases of it, no less!' And for those whose tastes ran
to milder forms of imbibing, there was punch, as well as as-
sorted hors d'oeuvres for a hungry snack. To top off this lar-
gesse, expensive gifts were distributed to more than one hundred and fifty guests.

Typical of the formal affairs which highlight the winter
social season that starts on Thanksgiving Eve and ends with
the beginning of Lent, is the gorgeous ball of the Comus Club,
café-au-lait society's most conservatively fashionable and
firmly established social organization. Its annual functions,
which mark the apex of the social year, are characterized by a
strict decorum and an air of elegance. Men in white tie and
correct tails, and women stunningly gowned in a brilliant
array of colors, provide one of the irresistible sights of Negro
life. At these affairs, the dancers staidly refuse to truck,
boogie-woogie, or Lindy hop. The parties nevertheless are exciting and picturesque. By employing a caterer at a recent
affair — thus doing away with the proletarian practice of
bringing shoe-boxes stuffed with sandwiches, fried chicken,

and deviled eggs to formal functions — the Comus Club thereby scored in a big way with those of social importance.

Negro society is rapidly losing its social pretensions, in the opinion of social experts. For its members are becoming a class of professional and white-collar workers, and as such are beginning to regard themselves not as a 'wealthy' Negro upper class, but as intellectual workers. This fact is being reflected in their changes of consumption, character of family life, and in their social outlook.

Chapter XIV

*It is not his money or the power of his muscles
which make him great ... (but) desirable traits
in any race or any station. ...*
— JOHN G. VAN DEUSEN

JOE LOUIS AND HIS PEOPLE

THE night of June 25, 1935, was a memorable one for Black
America, and marked a dramatic highlight in the race's march
along the glory road. Joe Louis, a Negro born of poverty-
stricken parents in the cotton patches of Alabama and a few
short months away from the assembly line of Ford's Detroit
factory, entered the prize ring at Yankee Stadium to battle
Primo Carnera, a massive Italian gladiator standing six feet
five inches. Louis was meeting the acid test as a pugilist!
His opponent was a seasoned veteran who looked very much
like a grizzled gangster capable of handily beating anyone.
Scheduling of the engagement had stirred much racial feeling, and among whites there was talk of an aftermath of
rioting by Negroes. Westbrook Pegler, the Scripps-Howard
columnist, was most vocal on this point. To the sporting
world, however, the match had the competitive glamour and
romance of a David-and-Goliath sort. ...

Negroes thought little about the event at first. For things
were going badly for them, and they were concerned with the
stern affairs of day-to-day living. The Depression had silenced
their songs and happy laughter. The insecurity of the times
had produced widespread discouragement, apathy, and indeed

cynicism. Negroes had little to shout about. This attitude was somewhat reflected in the trickle of pre-fight comments. Few Negroes — those who thought about it — believed that the young Midwesterner was anything more than a run-of-the-mill fighter despite the publicity lavished on him by the Chicago *Tribune*, which had proudly sponsored the young Negro as a glittering product of its Golden Gloves tournaments. Had Jack Johnson, the first modern Negro heavyweight champion, not said that Joe Louis was a second-rater? A good slice of the Negro population even scoffed, in a reference to the young fighter's light complexion, 'No high yaller has the guts to make a good fighter — too much *white* blood!' In support of this dubious color chauvinism, they pointed to the fact that most of the immortal Negro boxers had been *black* men.

Yet, suddenly, as the big battle approached, Negroes dropped what they were doing to listen to the radio reports. Some began rooting for Louis because he was fighting an *Italian* — the race was already stirred over the fate of Ethiopia — and others because Joe was in combat with a white man. But all Negroes joined in his corner because he was a *Negro!* Whether it was the South Side of Chicago, St. Antoine Street of Detroit, or the Hill District of Pittsburgh, Negro communities throughout the country seethed with excitement. Harlem was frankly and obviously on edge — the feeling was almost tangible. The night was hot and sultry, but the people of the Black Metropolis were glued to radios indoors. From every apartment and tavern window, from every candy store and barber shop, shadows of Negroes could be seen in various anxious poses, many rigidly hunched over the instruments that would bring the news. The streets, whose colorful neon signs seemed to give a festive air to the community, were suddenly deserted, except for a few policemen idling within the rings of the lampposts' lights. The atmosphere was tense, expectant, thrilling!

Then, Clem McCarthy's rapid breathless voice was heard

and the fight was on! Negroes hung on every word. For five rounds they heard Joe cut and slash at the huge hulk before him. But the white man was a dangerous foe. In the sixth and fatal round, Louis hammered him to the canvas three times. Each blow was delivered with the flash of a cobra's strike; each time the two-hundred-and-sixty-pound mammoth crashed to the floor, his battered face smeared with streaming blood; and each time he gamely rose. But after the third time down he was groggy and helpless and unable to raise a hand. The referee stopped the fight and lifted the Negro's hand in the traditional token of victory.... Then the winner was introduced to the radio audience — and for the first time Black America heard the thick, blurred voice of Joe Louis.

'He was a good boy,' he said of his opponent.

And with that a terrific roar went up in Harlem — the reverberations shook the very rafters of the community's tenements. Immediately men, women, and children, unable to contain themselves, streamed into the streets. They seemed to come from every doorway and basement, shouting with joy: 'Yeah, man!'... 'I knowed it, I knowed it!'... 'What a man!'... 'He's a killer-diller!'

Pandemonium broke loose. Tens of thousands marched through the streets, slapping backs, shaking hands, and congratulating each other. There was shouting, clapping, laughing, and even crying. Youngsters who should have long been in bed were on the streets pounding dishpans and yelling. The din was deafening. Thousands stormed through the streets chanting, 'We want Joe! We want Joe!...' Horns were tooted, cymbals crashed, and radios shrieked. Much whiskey was guzzled. To the music of jukeboxes which blared forth from every barroom, young couples on the sidewalks broke away from the crowds and went into furious Lindy Hops and Susy Q's, while the old folks capered happily. Urchins climbed aboard automobiles and busses, unable to pass through the dense crowds, and good-naturedly screamed their happiness. The hilarity lasted until the early hours of the morning.

To understand this collective behavior of Black America, we must try to grasp the meanings of the immense prestige that the Negro community attaches to those who are successful; and to grasp, as well, the social factors operating in the background. For one thing, the Negro is vastly concerned with the individual. When a Negro is a success, it is credited not only to him, but to the whole race. Close track is kept of Negroes who have been successful in all fields, but especially in those fields in which Negroes excel in competition with white men. For another thing, the Negro feels that achievement by a Negro breaks down the prevailing opinions of the Negro's inferiority. Actually, though, Negro achievement has an even more positive effect upon Negroes themselves. It is indeed a shot in the arm which helps to tear away inner feelings of inadequacy, and thus to quicken the social advancement of the entire race.

Joe was acclaimed by Negroes everywhere — even indeed by black men in the West Indies, South America, and Africa. All manner of honors were showered on him. He was made a director of the Victory Life Insurance Company, a Negro corporation, and a popular brand of bread, sold by a Negro company, was called 'Brown Bomber,' a title given him by the press. Clubs, societies, and babies were named after him, and from Harlem to Atlanta, testimonial dinners were given in his honor by members of his race. The Southern Negro Youth Congress awarded him a plaque as the country's most outstanding Negro youth. Enterprising men did a profitable business selling pictures, buttons, busts, and statuettes of Joe. From the Deep South came streams of letters. 'God bless you, Joe Louis,' a typical one read. 'You've given us hope. Keep on.'

His physical prowess represented lure, color, and glamour,

which every black boy has enjoyed vicariously through his identification with Joe. He gave the little fellow of the race the long-awaited chance to shout and yell — and indeed to brag and boast. But he also gave Negroes confidence which enabled them to meet with increased authority their day-to-day problems. He encouraged and inspired, moved and stirred, and set for them examples of exemplary conduct. He made them unafraid of tomorrow. Many Negroes came to feel that the door of opportunity in American life was not actually shut; with a little pushing it would open to the humblest member of the race. For, after all, had Louis not risen from humble beginnings to a position where white America heaped praise and wealth upon him?

He was hailed by Black America as a great symbol. The porter, the handyman, the domestic, the unemployed man, the lowliest black boy of the slums, now envisioned new hope. The Pittsburgh *Courier* held that Louis 'lifted an entire race out of the slough of inferiority, and gave them a sense of self-importance.' There is perhaps a little yeast contained in that statement, but it is a fact that Joe gave a decided lift to the Negro's morale by stimulating a more positive outlook on American life.

Negro scholars industriously began to dig up Negro prize ring champions of the past, to give historical perspective to the present-day development, and thus to reinforce Joe's accomplishments. One of these figures unearthed was the 'Tremendous Tom' Molineaux, who, back in the early part of the last century, drifted into New York City and became the first acknowledged boxing champion of America. As a porter at the Catherine Market, a place long frequented by white and Negro sailors and longshoremen, he demonstrated fighting ability. Newspaper references to Molineaux as a prize-ring champion first appeared in 1809.

A sea-captain then induced him to go to England, where boxing was a popular sport. On his arrival in London, he went directly to his compatriot, the American Negro Bill Richmond, who was conducting an inn, known as the Horse and Dolphin, and a boxing academy for the nobility at the Royal Tennis Courts, where one of his patrons was the poet, Lord Byron. Richmond, himself a boxer, became Molineaux's sponsor and coach. Tom met the famous Britisher, Tom Cribb, one of the greatest bare-knuckle fighters of all time, on December 10, 1810, at Caphorn, near Essex, and lost after forty blistering rounds. Following another losing engagement with Cribb, ill-fortune dogged the steps of the black boxer, and he met death by violence in a barracks at Galway, Ireland.

There is considerable speculation as to how Molineaux became a fighter. Information is scanty, perhaps, because he was a runaway slave and as such had to hide his true identity. At any rate, legend says he was born in 1784 at Georgetown, Maryland, and was reared on a Virginia plantation. He began fighting at the time the sport was first introduced into this country by sons of wealthy Southern planters. In those days the young men of the well-to-do Southern familes frequently traveled to England for their education, and while there many acquired a taste for boxing. They continued the sport after their return home, matching their slaves and wagering money on the outcome. It is just possible that Molineaux was one of these early slave-fighters.

The Golden Age of Negro pugilism was ushered in when Peter Jackson won the Australian championship in 1886, and came to America and fought James J. Corbett to a sixty-one-round draw. The later period saw such fighters as Joe Gans, George Dixon, Joe Walcott, Sam Langford, and Jack Johnson. Great as these men were, they never knew the feeling that out beyond the ring the tumbling roars were for them. In their day, Negro prize-fighters ran up against the crackling hostility of white crowds, and frequently received some pretty bad decisions. The burning hatred, which hung over the ring like a pall whenever a Negro met a white man, was so real a handicap that only the most stout-hearted overcame it.

But few black boxers felt the lash of prejudice as did Jack Johnson, who came into prominence after winning the heavyweight championship from Tommy Burns in 1908. Almost immediately a frantic search began for a 'white hope' to dethrone him. Jim Jeffries, a former heavyweight champion and then past thirty-five, was goaded into coming out of a well-deserved and prosperous retirement to meet the Negro. A large section of the press had whipped up the sentiment that the security of white civilization and 'white supremacy' depended upon the Negro's defeat, but Jeffries failed to rise to the occasion. When he squared off with Johnson at Reno, Nevada, July 4, 1910, he took one of the most awful lacings a fighter had ever received in the city. Jack London was at the ringside. 'The greatest battle of the century,' ran his dispatch to the New York *Herald*, 'was a monologue delivered to twenty thousand spectators by a smiling Negro. From the opening round to the closing, he never ceased his witty sallies, his exchange of repartee with his opponent's seconds and with the audience.' The next morning the old *World* observed slyly, 'That Mr. Johnson should so lightly and carelessly punch the head off Mr. Jim Jeffries must have come as a shock to every devoted believer in the supremacy of the Anglo-Saxon race.'

The fight caused considerable excitement — excitement which did not end with the final round. While the *Herald* wondered as to 'the effect of Johnson's victory on the colored population,' Negroes were being attacked by whites in various sections of the country. The following day the *Herald* acknowledged this fact in reporting race rioting in New York City as elsewhere. The story carried this headline: 'HALF-DOZEN DEAD AS CROWDS ATTACK NEGROES; REIGN OF TERROR HERE.' Showings of the fight pictures provoked further disorders. Mob passions reached such a point of violence and destruction that Congress, to forestall further incidents, passed a law — later repealed — prohibiting the inter-state shipment of moving pictures of prize-fights.

The Texas-born Johnson finally lost the title to Jess Willard, in Havana, Cuba, in 1915. Pictures of the fight show the fallen champion taking the knockout count while shading his eyes from the scorching tropical sun. Perhaps it was his sense of humor that carried him over many of the rough spots in his rather stormy career. Yet his conduct brought him disfavor, even persecution, and indeed increased prejudice toward his race. Following his marriage to a white woman — the first of three such relationships — virtually identical bills against interracial marriages were introduced in Wisconsin, Iowa, Kansas, Minnesota, New Jersey, Michigan, and New York. Similar bills were introduced in Congress, with penalties varying from imprisonment to enforced surgical operations. However, few of them came to a vote, but they reflect the temper of the times.

Johnson was, after all, a product of a boisterous and rowdy era, and as such one of its gaudy expressions. He drove about recklessly in big high-powered automobiles, wore flashy clothes, spent money lavishly, and generally led a fast life. Perhaps he mistook liberty for license — a distinction against which Negroes even today must be on the alert. Trevor C. Wignall, the famous English sports writer, who looked at Johnson more dispassionately than Americans, found him to be no better and no worse than other boxers. The fact is, Johnson's behavior lacked good taste and offended many people, both Negro and white, in a period when prize-fighting was outlawed in many states as 'a brutal exhibition.' The man who staged the Jeffries-Johnson encounter, Tex Rickard, vowed never to promote another interracial heavyweight championship contest — and he kept his word.

'If we had more Negroes like Joe Louis,' I overhead one Negro say to another, 'things would be better for us.'

'Sure 'nuff,' countered the other, 'but if we had more white folks like Joe, things would be better still. . . .'

Louis's phenomenal rise — contrary to the Johnson era — was met by a conspicuous liberality in the white population, an attitude that lately has been extended toward Negro fighters generally. Perhaps Louis earned it by his own deportment in defeat as in victory, and by his clean habits and total modesty. Nation-wide publicity never turned his head. He neither strutted, bragged, nor gloated over a fallen foe. He remained the unassuming boy who first came roaring out of the West to stand Black America on its head. . . .

Born Joseph Louis Barrow on May 13, 1914, the fifth child of poor tenant farmers, near Lafayette, Chambers County, Alabama, the future champion was a little over twenty years of age when he gave up a five-dollar-a-day job in the Ford motor plant in Detroit to gamble on professional fighting as a career. Previously, he had won the National A.A.U. light-heavyweight championship, and after definitely deciding on the ring as a means of livelihood, he placed himself under the management of John Roxborough, also of Detroit, who induced his Chicago friend, Julian Black, to become co-manager. To train their charge, they selected Jack Blackburn, a veteran fighter with a thorough knowledge of boxing; and together, they piloted Joe through the maze of angles, intrigues, and prejudice that clutter the road to a world's heavyweight championship.

The defeat of Carnera was the major leg in Louis's race to the crown. During the next year he polished off four more contenders by knocking out King Levinsky, the happy-go-lucky Max Baer, Paulino Uzcudun, and Charley Retzlaff. Joe was on the threshold of a fight for the world's championship when he experienced his first adversity at the hands of Max Schmeling, the German boxer, whom he met at the Yankee Stadium on June 19, 1936. The contest had stirred considerable debate and once again threw the racial issue into the public scene.

The German authorities were opposed to an Aryan fighting a Negro. Doctor Paul Joseph Goebbels, Nazi Minister of Propaganda and Public Enlightenment, forbade the German press to accept articles by Arthur Buelow, German boxing expert and former manager of Schmeling, because Buelow had predicted that Joe would trounce the Black Uhlan, as the Nazi fighter was called.

Forty thousand people were present to witness the fight — though it had been boycotted by many Jews and the Anti-Nazi League. As it turned out, Louis lost to Schmeling by a knockout in the twelfth round — the only one in his professional career. Goebbels immediately wired his congratulations. The *Schwarz Korps*, according to the Associated Press, exulted that Schmeling's 'shattering fists had smashed all adversaries of National Socialism in the face,' and had 'saved the prestige of the white race.' The Nazi pugilist, on his return to Germany, was saluted by Hitler as an inspiration to German youth and he and his wife were entertained officially.

The defeat of Louis was one of the most astonishing upsets in recent ring annals. The Negro public was flabbergasted. The downfall of their idol brought cries of 'doping,' implying that Joe had been the victim of foul play. Negro newspapers investigated the circumstances of the fight but were unable to reveal any double-dealing. So bitter was the feeling in Harlem — as elsewhere among Negroes — that Jack Johnson, who predicted Joe's defeat and boisterously flaunted his winnings on the fight, had to seek police escort to escape the wrath of angry Negroes.

Louis took his defeat philosophically, and redoubled his efforts to improve his ring technique. 'Me and Chappie's goin' back to school,' Jack Blackburn said. Joe hit the come-back trail, and within two months was scheduled to meet another opponent. About this time Louis was approached by the American Olympic Committee, which was meeting great difficulty in raising money to transport a team to Berlin, where the Olympic Games were to be held. 'They asked me for somethin' to help them out,' Joe admitted, 'but I sure done feel like doin' it.' He was feeling keenly the German gibes at his race. 'Any American,' he declared, 'that believes in fair play and the rights of people ought to feel that way. 'Course I'm a Negro, but it's not only that. . . .' Joe was clearly opposed to American participation in the Olympic Games in Nazi Germany.

By a curious irony the American Negro reached the peak of his athletic achievement in the summer of 1936 in Berlin — two months after Louis's defeat and Nazi bragging. In that most arrogant state in the world, the Nazi leaders were left stuttering, as Jesse Owens, Ralph Metcalfe, Johnny Woodruff, and Cornelius Johnson, Negro members of the American Olympic Team, swept to scintillating victories in running and jumping. Hitler, who was present in the Reichssports Field when this racial disaster occurred, beat a hasty retreat to avoid congratulating the Negro Americans before the German people. Next morning the Nazi newspapers attempted to persuade the Germans that what they had witnessed at the stadium was nevertheless not true. Editorials pointed to the amazing decline of the *white* American athletes and particularly noted the gratifying rise of the Germans. They baldly declared that the United States had not won the games at all — the record to the contrary — but largely its 'black auxiliary force.' In an unsporting manner, the German writers insinuated that white Americans had brought over the Negroes to steal the show. 'Actually,' *Der Angriff*, a leading Nazi organ, contended, 'the Yankees, heretofore invincible, had been the great disappointment of the Games, for without these members of the black race — their 'auxiliary helpers' — the Germans won.

Maybe this double-talk was not quite so much nonsense as it seemed at first glance. Even then, it appears, the Nazi-controlled press was attempting to divide the American people. But let's skip the moral and return to Louis. The feats of

Jesse Owens and Company served no doubt to inspire and restimulate Joe. He toppled seven opponents by knockouts —
among them Jack Sharkey, a former champion — before he
moved into Chicago on June 22, 1937, to tangle with that
sturdy Irishman, James J. Braddock, holder of the world's
heavyweight title. He took the crown by knocking him out in
the eighth round. But this engagement was only a rehearsal
for the event on which the whole world had its eyes focused —
the return match between the Brown Bomber and the Black
Uhlan. The Nazi boxer heightened interest in the bout on
his return to the United States by spouting nonsense about
his Aryan superiority over Louis. Joe said nothing.

When the floodlights set the ring ablaze in Yankee Stadium,
the night of June 22, 1938, there were seventy thousand people
in the stands. Among them were one thousand Germans who
had traveled here especially for the fight. Every train into
New York had disgorged thousands of fight fans. For days
people had been pouring into the city by airplane, ocean
liner, bus, and private car. Betting was brisk; Louis was
favored but plenty of Schmeling money was about. Black
America was in a rare pitch of excitement.

Three winning bouts — after his taking the title — had
given Louis a nice edge for this second encounter with the
Nazi. For the only time in his life, Joe entered the ring
with hate in his heart. When the bell clanged, and the long-
expected battle was under way, Louis advanced from his
corner, eyes narrowed into slits, arms poised in deadly precision. He quickly attacked the German with a fusillade of
terrific blows, which three times sent the Nazi invader to
the canvas. The bewildered Schmeling countered with exactly four punches. Louis crushed the Nazi Aryan within one
vividly savage round. . . .

A delirious celebration took place in Black America, rival-
ing the one following the Carnera fight, for a good deal of
emotion was tied up with this fight as with the others. But

many responsible Negroes came to view these demonstrations
of emotionalism with alarm, aware that many Negroes believed that Louis was a superfighter — especially after his
slashing one-round defeat of the Black Uhlan. So prevalent
was this attitude that the worried Negro leaders began to feel
that certain elements might try to make an issue of a Louis
defeat. Manifestly disturbed, Harlem's *Amsterdam-Star News*
published a series of editorials and cartoons warning the
Negro population against displays that would prove injurious
to the whole community.

This wholly dangerous feeling was particularly in evidence
the night that Joe met the handsome, cocky Irish lad, Billy
Conn, at the Polo Grounds in Harlem, on June 18, 1941. As a
precautionary measure, a special detail was assigned to aug-
ment the regular police force in Harlem. That night when
Conn put on a brilliant exhibition, and in early rounds appeared about to knock Louis from his throne, Black America
was stunned. The atmosphere in Harlem was extremely tense.
As the fight progressed, there were ominous grumblings, with
some near hysteria. The cheers of fifty-five thousand white
people in the Polo Grounds, which echoed down the streets of
Harlem, heightened the distress. Louis finally won by a knockout in the thirteenth round — and Black America relaxed.

William G. Nunn, managing editor of the *Courier*, who
recognized the danger signals, wrote a remarkable editorial the
next day, which indeed is a social commentary.

> Can Negro America 'take it'? [he began.] Frankly I don't
> believe they can. And if they can't take it, I'm preparing them
> right now for something which might happen at any time. . . .
> White America has been grand to Joe. They've made him a
> millionaire. They've been for him — they've admired him
> for a clean-cut young American, representing the very finest
> in powerful, young manhood. They've cheered him, and they
> rooted for him. Very few times has it been the lot of Joe Louis
> to hear the boos of the crowd. . . .
> We've built out of the mists a 'superfighter' — a man who

just can't be beaten. We've been selfish in the perpetuation of
an ideal which few of us would be willing to live up to. . . .
   Remember that he's helped you . . . and you . . . and you . . .
and all of us. . . .
   If — and when — he loses, Joe will take his defeat in his
stride!
   So will we!
   And so must you!

Everything in Joe's life has not been home-cooking. He
has known the little indignities which Negroes meet day after
day. But such experiences have not embittered him. Instead
he feels keenly the responsibility of being a sort of Negro am-
bassador in the white world. Frequently he has said, 'If I ever
do anything to disgrace my people, I hope I die!' It is this
quality which has helped to certify his greatness. For Louis is
well aware that he is a symbol of his race rather than a fighter,
and the high plane on which he has conducted himself indicates
how seriously he has accepted his unique rôle. Even while he
was training for his first fight with Max Schmeling, he revealed
this turn of mind.

I had been assigned by a newspaper to cover his training
camp, and while we played pool and lounged around the
camp, Joe talked volubly of many things — his hopes, ambi-
tions, racial problems, jobs, school, and the like. He often
said to me, in a half-musing way, 'You know, I gotta prove
myself!' Then he would think for a moment, and add, '. . . all
Negroes do!'

About this time, the white sports writers were making much
of Louis's impenetrable silence. Actually, before he got into
the important money he had had little contact with white
people and was very shy of them. Evenings, however, after
they had gone, he expanded among his Negro associates —
managers, friends, stable-mates, and the camp hangers-on.
He was alert to what was happening about him, and possessed
of a sense of humor expressed in Negro idioms. Travel and
experience have since developed him considerably. His shy-

ness has disappeared, and he has even mastered the radio micro-
phone. Perhaps his lack of formal education caused his silence.
In any case, one of the first things he did when he could afford
it was to employ a tutor, a Negro chap named Russell J.
Cowan, a graduate of the Detroit School of Technology. For
two hours every morning he taught Joe history, grammar,
mathematics, and geography. When Joe discovered golf, much
to the dismay of his teacher, he skipped classes and went off to
witness matches.

Louis is a big, good-natured boy, reflecting the homely
training of an honest, hard-working, ambitious mother. He
has not sought the spotlight nor wished cheap notoriety.
Beyond a splendid wardrobe, he has spent little money, and is,
in fact, one of the thriftiest of the Negro boxers. He made his
first bank deposit of seventy-five dollars in 1934. Today his
account runs into six figures. Yet he is very generous. Just
before the Carnera match, he bought and furnished a home
for his mother, and sent his sister off to Howard University in
Washington. Later he established a Joe Louis Fund for the
race relations department of the Federal Council of the
Churches of Christ in America. 'Before I retire,' he wrote to
the council, 'I want to put up one more fight — the best of
my career — to help my people.'

A few hours before he entered the ring to knock out Max
Baer in four rounds, in New York City on September 24, 1935,
he was married to Marva Trotter, an attractive brown-skinned
girl of Chicago. They have an heir. He provides for them
handsomely, and she leads an active life in sponsoring movements and benefit functions for the betterment of the race.
Mr. and Mrs. Louis own their own home in Chicago, two automobiles, and a dude ranch in Michigan where — before the
war — he worked at his hobby of raising show horses. But
Joe has put the greater portion of his earnings into fixed se-
curities. He also has financial interests in Chicago apartment
houses, which incidentally contributed materially to lifting the
living standards of Negroes in that city.

During his eight-year boxing career that began in Chicago July 4, 1934, with a fifty-dollar purse, he has fought fifty-seven fights, won forty-eight by knockouts, gained seven decisions, and won one by a disqualification. He has lost but one fight, and defended his crown twenty-one times. His shares of the purses have totaled approximately $2,228,000.

Louis enlisted in the Army as a private on January 12, 1942, while at the pinnacle of his career as one of the greatest fighters of modern times. The reaction of Black America was illustrated by an editorial which appeared in the *Amsterdam-Star News*. It said: 'Joe Louis is one of the Great Americans of our time. His deeds and his words have made him so. In heroic mold he has stood forth head and shoulders above men of sport in giving all and offering all for his native land.' Later he donated his share of two title defenses to Army and Navy relief — the amount totaling more than eighty thousand dollars. To cynics who criticized his fighting without pay, in the face of the racial-discrimination policy maintained by the Navy, Louis countered, 'I'm not fighting for nothing, I'm fighting for my country.' When he appeared soon afterward at the New York Boxing Writers' dinner to receive their award as the fighter of the year, former mayor of New York City James J. Walker, in presenting the award, praised him with: 'Joe, in what you have done you have shown you are a great Negro. You showed, too, you are a fine American. But you've done something more. You laid a red rose on Abe Lincoln's grave.'

Shortly after that speech, Louis appeared in Madison Square Garden in his own most eloquent rôle. He made a speech at the Navy Relief Show. Called from the stands, the heavyweight champion mounted the stage wearing his gold-buttoned army uniform. Under the spotlight he looked like a hulking schoolboy bursting out of his clothes. He spoke to his audience with deep emotion. Private Joe Louis is no master of the King's English. He fumbles his tenses and drops his final consonants. He was never trained as an orator. But in a slow, soft drawl, he brought forth one of those simple statements of faith that well up in Negroes as naturally as the spirituals. He said:

'We'll win because we're on God's side!'

Chapter XV

Only by preserving a voice in the councils of each political party can Negroes hope to share in the benefits of a victorious campaign. Whoever wins then must give the Negro vote consideration.

— HARLEM'S 'AMSTERDAM-STAR NEWS'

THE NEGRO'S BALLOT

'NEGRO VOTERS: YOU MUST REGISTER TO VOTE!' appears in streamers across the top of nearly every Negro newspaper in the months before elections. This call to political arms is indicative of the Negro's aggressive drive for political power as a means of improving his lot. The Negro has considerable confidence in the democratic processes, and to him the ballot is more than a sentimental symbol — it means freedom and progress! What gains have been made may be attributed in a large measure to his activities in the North, propelled by an increasing race-consciousness.

Every Negro in the North may vote, and Negroes have taken eager advantage of the privilege. The race's growing political strength is being rapidly increased by the migration North of Southern Negroes, and together they vote pretty much in a bloc. As ever, feverish efforts are made by the white politicians to corral these ballots. They have never forgotten that without the Negro vote the Republican Party would have lost the Presidency on at least two occasions. When inventory was taken, following the Democratic victories

of 1932, 1936, and 1940, the political strategists estimated that
the shift of the Negro vote away from the Republicans was a
major factor in the triumphs.

In seventeen Northern states the Negro controls 281
electoral votes of a possible 531, which is potentially the balance of power. In short, a solid vote may conceivably have
tremendous influence upon the fretful future of American
politics. The fact is that the Negro is not tied to any party, as
the last three national elections have demonstrated. The
Negro's political evaluations are realistic, and he is voting for
persons who, in their daily lives, have shown concern about
the Negroes' problems long before election day. The yard-
stick is as exacting for Negro as for white leaders. The most
significant development recently is the passing of the Negro
ward politicians as leaders of the race. Although there are
few outstanding Negro political leaders, the race has nonetheless great cohesion in pursuit of political objectives.

Today, the social and economic condition of the race is the
weather-vane of the Negro vote. For one thing, the Negro has
learned that politicians — white or black — are not idealistic;
nor are they responsive to the demands of constituents if
machine-controlled; also, they are not above sacrificing the
Negro for political expediency. Thus, the Negro vote goes to
the highest bidder in terms of concrete social and economic
offers. The measure of a Negro politician is determined by his
ability to achieve social gains. To survive as an influential
leader, he must be attuned to the aspirations of the race.

Moreover, the day has passed when a white man can choose
the Negro's political leaders. The Negro has learned the lesson
of racial solidarity, and is using it to go places. This fundamental shift in sentiment — coincident with the rise of race-
consciousness, or perhaps because of it — is the key to the
Negro's political development and strength, and reveals a
brand-new era in Negro politics. By alternately supporting
the best candidates of all parties the Negro has made major

advances. Today Negroes send representatives to at least twelve state legislatures in the North. The municipal g ins have been equally heartening. Chicago elected the first Negro to sit in Congress in twenty-seven years and has a Negro on the municipal bench; Harlem has five Negro judges serving in the courts of New York City and three Negro commissioners; and Black America is represented by a Negro in the diplomatic corps.

The Negro's first experience in politics was gained soon after New York's constitution, adopted in 1777, granted the franchise to free Negroes. Almost immediately the Negro became a pawn in state politics, though to begin with he had but three hundred votes. The rapid growth of the black voting population made many Democrats fear an independent Negro vote which would tip the scales in close contests. The Democrats — then called Democratic-Republicans — were a party of small farmers, artisans, and laborers, who rightly regarded their aristocratic opponents, the Federalists, as a party of the wealthy whose interests conflicted with their own. Negroes leaned toward the Federalists who, over the protests of Democrats, put through legislation in 1799 emancipating the blacks in New York State. Tammany Society, the organized Democrats of New York City, denounced the Negro as a tool of the aristocrats, and the cause of low wages and long hours. General Root, a prominent Democratic leader, indignantly complained that the Negroes would 'change the political condition of the whole State,' and the Democrats resorted to terror and violence to drive blacks away from the polls.

The Federalists found the Negro votes strategically important to maintain political power and amended the state laws so as to improve the social and legal status of the race. 'How important, then,' declared a Negro politician, Joseph Sidney, addressing a Negro audience in Liberty Hall in 1809, 'that we, my countrymen, should unite our efforts with those of our

Federalist friends.' When the Democrats were returned to power in 1821, they immediately started action to disqualify Negro voters. At the state convention that year they were successful in pushing through a special property qualification for black suffrage, which eliminated the Negro as a large voting factor until 1870, when three fourths of the states ratified the Fifteenth Amendment.

Except in the New England states, where there were no race stinctions in suffrage, free Negroes were deprived of the vote all other Northern states. From time to time, a few well-to-do Negroes were allowed to vote, but free Negroes all told hardly numbered more than ten per cent of the total Negro population, and their political influence at the polls was negligible. The indirect political influence of the Negro was nevertheless considerable.

Negroes resumed political activity with the antislavery movement and also kept up the drive to increase the number of voters. The *Colored American*, a leading Negro newspaper, agitated constantly for the Negro's participation in politics. Twenty-nine articles appeared in its columns within a three-month period before the elections of 1840. It not only discussed the question, but also gave advice to those Negroes qualified to vote and urged them to register and support the newly formed Liberty Party, which was running a candidate for President.

Alarmed by the growing activity of the proslavery politicians of the North, Negroes joined in the organization of the Liberty Party and supported the adoption of a radical platform, declaring slavery unconstitutional. Significant planks also included the free distribution of land, limitation of landownership, free suffrage, and the abolition of monopolies. However, Negroes were not finally united on action through political parties until Frederick Douglass made his historic decision. Previously, he had supported the Garrison faction of abolitionists which opposed using the ballot as a political weapon be-

cause, in its view, the Constitution was a 'proslavery instrument.' Douglass broke with Garrison and brought his immense prestige into the political arena. This move proved to
be a prelude to the Negroes' affiliation with the Republican
Party, and Douglass's emergence as the outstanding political
leader of the race.

Suffrage nationally followed Civil War and thrust Negroes
into the Reconstruction scene as an important political faction, at a time when the Republican Party needed votes desperately. Negroes now had their first real taste of political
participation in both state and federal governments. They
eagerly began by helping to reorganize the state governments
of the South. In Arkansas, for instance, J. T. White became
Commissioner of Public Works and Internal Improvement,
and J. C. Corbin, the State Superintendent of Schools. F. L.
Cardozo, educated at the University of Glasgow, Scotland,
was State Treasurer of South Carolina. Florida elected a
Negro Dartmouth graduate, Jonathan C. Gibbs, as the first
Superintendent of Public Instruction. A Negro, P. B. S.
Pinchback, served as Acting Governor of Louisiana.

When the Mississippi state legislature convened in January,
1870, a Negro minister, Hiram R. Revels, opened the Senate
with a moving prayer which helped to make him a United
States senator — the first Negro to be elected to that body. He
was nominated for senator by a Negro conference, which then
put him forward at the Republican Party caucus, and he was
elected in a joint session of the state legislature.

Considerable excitement attended his appearance in the
United States Senate, though some doubts arose as to his
eligibility. While the newspaper editors worried over the
technicality of his citizenship, the Negro statesman went to
Washington, where he was sworn in and seated. He immediately plunged into the routine of the Senate. Ten days later,
with much Republican fanfare for the party's Negro protégé,
Revels made his maiden address. 'Never since the birth of

the republic,' one observer remarked, 'has such an audience
been assembled under one single roof.' Revels was said to be
self-possessed, dignified, and lucid, some people comparing
his manner with that of Jefferson Davis, the Confederate
leader.

The Negro senator was an industrious legislator. He took
especial interest in the freedmen's welfare, introduced bills to
construct levees on the Mississippi River, and appointed a
Negro to West Point. Back home, meanwhile, Negroes were
increasing their influence in the political affairs of his state. A
former slave, Major John R. Lynch, became Speaker of the
Mississippi House of Representatives. He later served three
terms in Congress and was considered one of the most forceful
speakers in politics during the seventies and eighties. Besides
Revels, Mississippi sent another Negro to the United States
Senate — B. K. Bruce, a graduate of Oberlin College. From
1868 to 1895 twenty-three Negroes were elected to Congress,
representing Virginia, Georgia, Florida, Alabama, Louisiana,
Mississippi, and North and South Carolina. At one time all
the representatives of South Carolina were black men.

The Negro legislators were earnest, ambitious men whose
conduct, according to James G. Blaine, a white colleague,
would honor any race. He particularly praised the representatives, James T. Rapier of Alabama, Joseph H. Rainey of South
Carolina, and Lynch of Mississippi; and the two Mississippi
senators, Bruce and Revels. The failure of these men to accomplish much of importance may be attributed to the hostility of their Southern colleagues. A white Solid South had
formed for the purpose of ending the Negro's participation in
the section's political life. When the federal troops were with-
drawn from the South in 1877, the Ku Klux Klan spread terror and dismay among Negroes. Violence, intimidation, legal
obstacles, and arbitrary administrative practices were used to
keep Negroes from the polls. These proving insufficient, restrictive measures were enacted. One, for instance, was the

'grandfather clause,' which allowed only descendants of persons who had voted prior to 1867 to exercise the franchise. To restore the caste system, whites closed the doors to schools, hotels, restaurants, and public places of amusement. The process of reducing the Southern Negro to a second-class citizen was completed by 1910. Though Negroes protested, the moral conscience of the nation was unmoved!

With the collapse of the reconstructed governments in the South, Negroes sought to re-establish their political prestige through activity within the Republican Party and by securing federal appointments. Beginning with President Grant a number of jobs of importance were given Negroes, which incidentally helped to steady their wavering loyalties. Douglass was successively a commissioner of Santo Domingo, Minister to Haiti, counsel for the government, and recorder of deeds for the District of Columbia. A number of others held such positions as register of the Treasury, consular agent, and collector of internal revenue. There were also collectors of ports, collectors of customs, and postmasters of small cities. Major Lynch was elected temporary chairman of the Republican National Convention.

The political arena for the Negro shifted to the North, where the race was becoming increasingly active in ward politics. The developments in New York are illustrative. Here the Democratic Party had been aggressively proslavery during the Civil War and spoke of the 'political supremacy of the white race.' Yet, with the close of the war, Boss Tweed of Tammany Hall, who had shrewdly contributed money to the Anti-Slavery Society and had been seen on platforms with abolitionists, promptly sought to bring Negroes into the Democratic fold. But Negroes still felt a moral indebtedness to the Republicans. Tweed made little headway beyond winning over a few underworld figures, from whom he exacted tribute for the privilege of conducting disorderly houses without being raided by the police. For many years the Negro neighborhoods were plagued by such Negro criminal characters as 'No-Toe' Charley, 'Black Cat,' and 'Jube' Tyler, who strode about with the arrogance of those under corrupt protection. Hank Anderson, Tweed's valet, was strong-armed boss of the Negro underworld, and was said to be the 'man' for those who 'coveted the colored vote.'

This sort of politics was hardly attractive to Negroes who had participated in a more or less revolutionary movement. The abolition crusade had created high expectations. But in the closing years of the century, many Negro Republicans began to express discontent with the treatment meted out to them by their party. Actually, the Republican Party leaders had sold the race down the river in an attempt to crack the Solid South. Negroes were placed in the dilemma of having to choose between backsliding Republicans and Southern politicians — those avowed enemies of the race. Negroes continued to vote solidly for Republican presidential candidates, but the liberal leadership of President Grover Cleveland made them take a second look at the Northern Democrats. Now under the leadership of Richard Croker, Tammany Hall gained the support of a large bloc of Negro votes. A committee of Negro leaders visited Croker and asked him what pledges he would make to the Negro community. He is quoted as saying, 'A colored man will be placed in every department of city government.' To consolidate the party's gains, Croker organized the United Colored Democracy of Tammany Hall, designating 'Chief' Edward E. Lee as its leader. He set Lee up in a clubhouse on West Fifty-Third Street, this making him New York's first Negro machine boss.

Lee, a native of Virginia, was head bellman of the Murray Hill Hotel — which incidentally gave him his title. This popular hostelry was frequented by prominent New Yorkers. Among those often seen there was Richard Croker, who soon recognized the Negro's ability to handle men. In time Lee was referred to in political circles as the 'Black Croker' — a name

he hardly deserved. He was without voice in the councils of
Tammany Hall, and only a few crumbs fell to Negroes, beyond
the appointment of James D. Carr as the first Negro deputy
assistant district attorney. Almost immediately Negroes deserted Tammany and remained away for the next thirty years.
Police brutality — in a Tammany-controlled city — did much
to embitter Negroes and to drive them away from the party.
Memories of Southern injustices were still fresh in many
others. Douglass was right, they said: 'The Republican Party
is the ship. All else is the open sea.' As late as 1915 there were
less than a thousand enrolled Negro Democratic voters in New
York City.

In the last twenty-odd years the Negro politically has re-
gained something of the importance he enjoyed during the
early Reconstruction era. A prime factor is the heavy Southern migration to Northern cities, giving the race a voting
preponderance in many areas. This migration also brought a
great change in the outlook of Black America, a change which
is destined to have a profound effect on American life. The
city had indeed become Black America's frontier. Here the
people are restless and ambitious. Here, too, the race is
politically adventurous, even to the point of occasional shifts
to the radical parties.

By and large, ward politics produced a hard-bitten, cynical
crew of Negro politicians. Some of them were none too
scrupulous, associating quite frankly with the underworld,
and winking at police attempts to regulate vice. They were
solid realists who inherited little of the idealism of the Reconstruction leaders. Men like 'Mushmouth' Johnson and
'Teenan' Jones in Chicago, and R. R. 'Bob' Church, Beale
Street boss of Memphis, were extraordinarily powerful politicians. Tammany Hall attracted men of a similar stripe, whose
sole purpose in politics was the gravy. But on the whole, these
men were faithful to friends and respected by enemies, and
many of them gained a dignity and importance far beyond

their personal worth, because Negroes associated them with the struggle for civic and political rights. The Depression — and the consequent need for change — terminated the behind-the-scenes rule of many of the ward politicians and ended the careers of some.

Black America's largest political figure in this period was Oscar De Priest, a Chicago ward politician who was elected to Congress in 1928. He immediately became a national leader and Black America turned its eyes toward Washington, where Negroes hoped his unique position would enable him to render service to the race.

The future congressman was born in Florence, Alabama, on March 9, 1871. With a normal school education, he started life in Chicago in 1899 as a laborer. When he arrived there were only fourteen thousand Negroes in the city. Almost immediately he plunged into ward politics. With rare skill as an organizer and propagandist, his rise in politics was rapid and indeed profitable. He never lost an opportunity to drive the Negro's cause forward, and with a courageousness that won him many friends. At a meeting of both white and Negro persons, during the period when new Negro homes were being bombed in Chicago, De Priest is quoted as saying: 'Negroes are going to move anywhere they can pay rent and if the white people don't like it, we'll run them into the damn lake.'

Negroes like such talk from their leaders. Politically, however, he made many a somersault. He alternately supported the Republican and Democratic Parties, but made his greatest gains as a supporter of the Mayor Thompson faction of the Republican Party. He was the first Negro to be elected as an alderman in Chicago. Whatever his critics may say of his career in the jungle of ward politics, his election to Congress undoubtedly represented a symbol of Negro achievement.

De Priest was succeeded in Congress in 1934 by Arthur W. Mitchell, a Democrat, who four years before had been a registered Republican. De Priest's vote against the W.P.A. was perhaps a reason for his defeat. His successor, once Booker T. Washington's office boy, was a novice in politics and as such was buffeted about by the old-line politicians in Congress.

With the election in 1942 of William L. Dawson, Chicago already has sent three Negroes to Congress, and has men of the character of Alderman Earl B. Dickerson, a rising political figure, to take the helm. But Harlem, even without congressional representation — because of gerrymandering — is still the scene of the race's most fundamental political progress. The resurgence of Negroes in New York State politics began in 1917 when they elected Edward A. Johnson, a Republican, to the State Assembly. The next year, George Harris, a Harvard man and editor of the New York *News*, became the first Negro alderman. He had a useful career as a public servant, and, among other things, was instrumental in having Negro physicians appointed to Harlem Hospital and Negro nurses employed by the city. Black men have since represented Harlem in the City Council and State Assembly.

Not until 1930, however, was control of the Negro districts wrested from white men. That year Negroes launched a campaign to elect their own district leaders, hoping thereby to snatch a larger share of the spoils. The Republicans were first to recognize the Negro's new aspiration and nominated Colonel Charles W. Fillmore, a lawyer and World War veteran. He won handily, but at best it was a profitless victory, for New York was under the control of Tammany Hall. Negro Democrats soon started whooping it up for Negro leadership, but the Tammany sachems were in no mood to have Negroes in their inner circle. To divert the Negro's attention, they created a new judicial district and allowed Ferdinand Q. Morton, a Negro civil service commissioner who had succeeded to the leadership of the United Colored Democracy — largely a paper organization — to name two Negro candidates for municipal judges. He chose James S. Watson and Charles E. Toney, and they were elected over two Negro Republicans.

This honor failed to cool the ardor for Negro district leadership. Negroes again began agitating in the predominantly Negro areas — raising the question as a purely racial issue. Harlem quickly responded to the plea for race loyalty. Today, there are two Negro members of Tammany Hall's executive committee — Herbert L. Bruce and Daniel L. Burrows, also a state assemblyman. Burrows, a young man in his early thirties, was elected at a stormy session in 1939, suggesting something of the heat engendered by political affairs. The Tammany bigwigs were on hand to see that proper parliamentary procedures were observed! They looked on while fifteen patrolmen and two mounted policemen kept disorder from breaking into open violence. Three men were running for the leadership of the Nineteenth Assembly District — Burrows, who received 185 votes on the first count; James Ravenell, also a Negro, who won 253 votes; and Harry C. Perry, a white man and former leader, who obtained 131 votes. When Perry threw his votes to Burrows, one hundred of Ravenell's supporters moved down the aisles, aiming to do battle for their man. They set up a din in the process that could be heard blocks away, and it was with difficulty that the police restored order.

When the other Negro member of the Tammany executive committee, Herbert L. Bruce, leader of the Twenty-First Assembly District, made his bid for leadership, he was a restaurant proprietor, without political experience, but possessed of a driving racial passion. Negroes rallied to him, and after more than three years of heated campaigning, he was elected in 1936. He brought an honesty to politics that amounted to gross impertinence in the eyes of some white politicians. Stocky and bulldoggish in appearance, his tenacity of purpose and loyalty to friends are almost legendary. Born in Barbadoes, and educated in the public schools of Harlem, Bruce is something approaching a literalist. This seems to have been the case when he broke up a partnership with Miles Duncan, co-owner of the Monterey Restaurant, one of Harlem's popular cafés.

The two men, who met as fellow redcaps at Pennsylvania Station, opened the Monterey with an initial investment of six thousand dollars. Three years later they remodeled the establishment at a cost of eighteen thousand dollars. Duncan, an ardent Republican, began to disagree with the Tammany leader. When Duncan tried 'to freeze Bruce out' of the partnership, Bruce decided to dissolve the business on a share-and-share-alike basis. Early one morning, following months of strained relations, Bruce called in the 'boys' from his political club and they calmly proceeded to partition the place completely. The job was executed with mathematical precision. Not a single item was overlooked. Tables, chairs, doors, windows, lighting fixtures, cutlery, dishes, glassware, liquor, food — even the plumbing, toothpicks, and napkins — were split on a fifty-fifty basis. Objects that could not be divided equally — such as a discarded straw hat, a twenty-foot counter with a concrete foundation, and a red-blue-and-gold circular bar — were sawed into two parts. After several hours of division and demolition they carted away Bruce's half of the Monterey Restaurant to a warehouse.

In this manner, Bruce divides the spoils between his white and Negro constituents. Lately, though, there has been little to share. Tammany Hall has been on famine rations. For Bruce — like other Tammany leaders — was unable to stem the tide toward reform government.

There are roughly three hundred and fifty thousand Negro voters in New York City. In the last ten years this vote has shifted from the Republican to the Democratic Party in national elections, but again seems on the verge of another significant shift. Locally, Negroes have supported independent candidates. In the last three elections for mayor of New York City, Negroes voted ten to one for Fiorello La Guardia, a reform candidate whom they call 'Shorty George.' This has paid off high dividends. Besides making reforms in the relief system and providing low-cost housing for Negroes, Mayor La Guardia has made some historic Negro appointments. He appointed Hubert T. Delany, a former tax commissioner, and Jane M. Bolin, a Wellesley and Yale Law School graduate, as judges in the Domestic Relations Court; reappointed Ferdinand Q. Morton, a Harvard graduate and Tammany holdover, as a civil service commissioner; elevated Samuel Battle from the police ranks to parole commissioner; and made Myles A. Paige a judge of the Special Sessions Court. Today, some five thousand Negroes hold civil service positions in New York City and earn more than six million dollars annually. The higher brackets of Negro civil employees earn salaries ranging from five to twelve thousand dollars a year.

Under the revamped civil service system Negroes have risen through the ranks to jobs of honor and responsibility. Wesley Williams, standing high on the competitive list, was promoted to battalion chief of the Fire Department. Mrs. Gertrude E. Ayer, a popular educator, was made a principal of a large public school, and Mrs. Vivian Mason was advanced to administrative district supervisor in the Department of Welfare. Besides, Negroes hold positions ranging from district attorneys and city marshals to insurance superintendents, physicians, architects, and purchasing agents. The federal and state payrolls in New York City contain another five thousand Negro employees — distinct from the war agencies — with Elmer A. Carter the top person as a member of the state's Unemployment Insurance Appeals Board.

These developments on the top-drawer level, while acclaimed, are chiefly class honors rather than major advancements of the whole Negro community. Broadly speaking, the danger in the top appointive jobs is that the Negro recipients are beyond the control of the Negro rank-and-file. What often happens to these people is that they tend to form an aristocracy within the race and become jealous of their privileged position, and become chiefly concerned with maintaining it. They are unresponsive to the aspirations of the little fellow, and, in racial crises, frequently fail to speak out in behalf of their race, conscious perhaps that the security of their positions is dependent on the goodwill of the white folks. This, in its modern dress, is called Neo-Uncle Tomism.

The Southern Negroes, more so than Northern Negroes, are plagued with such leadership among the state-paid teachers, professors, and college presidents. But such leaders in the South can be by-passed if the rank-and-file once secure the ballot. Actually, the whole condition of the Southern Negro is directly a result of his lack of the ballot. Without it, he is denied the right, along with whites, of ousting such flagrantly anti-Negro elements as the 'white trash' bloc of Southern politicians, who perpetuate and impose segregation. In such heavily Negro-populated states as Mississippi with forty-nine per cent, South Carolina with forty-three per cent, Alabama with thirty-five per cent, Louisiana with thirty-six and Georgia with thirty-five per cent, the Negro is completely unrepresented.

In the 1940 elections, in which seventy per cent of the electorate of forty states went to the polls, only twenty per cent of the electorate voted in the eight poll-tax states — Virginia, South Carolina, Georgia, Mississippi, Tennessee, Arkansas, Texas, and Alabama. Today, with loud talk current about democratic rights, the poll tax has become a national issue. It was designed originally to maintain the supremacy of whites over Negroes, but like most racial legislation, has succeeded only in maintaining the power of a few over both Negroes and poor whites. So today almost five million white people are barred from voting.

The poll-tax requirements in a cursory reading do not seem excessive. The tax ranges, in the eight poll-tax states, from one dollar in Arkansas to two dollars in Georgia and Mississippi, payable annually a few months before election time.

But one dollar is an enormous amount when the average per-capita income of the poll-tax states is three hundred and seven dollars annually — this figure being based on the total earnings of the South. In four of the states, the taxes are cumulative. In Alabama, for instance, a man born in 1900, about the year the poll tax was passed in that state would have had to pay thirty-five dollars to vote for the first time in 1942. In Georgia he would have had to pay nearly forty-five dollars. The poll tax, according to the Southern Electoral Reform League, is actually a vehicle for political corruption. Elections are matters of buying and selling poll-tax receipts and absentee-voter ballots.

Abolition of the poll tax, Negroes say, will not of itself enfranchise the Negro and poor white of the South. They point to the fact that there are no poll-tax laws in Louisiana and Florida, yet Negroes there are not allowed to vote in any great numbers. There is a poll tax in Vermont, but Negroes in Vermont vote. The South has other devices for keeping the Negro from exercising the right of suffrage. There are the notorious 'educational tests' and 'white primaries' which effectively bar Negroes from the polls. The story is told, concerning the 'educational tests,' of a Negro who had received his Ph.D. in Romance and Classical Languages at Harvard and had traveled abroad widely, and later sought to vote in Alabama. In taking the test, the white clerk put a number of newspapers before him — German, French, and Russian — and asked him to read them as proof of his literacy. This he did without one error. Finally, the clerk reached under his desk and brought forward a paper printed in Chinese.

'What does it say?' urged the clerk impatiently.

'It says,' began the Negro, 'that in Alabama they don't let Negroes vote.'

In the fight against the primary laws in Texas, Negroes took their case before the United States Supreme Court four different times. Each time the court ruled in their favor, the Texas legislature amended the existing statutes. In 1923 — to cite one occasion — it specifically provided that 'In no event shall a Negro be eligible to participate in a Democratic primary election held in Texas. . . .'

'Let us not delude ourselves,' said the Pittsburgh *Courier* editorially, 'that those fighting the Civil War will not find other means of defying the federal authority.' In brief, what Negroes want is the right to vote, implemented by tangible safeguards. Maybe, federal supervision of elections! The inability to use the ballot has discouraged a considerable section of the Negro population, but the migration of Southern Negroes to the Northern cities may very well put the mass power of the race into the hands of the aggressive Northern leaders, and finally bring the issue to a life-and-death struggle.

Among the intellectuals, there are those who have turned to the Communist and Socialist Parties, but these groups have never mustered any great voting strength among Negroes. Perhaps Negroes, a minority group seeking governmental protection, are instinctively aware that they cannot always afford to be out of touch with the major parties. During the Depression, however, the radical parties made deep inroads, but the rank-and-file of Negroes are not likely to go all-out for radicalism until they completely despair of the democratic processes. Nevertheless, the Communist Party has had a profound effect upon the political thinking of Negroes.

What seems to be taking place in Negro life is a transfer of power from the politicians to the leaders of the labor and militant civil rights organizations, and the emergence of new types of men who are taking positions toward the left.

Chapter XVI

Young man, young man,
Your arm's too short to box with God.
— JAMES WELDON JOHNSON

GLAMOUR BOY

BIG, booming Adam Clayton Powell, Jr., preacher, editor, and legislator, is one of the handsomest men in Black America. Women sometimes call him 'Mr. Jesus.' Therein lies the source of his extraordinary popularity. He is six feet three inches in height, and weighs two hundred and ten pounds. Sloppy tweeds hang on his powerful frame with *Esquire* distinction. He is a white man to all appearances, having blue eyes, an aquiline nose, and light, almost blond hair. At thirty-four years of age, he is going places in a rush. Impatiently ambitious, he seeks to lead the working-class whites as well as Negroes in a 'People's Movement,' and is one of the first Negroes to aspire to the leadership of both people. Such a leadership, should he realize his ambition, would be noisy, militant, and opportunistic. 'Do it, Brother Powell!'

Somewhat the careerist — aggressive, articulate, unpredictable — no more contradictory character exists in Negro life. He is an incredible combination of showman, black parson, and Tammany Hall. He is at once a salvationist and a politician, an economic messiah and a super-opportunist, an important mass leader and a light-hearted playboy. This young man on horseback — with a love for pleasure, quest for power, and unusual capacity for work — combines qualities which defy clear pigeonholing. To some he is a demagogue; to others the anointed leader. To all, though, he is a thoroughly engaging personality, whose weaknesses as a man are his virtues as a public figure.

If personal qualities alone are not sufficient to snatch the national Negro leadership, he possesses the instruments for pushing himself forward. As pastor of the largest Negro church in America, the Abyssinian Baptist, with a membership of fourteen thousand, he has a platform and to all practical purposes a powerful, cohesive political bloc. As the only Negro member of the City Council, he has prestige and a public sounding-board with echoes in the metropolitan press. As editor and co-publisher of a newspaper, the *People's Voice*, he can reach those thousands of Negroes who never darken the doorways of churches or political clubs. And as the leader of the Greater New York Coordinating Committee for the Employment of Negroes, a mass organization which has obtained hundreds of jobs for Negroes, he is provided with a mobile pressure group.

In short, he is the new and different kind of leader that the Negro church has produced — as modern as jive talk!

There are approximately four million Negro Baptists and about one and a half million Negro Methodists in the United States. The Baptist Church attracts the great masses. The Methodist with its hierarchy and formal ritualism does not have quite so strong an appeal. The other religious denominations trail in Negro attendance, though in recent years the missionary work of the Roman Catholic Church has made pronounced headway. However, those denominations which are controlled by a white hierarchy are at a disadvantage in attracting Negroes, for the Negro church, developed by the Negro in slavery, is his very own to an extent equaled by few other institutions. Not alone is the church the center of the Negro's independent existence, but it is one of the most important tools the Negro has in his struggle for status.

By fostering race-consciousness the Negro church helps to solidify the race, a function the white church can hardly perform. There was talk some years ago by Negroes, when Saint Benedict, the Moor's Roman Catholic Church, was being redecorated, to have the pink cherubs pictured on the ceiling painted *black!* The church being led by a white priest, this business never came to pass.

In recent years the Negro church has been sharply criticized for assuming a passive, sometimes indifferent rôle toward the Negro's social and economic problems, even indeed advocating submission to white domination. Some Negroes declare that the church exploits its members. H. L. Mencken, none too generously, called the Negro clergymen 'barnyard theologians' and the church a 'hogwaller of Christianity.' While the Negro church of today does not approximate the vigorous instrument it was in the antislavery period, individual ministers nonetheless have spoken out clearly and have frequently mobilized forces for aggressive action in the Negro's cause. By writing letters, holding mass meetings, and threatening economic boycotts, certain ministers have helped to break down economic discriminations against the race. A survey conducted recently by Jerome H. Holland, a Negro professor at Lincoln University, to determine the attitude of the Negro clergy toward social injustice, showed that only 23 were opposed to any action being taken by the Negro ministers out of a possible 776 answers. Asked whether they thought immediate action was imperative, 597 replied in the affirmative.

For a number of years following the first World War, the press rivaled the church as a medium of racial self-expression, concerned as the church was with purely religious functions. Today, the Negro church is attempting to recapture its former place in the secular life of the black man. New types of leaders are taking over — men who are trained, socially conscious, and forward-looking, with their fingers on the pulse of the Negro. First-rate seminaries are turning out men prepared not only in the Scriptures but in the importance of health, employment, and housing, from such institutions as Gammon Theological Seminary, a Methodist school in Atlanta, and Howard University in Washington.

It was, for instance, J. C. Austin, pastor of Pilgrim Baptist Church, who first led the Jobs-for-Negroes campaign in Chicago; and in New York it was John H. Johnson, pastor of Saint Martin's Protestant Episcopal Church, who took the helm in Harlem's jobs campaign. Stanley High, a white journalist, visited the Chicago church and there saw a huge sign hanging beside the entrance which, in the distance, he took to be an announcement of revival meetings. The first sentence read, 'What Must We Do to Be Saved?' The answer surprised him. It was this: 'Beset by Rent Hogs, Overcrowded in Hovels. Come to the Housing Mass Meeting on Thursday Noon. The United Front.'

For a number of years, the only Negro member of the Pennsylvania state legislature was Marshall L. Shepard, pastor of Mount Olivet Tabernacle in Philadelphia. He attracted national attention in 1936 when he rose to deliver the opening prayer at the Democratic National Convention in Philadelphia and Senator Ellison D. ('Cotton Ed') Smith of South Carolina marched out in protest — 'racial pandering,' the Southern politician called it. Two years later Shepard was awarded a medal for meritorious service to his state.

Twenty years ago it is doubtful if any Negro church anywhere would have opened its doors, much less given the freedom of its pulpit, to a Socialist. Today, there is indeed a Socialist minister — the Reverend Ethelred Brown of Harlem. Moreover, James W. Ford, the Negro Communist candidate for Vice President, has spoken in Negro churches all over the country. He attracted two thousand in 1934 at the Ebenezer Baptist Church in Pittsburgh, and similar numbers at the Abyssinian Baptist Church. The Scottsboro boys, who, after their release, made a triumphal tour through Negro communities under the wing of the Communist Party, had church pulpits offered them wherever they went.

'We've had enough,' one young preacher was heard to say, 'of the gospel of "dem golden slippers." What we want is the gospel of thick-soled shoes.'

What is happening to the church is a reflection of what is happening to Negroes. Though the Negro church appeared to be slipping some years ago, it will never completely lose its place in the Negro's life so long as the race is discriminated against. For, within its portals, Negroes find entertainment, culture, and self-expression as well as political guidance and spiritual nourishment. The fact that the ministers have again stepped to the front has reinforced the church's hold on the Negro. Yet, curiously enough, not one clergyman can be called a national leader.

To corral the Negro vote, though, the Democratic Party crowds its stationery with the names of oustanding Negro clergymen. Topping the list is Doctor R. R. Wright, bishop of the African Methodist Episcopal Church. During the 1936 campaign, Bishop Wright was given permission to delay his sailing to his African mission in order to labor in the political field. Another bishop, Doctor Reverdy C. Ransom, is a very large figure among Negroes in the Midwest — both as a clergyman and as a politician. Elder Solomon Lightfoot Michaux, famed radio preacher of Washington's Church of God, is something of a pet among Democratic politicians, and is frequently called out to beat the drum in campaigns.

Adam Clayton Powell, Harlem's crusading preacher, was born with a silver spoon in his mouth which he is using as a lever to lift himself up in the world. His father, Doctor A. Clayton Powell, Sr., born of Virginia slaves and today a man of considerable means, was pastor for some thirty years of that great Gothic structure of New York bluestone which is the Abyssinian Baptist Church. Before he moved the church to Harlem, it occupied a building on West Fortieth Street, opposite the site of the present *Herald Tribune*. In 1921 the church sold the site for $190,000 and erected the present edifice at a cost of $350,000. It has an amphitheater auditorium seating two thousand, a pulpit constructed out of Italian marble, and a community house with offices, lecture rooms, gymnasium, showerbaths, reading-rooms, and a roof garden. The mortgage was publicly burned in 1928, after the church's membership had observed a rigorous tithing system. Today, the cost of maintenance and manifold activities is estimated at seventy-five thousand dollars annually.

The Abyssinian Baptist Church, organized by eighteen Negroes in a building on Anthony Street, was one of those religious bodies which separated from the white churches at the turn of the last century. With the migration of Negroes to Harlem the downtown churches were forced to pursue their flocks, and an era set in of large-scale buying and building. Today, scattered throughout New York are more than two hundred and fifty established Negro churches. The most significant commentary on this phase of Negro life is the fact that ten million dollars is invested in Harlem temples of worship, and some seventy thousand Negroes — most of them women — are members.

Before the government launched the public-relief program, during the Depression, the elder Powell established a relief

bureau in the Abyssinian Church and appointed his son as
director. This brought young Powell to the front for the first
time. Suffering thousands were given clothes, coal, kerosene,
and medical care, and two thousand persons were fed daily
in a free food kitchen conducted in the gymnasium of the
community house. The newspapers reported that Powell
père had contributed one thousand dollars to start operations.
When he publicly called upon the Negro ministers throughout
the country to do likewise, if they could afford it, a bitter and
acrimonious battle began to rage within the Negro church.
One clergyman, manifestly resentful of the publicity that
Doctor Powell had received, said that 'It is a mooted question
whether the church should actively engage in making medicine, serving soups, and juggling jobs.' To which another
preacher replied, 'If the newspapers don't publish what you
do, remember that "Thy Father which seeth in secret, Himself shall reward you openly."'

'My father,' young Powell once told an audience, 'said he
built the church and I would interpret it.' The Abyssinian
Baptist Church is indeed a Powell institution, unaffiliated as
it is with any denomination. This fact, perhaps, is the secret of
its challenging policies. At any rate, the elder Powell forged
the instrument, and young Powell has streamlined it. The
church's letterhead speaks of it as 'The Church of the Masses.'
One Sunday morning he said to his flock: 'At times it seemed
as if we were going to become a society church with a so-called
mythical Negro upper class. At other times we drifted into
what seemed to be an intellectual church, then again a church
for radicals, but today we have come of age, we are *The
People's Church*. All classes, all races, all schools of thought —
that is our parish.'

That boast is supported by a vast institutional program,
which attracts all sections of the population. The church has
become a complex organization of men's clubs, women's societies, and young people's groups sponsoring a host of activities

for children. The church's bulletin boards are fair indexes of
the activities. They are loaded down with announcements of
labor and political meetings, notices to those on relief, calls for
jobs, and a variety of social gatherings. The church provides
a clearing house for the multitude of community interests.
Powell, alert to social trends, sponsors forums with speakers
whose views range from those of James W. Ford, the Negro
Communist, and Margaret Sanger, the birth-control advocate,
to those of Evangeline Booth, the Salvation Army leader, and
Rabbi Stephen S. Wise, pastor of the Free Synagogue.

Before assuming the assistant pastorship in 1930, young
Powell was graduated from Colgate University and then spent
a year traveling in Europe and Africa. He attributes his
present progressive views to the oppression of colonial peoples
which he witnessed while in Africa. Perhaps the accident of
his having worked as a bellhop in the Equinox House, a summer resort in Manchester, Vermont, where he met Robert
Lincoln, son of the Emancipator, had a more profound influence upon him. Lincoln, it seems, manifestly disliked
Negroes. He even forbade any of the Negro help to touch his
personal possessions — luggage, clothes, even his automobile.
If one did, with his cane he soundly rapped the offender on the
knuckles. Powell, whom Lincoln mistook for a white man,
was the only Negro member of the help whom he would allow
to wait on him. The other Negro bellhops thought the incident humorous, but the future Negro leader never forgot
it.

Even more important in his development was the fight he
waged against his parents and the deacons of the church some
years after becoming the assistant pastor, to marry Isabel
Washington, a lovely and talented actress, who was then star-
ring on Broadway in Vinton Freedley's *Singin' the Blues*. He
told Richard O. Boyer, in an interview, that the affair revealed
to him the unreasonable formalism of the Baptist Church, and
from that day he learned to stand alone. Actually, he didn't

stand alone. She immediately gave up a bright and profitable career in the theater. The affair assumed the proportions of a public issue, with people taking vocal sides. There
were perhaps more people standing with him, supporting his
right to marry the woman he loved, than those who opposed.
He finally married her, with the applause of Harlem ringing in
his ears. The deacons relented and in 1937 formally called
him to the pastorate, to succeed his father, who today is pastor
emeritus. In winning out, young Powell gained considerable
confidence in his ability to meet a tight situation. But more
important is the fact that he won his first important following
beyond the corridors of his church.

From that day he really spread his wings. He joined the
Jobs-for-Negroes Movement, which was then languishing in
the hands of anti-Semites, and returned it to lusty life. In association with the Reverend William Lloyd Imes, then pastor of
Saint James's Presbyterian Church, and A. Philip Randolph,
president of the Brotherhood of Sleeping Car Porters, he
formed the Greater New York Coordinating Committee for the
Employment of Negroes. Before long, it had become a Powell
organization. In the spring of 1938 he led the committee in a
'Black-Out Boycott' of the Consolidated Edison Company
to force it to hire Negroes in capacities other than menials.
Every Tuesday night, in waging this unique economic battle,
in many Harlem homes electric lights gave way to two-cent
candles.

When the boycott tactic produced few gains, Powell geared
his organization for sharper action. At a mass meeting he
sounded the keynote of the new drive: 'Harlem is sick and
tired of promises. The hour has struck to march!' A bill-
payers' parade was staged in which hundreds converged on
the company's Harlem offices daily and paid their bills in
nickels and pennies — obviously a stratagem to disrupt service.
Simultaneously, action against other public utilities was taken.
Picket lines were thrown before their offices, led by Powell im-

. maculately dressed in a white linen suit. Attention also was again focused on the 125th Street merchants, with chanting picketeers loudly telling the world of their economic woes.

After months of intensified agitation from soapbox, newspaper, and pulpit — with, incidentally, the black nationalists rallying to his banner — the Harlem Chamber of Commerce, representing the white merchants, negotiated a contract with the Coordinating Committee which guaranteed jobs to Negroes on a basis of their numbers in the population. The *Times* commented favorably on the impressive gains. One thousand persons were employed over a period of one year. The Consolidated Edison Company capitulated and placed a number of Negroes in white-collar positions, ending the policy of hiring Negroes for menial tasks exclusively. The New York Telephone Company followed suit in handsome fashion. It staffed its entire Harlem office with a Negro personnel, and appointed a Negro as manager. The gleaming feather in Powell's cap, however, was the contract signed with the Fifth Avenue Coach Company and the New York City Omnibus Corporation which, for the first time in the history of the city, hired Negro drivers and mechanics. This was an achievement of no small proportion in the eyes of Negroes, and they loudly applauded. Every time they board a bus today and see Negroes at the wheel, they swell with pride.

The Jobs-for-Negroes movement is profoundly serious business to Negroes, but Powell always has an immense time. He enjoys himself so thoroughly that some are inclined to doubt his sincerity. Perhaps his vast sense of humor is discomforting. At any rate, he is too vibrant and happy to be a solemn reformer. Some people turn to gambling for excitement. Powell gets his in the daily rough-and-tumble of industrial strife. Once a movement bogs down, he soon wearies and turns to something else. If nothing is cooking, Powell discovers something that needs immediate action. For instance, take the letter he addressed to the thousands on his mailing list, calling them out for a mass demonstration:

My dear friend:
A crisis has arisen in Harlem.
A Negro — Wallace Armstrong, 168 W. 128th St. — was brutally beaten and then killed by over 15 policemen.
He was shot down like a dog.
This marks the third inexcusable killing this year in New York City of Negro people.

NOT ONE KILLER HAS BEEN ARRESTED.

IT IS OUR FAULT.

YOU MUST BE PRESENT, May 14, at 9:30 sharp at the Abyssinian Community House to stage a MONSTER CITIZENS' PROTEST MEETING for This Sunday, May 17, at 5 p.m., at the Golden Gate (Ballroom) and to PLAN A MARCH–ON–CITY HALL.

DO NOT FAIL THE PEOPLE. LAY ASIDE EVERYTHING.
Yours for People's Victory,
(Signed)   A. CLAYTON POWELL, JR.

What first comes to mind about Powell is his overwhelming charm, to which men and women alike succumb. He is boyish, affectionate, and playful. Once an athlete, he has never lost his love of sports. In the well-cushioned study of his Sugar Hill private home, he is relaxed, even reflective. He has a sharp, brittle mind, which is allergic to old ideas. In relating some new idea, he wags his head happily, chortles through his teeth, while gripping a pipestem tightly. In the midst of a conversation he will bounce out of his chair and say, 'How about a game of ping-pong?' Between strokes, the conversation continues as if never interrupted. He is never complex or ponderous. Hundreds of admirers flock in and out of his home, some hoping to bask in reflected glory.

He prides himself on being the perfectionist as an executive.

His half a dozen jobs keep him going at high speed, and over-
work two secretaries. His office is almost a confessional — he
is a political boss, economic consultant, and seven-days-a-week
pastor. Beside his desk is a dictaphone into which he delivers
his mail, and when he travels he takes the machine along, preparing speeches, notes, and directives for his office staff. His
study, too, is equipped with a dictaphone.

He works with his bare hands in the political pastures. He is
a man without a political party behind him — though lately
he has been close to the Communist Party. The Socialist
Party is openly suspicious of him. A lot of Democrats and
Republicans hate him because he is too far ahead of their parties, yet he has friends in both parties. He moves independ-
ently under the force of his own personality, his courage, and a
whole lot of insight into what is going on about him. He
preaches no Valley-and-Dry Bones sermons, but salts down his
speeches with nicely chosen Negro idioms about everyday
issues. But it is not so much what he says as the way he says it
— loud, dramatic, and often. He is perhaps the outstanding
orator in the race, and a spellbinder of no small proportions.
Sometimes he becomes entranced with his own words, and, on
at least one occasion, has been so moved as to weep publicly.
Negroes like their leaders emotional. Powell drips with
emotion. Yet thousands follow him because he has vigor,
brains, and understanding, and has identified himself with the
aspirations of the black rank-and-file.

But there are Negroes who complain that he is 'a stranger in
our midst.' Perhaps his light complexion is the source of this
feeling. For Negroes are very conscious, maybe envious, of
the fact that he can visit hotels, restaurants, and cafés run by
whites and not suffer any racial indignities. But to other sections of the black population, he is the idolized 'White Hope!'
Dan Burley, witty editor of Harlem's *Amsterdam-Star News*, is
not the least bit worried about Powell's color. He once remarked that Negroes need have no fear of him as a leader

because 'being *white* he constantly has to prove he's a *Negro* to Negroes.' If Powell is aware of this banter about his complexion, no one would know it. His racial patriotism is unquestioned. The unkind cuts at the race reach him as deeply as they do black men.

His every act is done with flamboyant suddenness. A Sunday morning late in the summer of 1941, for example, Pastor Powell mounted the marble rostrum of his church in an unusually serious mood. 'Brother pastor must be sick,' said one old woman. When he closed his sermon, appropriately chosen for the occasion, he walked down to the edge of the rostrum and rather intimately announced that he was running for a place in the City Council. For a few moments the packed auditorium was motionless. 'Then,' according to one newspaper report, 'as if blitzkrieged with religious fervor, the congregation suddenly turned the sacred meeting into a bedlam of hallelujahs and vociferous hand clappings, lasting twenty minutes, leaving no doubt that the pastor would have the full backing of his membership.'

When he flung his hat into the political pot, three other Negroes were already in the field — Doctor Channing H. Tobias, candidate of the Fusion Party; Doctor Max Yergan, president of the National Negro Congress and American Labor Party standard-bearer; and a lawyer, Herman C. Stoute, the Tammany Hall choice. Powell lost no time in persuading Doctor Yergan and Doctor Tobias to withdraw in his favor, and without the backing of any political party he launched a campaign which startled even old heads at the game. He first formed the People's Committee, with his Coordinating Committee as a nucleus, and selected an imposing list of white and Negro sponsors. He announced a platform which pledged a fight for 'Jobs! Jobs! Jobs!' He established headquarters, staffed by almost a thousand volunteers who worked with religious zeal. When he began to show strength, the American Labor, Republican, and Fusion Parties endorsed him — not, however,

without some behind-the-barn dickering. At a formal session
of the New York State Colored Baptist Convention, Mayor La
Guardia finally threw his support to the Negro minister.

Powell spoke every day and night to any group that would
listen. Always carefully groomed for these occasions, he wore
tweeds when he addressed white people and pallbearer blues
before Negro audiences. All during the campaign it was impossible to keep placards with his picture in their appointed
places — women cut them out as souvenirs! He waged an unorthodox political fight, even to turning out a parody on a
song popular in Harlem, 'Why Don't You Do Right?' The
heat churned up in this campaign was reminiscent of his
stormy job crusades. And he was elected — receiving the
third highest number of votes in the city. He received a
tremendously large white liberal vote. This opened his eyes to
the possibilities of becoming the leader of a people's movement! His election cost twenty-five hundred dollars, whereas
one losing candidate had spent twenty thousand dollars. The
job pays five thousand dollars annually!

Councilman Powell, measured by ordinary standards, has
been no flaming success as a legislator. Standing pretty
much alone, he is without organized support for any legislation
he would like to see enacted. But he does manage to make his
presence felt — however flamboyantly. His initial act as a
councilman was to charge the New York colleges with racial
discrimination, because of the absence of Negro professors on
the teaching staffs. The old-line Tammany politicians who
dominate the council, pinned back his ears on this one. Instead of tabling his motion as was no doubt expected, they
promptly supported his plea for an investigation. Nice boys!

A public hearing was held at which the college presidents
testified that Negroes had never made application for teaching
appointments! This closed the matter, and the Negro and
white press criticized Powell's impetuousness and baseless
charges. Actually, he was absolutely right. Of the 2232

faculty members of the city's four colleges, none are Negroes, but he presented few cases to prove racial discrimination — not because they did not exist, but because he had failed to take the trouble to consult with those responsible agencies concerned with this specific problem. He was vindicated in a measure when some months later City College made a gesture by appointing Doctor Abram L. Harris, Howard University professor of economics, for the summer session.

Possessed of amazing buoyancy, Powell was little dismayed by this setback. Unable to offer but few tangible accomplishments as a legislator, he insists that his *presence* there is sufficient. For, to the young leader, a public office is a platform and he sounds off regularly in behalf of the Negro. To further his political career, he entered into partnership with Charles Buchanan, manager of the Savoy Ballroom, to publish the *People's Voice*. It has become another platform from which he dins his name into the consciousness of the public. His editorials, captioned 'The Soapbox,' are the wordy diatribes of a speech-maker, but they also are forceful denunciations of the evils of our times and attract followers. Here is a sample:

> We are fighting FOR equality of races, blackout of discrimination, just economic opportunity, and decent housing anywhere, on either side of the tracks. . . .
> We are all men together. We are demanding a share in carrying this cross of world conflict, and just as strongly as we demand that, we demand a share of the crown of victory. . . .

Powell's immediate political aspiration is Congress. Once provided with this national platform, he will attempt to seize national leadership of the Negro people. He frankly says he has no program — beyond seeking the total integration of Negroes in the political and economic scheme of America. But already he has formidable enemies arrayed against him among the intellectuals and mass-organization leaders. While loudly applauding his achievements, Negroes frankly distrust him. They resent, too, his playing both ends against the middle. His frequently changing political alignments do not inspire confidence. Moreover, no one seems to know exactly what is his ultimate goal — beyond having power. He stirs the emotions, and drives people to action. But it is left to others to formulate concrete programs. Actually, Negroes are more dazzled than lifted by him — which indeed makes him a tough man to beat.

Chapter XVII

The issues are clear; the stakes are great; the path is straight; the tensions are tremendous; the pressures crushing.... This is the watchword that must go forward. We cannot give up the trust!

— ROY WILKINS

WHO ARE THE NEGRO'S LEADERS?

MEN and institutions beyond church doors, and without political labels, lead the race today. Both follower and leader, both servant and master of the Negro people, they are important cogs in the organized movement to set a 'constitutional revolution' in motion, through which, by orderly democratic processes, the black man hopes to bring about an end to distinctions based on skin color. The logic of such a movement compels its leaders to pursue a vigorous policy. Significant strides have been made already.

Stirred by the well-advertised slogans of freedom currently heard, Negroes are on the march. Spiritually aligned with the vast millions of oppressed colored peoples elsewhere in the world, giving American black men strength and numbers, Negroes are no longer in a mood to be placated by pious double-talk — they want some of the gravy of American life. The status of Negroes being what it is, they are, if anything, more ready than whites for immediate change. Today, the vast majority of Negroes are omitting no activity, or opportunity, to make the war the vehicle for rolling equality into American life.

Experienced in the techniques of mass action, Negroes are

better organized and better led than in the last war period. Their leaders are educated, intelligent, realistic, and international in outlook. Pearl Buck compares them to Nehru. Today only eight per cent of the Negroes are illiterate, as compared with thirty per cent in 1910. There were sixty-four Negro high schools in 1915; now there are twenty-five hundred. Between 1930 and 1940 almost twenty thousand Negroes graduated from colleges, more than twice the total of the preceding decade. There are two-hundred-odd newspapers which are keenly aware of their rôle in the struggle. Through the 'Black Cabinet,' a group of bright young men holding important positions in Washington, the race has pipelines into government circles. Besides the church already discussed, there are a multitude of labor and civil-rights organizations championing the Negro's cause. The 'Big Five' are the most powerful — the National Association for the Advancement of Colored People, the National Urban League, the National Negro Congress, the National Council of Negro Women, and the March on Washington Movement.

The growth of a militant racial sentiment, and thus of racial solidarity, has produced leaders different from any period in the Negro's history. The slave régime, for instance, offered little opportunity for the emergence of an independent type of leadership. Negroes who managed to achieve prominence during slavery were Northerners and active in the antislavery agitation, a movement largely directed by high-minded whites. Frederick Douglass was the most aggressive and conspicuous of the Negro leaders, but his appeals were directed not so much to his own people as to white society which he hoped to influence. In spite of his militancy, he was not a Negro nationalist, nor did he encourage any form of nationalism. Following the Civil War, the Negro clergy came into its own and constituted the most generally recognized group of leaders along with the Republican politicians, but they, too, made little appeal to nationalism.

Toward the close of the last century, new types of leaders ran up their colors unfettered by political commitments or religious connections, and began the trend to black nationalism by appeals to the Negro to pull himself up by his bootstraps. It was about this time that some Negroes began to regard themselves as 'a nation within a nation.' With the emergence of Booker T. Washington and W. E. B. Du Bois as national leaders, two general divisions, or schools of thought, developed for solving the Negro's problems, and Negroes arrayed themselves on either side. Washington, one of the most astute of the Negro leaders, was willing to accept, for the time being, less than the Negro's just rights, believing that these were impossible without economic independence. His messages of racial self-sufficiency and economic enterprise were directed to his own people. For, as he saw the future of the Negro, it rested finally on the ability of the individual Negro to make his own way in the world.

The followers of the Tuskegee educator today are mainly Southerners. Though more uncompromising than Washington — reflecting the trend of Negro thought — they essentially hew to his line. The principal figures who compose this body of leaders are Doctor F. D. Patterson, principal of Tuskegee Institute; Dean Gordon B. Hancock, of Virginia Union University; Doctor Charles S. Johnson, director of the Department of Social Science at Fisk University; Doctor Benjamin E. Mays, president of Morehouse College; Doctor Rufus E. Clement, president of Atlanta University; Doctor Horace Mann Bond, president of Fort Valley State College; and Doctor James E. Shepard, president of North Carolina College for Negroes.

These Southern leaders, sometimes called 'Uncle Toms' by the more radical Negroes, apparently have not made up their minds which way to turn in the present crisis. John Temple Graves sees their problem as ' . . . whether to follow the Southern white liberals or the Northern crusaders for all-

or-nothing.' Something, however, seems to be brewing. Late
in the fall of 1942, fifty of them met in Atlanta to prepare a
public statement on race relations in the South. Significantly
enough, Northern Negro leaders and Southern white liberals
were not invited to participate. The New York *Times*, in its
report of the meeting, observed that 'In view of the personnel
of the conference, it may be taken for granted that the document in preparation will be both dignified and amicable. . . .'
The statement, described as 'Articles of Cooperation' intended
to provide the basis for an understanding between the whites
and the Negroes in the South. As it turned out, the statement
was politely aggressive, but in the view of Northern Negroes a
retreat!

In dealing with the realities of the South, Southern Negro
leaders tiptoe with the angels. Rarely do they make frontal
attacks on a problem. Yet the militant trend of Negro life has
swept them into the progressive stream. Hence something
more can be expected in the days to come than a mere reci-
tation of the Negro's aspirations and an enumeration of the
injustices that hamper his progress.

Northern Negro leaders have pretty much taken the course
which Du Bois espoused. Inheriting much of the idealism and
radicalism of the abolitionists, he insisted that the Negro
should have, here and now, the rights to which he is entitled.
He held that Washington's program served to perpetuate the
inferior status of the race. Actually, Du Bois was concerned
mainly with the development of an intelligent, college-bred
minority, called a 'Talented Tenth,' to lead and elevate the
masses of the race. Such a group seems to have emerged, and
today constitutes the Northern group of intellectuals, who are
forwarding the Negro's cause with a vigor and skill hitherto
unknown in American life. Unlike Du Bois, however, they
have aligned themselves with the organized labor movement,
radical groups, and the 'left' elements of New Deal persuasion.
Vastly important, too, is the fact that these Negro leaders

make their appeals to the black rank-and-file. To put their objective briefly, they seek for Negroes unconditional equality with whites!

The men who are leading the Negro in this direction are, in the main, A. Philip Randolph, president of the Brotherhood of Sleeping Car Porters; Walter White, executive secretary of the N.A.A.C.P.; Mrs. Mary McLeod Bethune, president of the National Council of Negro Women; Lester B. Granger, executive secretary of the National Urban League; Doctor Max Yergan, president of the National Negro Congress; Doctor Channing H. Tobias, member of the National Council of the Y.M.C.A.; Doctor Alain L. Locke, professor of philosophy at Howard University; Roy Wilkins, editor of *The Crisis* magazine; and Willard S. Townsend, member of the Executive Board of the Congress of Industrial Organizations and president of the United Transport Service Employees. The Negro writers and artists might properly be brought into this group. Such people as Langston Hughes and Richard Wright have articulated the Negro's aspirations; and individuals like Paul Robeson and Marian Anderson, by their acts, inspire the masses to greater racial solidarity. Together, they have brought their great prestige to the Negro's cause.

One night in Kansas City — to illustrate — Paul Robeson interrupted his concert to deliver a spirited lecture against race segregation to a startled white audience. Said the baritone: 'I have made it a lifelong habit to refuse to sing in Southern states or anywhere that audiences are segregated. I accepted this engagement under the guarantee that there would be no segregation. Since many local leaders of my own race have urged me to fill this engagement, I shall finish the concert, but I am doing so under protest.' This sort of pluck has made much impression on Negroes. Later, when Robeson publicly defended the Russian invasion of Finland, the Pittsburgh *Courier* had this to say editorially: 'It is refreshing when a Negro of prominence disdains to follow the crowd for the sake of popularity and imperils his position for principle. So our hats are off to Paul Robeson.'

No less outspoken is Marian Anderson, whose statesmanship might well be emulated by other Negro leaders. Three years ago the Daughters of the American Revolution — those perverse ancestor-worshipers — refused her Constitution Hall in Washington for a concert. There was an outburst of protests, led by Mrs. Roosevelt and Harold L. Ickes, Secretary of the Interior. Through their efforts a concert was organized to be broadcast to millions as the world-famous contralto sang from the steps of the Lincoln Memorial to an audience of seventy-five thousand persons. When the D.A.R. sought to engage her to sing for Army relief, she stipulated that there was to be no segregation for this or any future concerts. The D.A.R., after prolonged consideration, agreed there would be no segregation for the one concert, but stated further commitments would not be made. The Negro artist finally agreed to sing, so that the war relief fund 'should not be deprived of the financial income' which her performance would bring.

The growth of racial sentiment has permeated Negro life. Though Marcus Garvey's philosophy for solving the Negro's problem — abdication of his rights and place in American life — was rejected by the masses of Negroes, he nevertheless demonstrated the striking appeal that race-consciousness has for the Negro. He stimulated and set it into motion, and it is these wild currents that the Negro leaders are riding today. His race missionaries, active since Garvey's removal from the American scene, have exhorted Negroes to repudiate white standards and wherever possible substitute black ones. Their day-to-day harangues from soapbox and pulpit have increased the prestige of all Negro leadership. The emergence of advanced leaders has helped to channelize this growing race-consciousness. In all likelihood it would have become fiercely anti-white had much of its heat and energy not been directed into the labor movement.

A fourth group of Negro leaders is already forming, stimulated by the growth of communism and socialism in the Negro
urban centers in recent years. Actually, it still is a part of the
Talented Tenth group, though its outlook embraces a world
view of the Negro's problems in Marxist terms. As yet, it has
no mass base among Negroes, but its influence in intellectual
circles is considerable. Most of its members are hardly known
to the masses of Negroes. This group is made up of James W.
Ford, the Negro Communist candidate for Vice-President in
1940; Ben Davis, Jr., former Amherst football star and leading
Communist Party figure; Ferdinand C. Smith, national secretary of the National Maritime Union of America; and Frank
R. Crosswaith, Socialist Party leader, organizer for the International Ladies' Garment Workers Union, and columnist for
Harlem's *Amsterdam-Star News*. These men, though personally
at political variance, are as one with the other Negro leaders
that Negroes must struggle for complete equality. But, in their
view, the vehicle is socialism or communism. Actually, though,
they are unable to make their point of view felt, for the Socialist Party has little following and the Communist Party —
though a tremendous factor in Negro life during the Depression — has lost ground steadily since the war began. Many
Negroes complain that in the Communist Party's quest for
national unity the struggle for Negro rights is being sacrificed.
A post-war depression may very well bring the radicals to
power.

The Communists first came into the consciousness of the
masses of Negroes during the famous Scottsboro case in 1931,
when an Alabama court sentenced nine Negro boys to death.
Caught stealing a ride on a freight train, they were charged
with raping two white girls found on the same train. The
International Labor Defense took up the case and carried
it to the United States Supreme Court, and secured a reversal
in 1932 on the ground that the defendants were not permitted
to have adequate counsel. The cases were retried and for

several years afterward furnished the Communist Party with a basis for nation-wide agitation, and an opportunity to present the party's platform to the Negro community.

With the Depression, Negro Communists came forward as leaders of the unemployed. In 1932 the party startled Black America by nominating one of its largest Negro figures, James W. Ford, as candidate for Vice-President of the United States. Ford, whose influence in Negro life rests on his strategic position in the party, had been a native of Gainesville, Georgia, where his father was a tenant farmer. He had witnessed the lynching of his grandfather by a white mob because of a dispute over the ownership of a pig. Soon after, the family moved away and both father and son went to work for the Tennessee Coal Company. Later young Ford graduated from Fisk University, and joined the Army. He served at the front with distinction, and upon his return entered the postal service, where he became active in the Postal Workers Union. He later began to give his entire time to these activities, finally joining the Communist Party. Today he is a member of its Central Committee.

The Communist Party, particularly vocal during the Depression, became a force in Negro life. But what is much more important, it seems to me, is the effect that its activities had upon the thinking of Negroes in this matter of race. The fact is, the party did more than any other agency in American life toward breaking down the rigid color barriers that once existed between the races, through organizations in which the party's influence was a factor — youth, labor, unemployed groups, and in the cultural movements. It is impossible to measure such intangibles, but generally speaking many Negroes discovered themselves, once given opportunities for self-expression beyond the Negro world.

One factor at least made a deep impression on Negroes — the ruthless manner in which the party fought in any form within its own ranks 'white chauvinism,' or race prejudice against Negroes. Public trials were held in Harlem, Chicago, Pittsburgh, and other large Northern cities throughout the country. Even where race prejudice reared up in any Communist affiliate it was promptly stamped out. These affairs, which served to dramatize the party's position, received considerable publicity through the Negro press. For instance, on one occasion the Chicago *Defender* commented favorably on this development. Heading its story, 'WHY WE CAN'T HATE "REDS,"' it said, 'We may not agree with the entire program of the Communist Party, but there is one item with which we do agree wholeheartedly and that is the zealousness with which it guards the rights of the [Negro] Race.' This statement pretty much reflects the attitude of the Negro press. As to the Communist Party's ultimate goal, the Negro's attitude is something else again.

The ticklish job of advancing the Negro's cause today is mainly in the practiced hands of two veterans — Walter White and A. Philip Randolph. Together, they work in easy association from New York headquarters. Two men who form a sort of supporting cast are conservative Doctor Channing H. Tobias and industrious Lester B. Granger, a former Dartmouth athlete. These men have the delicate task of negotiating gains for the race.

Walter White, a dapper, highly strung man, can pass for a white person. But his sympathies and outlook are those of a black man. He is a talented and shrewd negotiator and a quick-witted lobbyist — one of the best in the race. Any crisis that involves Negroes finds him on the spot — as in the case of the strike against Henry Ford, in which he called upon Negroes to support the union. Yet he is no radical. His politics may be summed up as 'Negro.' With a driving energy that gets things done, he is perhaps one of the ablest propagandists in America.

After graduating from Atlanta University, he studied in

France, later coming to the N.A.A.C.P. in 1918, where he eventually succeeded James Weldon Johnson as its head. He has perhaps more authoritative information on lynching than any living man. At the risk of his skin, he has investigated forty-one lynchings and eight race riots. For procuring the inside story on many race riots he was awarded the Spingarn Medal which was formally presented to him by Governor Frank Murphy. A writer of considerable ability, he prepared a documentary account of lynching, called *Rope and Faggot —— A Biography of Judge Lynch.* He has more than a nodding acquaintance with outstanding people in all walks of life, which has enabled him to get the off-the-record facts. He particularly has the ear of Mrs. Roosevelt and, before the war, corresponded with Nehru, the Indian leader. With the organized power of the association's six hundred branches —— with a membership of one hundred thousand —— and widely circulated magazine, *The Crisis*, at his command, he is a figure of considerable influence who recently has demonstrated a mature, comprehensive understanding of the trends of the times.

Under his leadership, the N.A.A.C.P. is carrying on a fight begun during W. E. B. Du Bois's day, to win complete equality for Negroes —— thus the association opposes all forms of segregation, discrimination, injustice, suppression, and special privilege. Quite recently it was successful in securing equal pay for Negro teachers in the South by legal action. It has waged unceasing war against lynching, and kept the anti-lynching bill before the public. It advocates use of the ballot as a political weapon, and militantly supports the fight to abolish the poll tax and 'white primaries.' The N.A.A.C.P. supports friends and punishes enemies. There was the time, for instance, when it successfully fought against the elevation of a man to the United States Supreme Court.

This happened during President Hoover's administration, when he nominated John Johnson Parker of North Carolina, a federal circuit judge, and sent his name to the Senate for confirmation as a Supreme Court justice. Immediately the N.A.A.C.P. sought to discover his stand on questions relating to the Negro. Word came from his state that he was opposed to the Negro's participation in politics. It seems that he had made a speech in 1920, published by the Greensboro *Daily News*, in which he said, ' . . . The participation of the Negro in politics is a source of evil and danger to both races and is not desired by wise men in either race.' Walter White wired and found that he did not repudiate this earlier stand.

Vastly concerned with the personnel of the Supreme Court, the machinery of the association was set into motion to defeat him. Since one of the association's cardinal methods of advancing the Negro's cause is through the courts, it was felt that Judge Parker's presence on the Supreme Court bench would greatly jeopardize the outcome of legal conflicts where the citizenship of the Negro was at stake. White appeared before the Judiciary Committee and filed a protest. Mass meetings were held in Chicago, Cleveland, Detroit, Kansas City, Los Angeles, Philadelphia, Baltimore, and St. Louis. Labor was persuaded that its rights would be endangered, and the A.F.L. went to town in opposing him. Senators were bombarded by Negroes with letters, long-distance telephone calls, telegrams, petitions, and personal visits. The Sunday prior to the final vote two thousand telegrams came from Chicago alone, putting the heat under the Illinois senators. In the midst of the campaign, the editor of the Greensboro *Daily News* wired Washington denying that his paper had published the anti-Negro speech by Judge Parker, which the association was quoting all over the place. The N.A.A.C.P. promptly had photostatic copies of the paper made, sending them to the President, senators, and the press. The upshot was that on a roll-call vote the Senate rejected Judge Parker's nomination.

For a time, according to Ben Stolberg, the N.A.A.C.P. was no more than a black Civil Liberties Union. Its leaders re-

ceived considerable criticism from Negroes because of the
association's failure to extend its activities. But with ominous
rumblings coming from abroad, the organization began talking in stronger terms. White asked this challenging question:
'How can a Negro believe whole-heartedly that the cause he is
asked to die for is worth dying for when daily he is confronted
by insult, discrimination, and segregation?' These were
strong words. But White was serving notice that race equality
was a war issue, and that repression of the Negro in the United
States would influence the colored races beyond our borders
and reduce the chances of ultimate victory. In his view, good
relations with the Latin American countries are hampered by
American attitudes toward colored peoples. To illustrate the
sort of thing he has in mind, White relates a curious episode
which took place in Washington some years ago. It seems that
M. Stenio Vincent, President of Haiti, a black republic, came
to this country for, among other purposes, a conference on
mutual action by Haiti and the United States in protecting the
Panama Canal. As he left the capital the United States
Marine Band, ordered to play a farewell in his honor, struck
up an old Broadway favorite, 'Bye, Bye, Blackbird!'

Color prejudice, in White's opinion, is the crux of the world
struggle. 'What is needed at this momentous period in our
history,' said *The Crisis*, organ of the N.A.A.C.P., 'is a sharp
and dramatic break with the past. War will not wait for slow,
educational processes. Not this war. While we fumble with
tradition, victory may easily slip from our grasp.' The
N.A.A.C.P. proposes no retreat from traditional policies. It
came through with an aggressive 'War and National Policy'
at its annual convention, held in Los Angeles in the summer
of 1942. In essence, this is the present position of the
N.A.A.C.P.:

> We Negroes of America demand no special privileges. But
> we do demand from America all the rights accorded to our
> white fellow citizens, the rights to which we would be entitled

if the professed democratic ideals of equal rights for all re-
gardless of race, creed, or color were really carried out.

We demand the right to live and work for our country in
defense industries and the right to die for our country without
segregation or discrimination in the armed forces and on the
same basis as all other citizens. . . .

We do raise and will continue to raise with all the vigor of
which we are capable, these issues of discrimination and segregation. . . .

Later, sitting in Walter White's office on New York's Fifth
Avenue, I asked him point blank what he thought could be
done by Negroes to stem the rising tide of race issues in the war.
'Whether this becomes a race war or not,' he told me, after a
moment's quick reflection, 'is in the hands of white people —
for the Negro sees through the Goebbels aspect of race propaganda.' Some months later, in answer to my question, 'What
can be done about the Southern bloc of politicians who fight
against the Negro's advance?' he said: 'The menace of that
bloc is much greater than most people realize. As for ourselves [N.A.A.C.P.], we are going to slap them in their noses
not only with the anti-poll-tax bill but with the anti-lynching
bill and certain other legislation and give them the opportunity of filibuster after filibuster until the country finally wakes
up and does something.'

The most self-effacing of public men, tall, dark, brooding
A. Philip Randolph, is today one of the outstanding Negroes in
America. For thirty years he has lived in the midst of the
hurly-burly of politics and bloody trade-union wars, and knows
the labor problems of the Negro exceedingly well. Free from
scheming or duplicity, honest to the point of being almost
naïve, he has nonetheless achieved a position of great strategic
importance at a crucial moment in our history.

He is unique among Negro leaders, in that he is neither
preacher, educator, nor rabble-rousing politician, but a labor
organizer — which perhaps suggests the trend of Negro

thinking. He is a man of great eloquence. Talking with him in the confines of his office is an experience, as his rumbling voice fairly vibrates the room. He is indeed no conversationalist — but always the public speaker with a vast audience. What seems to captivate Negroes, is the impression he gives of being all *soul*. His present leadership of Negroes seems to be based on this somewhat nationalistic statement. 'The old policy of defending Negroes' rights is well-nigh bankrupt and is of limited value,' Randolph declared. 'Fundamentally, rights don't mean a thing if you can't exercise them. The solution, then, is for the Negro to take the offensive and carry the fight for justice, freedom, and equality to the enemy. No minority group, oppressed, exploited, and discriminated against, can win its rights and place in the sun on the defensive.' Perhaps the real clue to his outlook today is revealed in his resignation from the National Negro Congress because, as he stated, it was dominated by the Communist Party, and thus by white people.

Randolph was born in 1889 at Crescent City, Florida, son of a poor Methodist minister. As a young man he joined the migration North and entered New York's City College. The problem of earning enough to eat interfered with his studies, and he applied for a job as a waiter on the Fall River Line, and was fired on his first trip for having organized a protest against the miserable living quarters for the workers. Impatient with the views of the Negro leaders during the last war, he joined the Socialist Party, and later edited the radical *Messenger* magazine along with Chandler Owen. A few days after Eugene Debs's arrest, Randolph was also put in jail because of his stand against this country's participation in the first World War. He later was released.

He is a zealous and indefatigable worker — the successful organization of the Brotherhood of Sleeping Car Porters was no mean job and is a key to his organizing powers. Talk of organizing the Pullman porters had been heard for a number of years, but no serious attempts were made until Randolph turned his attention to the matter in 1925. One of the difficulties in organizing porters was the fact that as a class they had fairly steady work — and in those days rated highly in Negro society. He held a mass meeting in Harlem and formed a tentative group. The *Messenger* magazine furnished the movement with an organ already well known in Negro and white labor circles, and by 1927 more than fifty per cent of the five thousand eligible workers in New York carried union cards. But an abortive attempt to strike in 1929 shook the confidence of the porters, and the Depression further discouraged the leaders. Membership fell off, and dues dribbled in so slowly that the telephone had to be discontinued and the lights were finally turned out at the headquarters.

Randolph rose to the occasion. He launched a terrific membership drive, and by 1935, with activities being stimulated by the N.R.A., he was able to count five thousand union heads. Two years later, October 1, 1937, the Brotherhood was finally recognized as the porters' bargaining agent, after years of bitter struggle with the powerful Pullman Company. An agreement was signed which increased the rates of pay, improved working conditions, and established machinery to handle grievances. The salary increase amounted to more than a million dollars annually.

Randolph has fought for years to persuade the A.F.L. unions to drop their barriers against Negro workers. His effort in 1941 was made under uniquely auspicious circumstances — the Seattle Convention at which the A.F.L. leaders bellicosely bludgeoned Naziism on the eve of war. When the Negro leader rose to speak, the hall became very quiet. He told tale after tale of how Negroes were excluded from 'all but menial jobs' in occupations controlled by the A.F.L. unions, and charged that this hampered the war effort. He then called upon the convention to 'make one step toward progress' by surveying the situation — at least. The delegates conceded, as does virtually everyone else, that he was telling the truth, and Randolph received a long ovation from a big part of the auditorium. It looked momentarily as if he had won. But the hard-headed realists of the A.F.L. went into action, the matter was tabled, and Randolph was once again rebuffed.

'Randolph has an advantage over others here,' one delegate remarked; 'he studied at Harvard!'

Randolph believes that only in periods of great social upheaval can Negroes make fundamental gains. Thus, a year before the war began he threw in his lot with power politics and formed the Negro March on Washington Movement, to mobilize Negroes nation-wide for a demonstration in Washington if the need should arise. The N.A.A.C.P. and the National Urban League sponsored the movement. Rallying Negroes on racial sentiment, a thing he opposed in Garvey, he has welded a powerful organization of nearly fifty thousand persons. The movement excluded *white* Communists. The Left attacked him for this back-watering on his early declarations that 'only solidarity can save the black and white workers of America, and this solidarity must be developed in mixed unions, composed of black and white, Jew and Gentile, native and foreign, Republican and Democrat, Socialist and Communist.' The Negro leader explained his position this way·

'The March on Washington Movement is an All-Negro Movement, but is not anti-white. We believe that Negroes need an All-Negro Movement, just as the Jews have a Zionist Movement and the Catholics have an All-Catholic Movement of which only workers are members. . . .

'The purpose of the March-on-Washington Movement is to stress definitely and emphasize that the main and basic responsibility for effecting the solution of the Negro problem rests upon Negroes themselves. We believe that the Negroes should supply the money and pay the price, make the sacrifices, and endure the suffering to break down the barriers to a realization of full citizenship rights in America.'

In the spring of 1942, Randolph rallied twenty thousand Negroes in a mass demonstration, held at Madison Square Garden, to protest discrimination in industry and the armed services — the first of a series that was duplicated in nearly every city in the North having considerable Negro population. Harlem merchants were urged to demonstrate their sympathy by participating in a blackout from 9 to 9.15 in the evening, while the meeting was in progress. The nation's most militant leaders appeared on the platform — White, Powell, Granger, Crosswaith, Tobias, and Mrs. Bethune. One after another, they declared that Black America's destiny lay in the defeat of the Axis, but that Negro Americans were dedicated to the task also of 'crushing the foes of liberty within the confines of their native land.' The crowd's approval was tremendous. Every Negro newspaper in the country enthusiastically reported the meeting in front-page stories with accompanying pictures. The *Courier's* man saw 'a vast audience, twenty-five thousand strong, voice lusty approval of A. Philip Randolph's March on Washington Movement and participate in the greatest race meeting in this city's history.' Harlem's *Amsterdam-Star News* carried this headline:

20,000 STORM MADISON SQUARE GARDEN
TO HELP BURY RACE'S 'UNCLE TOMS'

Randolph, curiously enough, never got a chance to speak that night — he allowed all the other leaders to have their say! But in a formal statement to the press, a speech he later made, he said: 'American democracy is a failure. It is a miserable ailure. It has failed because it is a limited and racial and divisible democracy.' He warned that 'America will have to answer to the colored peoples everywhere before the bar of world opinion.' Finally he asked, 'How can we fight for democracy in Burma, a country we have not seen, when we don't have democracy in Birmingham, a city we have seen?' When Lester B. Granger, executive secretary of the National

Urban League, rose to speak, he coined the slogan to which Negroes are being rallied today: 'Democracy in Our Time!'

What amount to the Negro's ultimate aims were formulated in an 'Eight-Point Program' adopted at that and similar meetings throughout the country, and recently presented at the White House:

> 1. Abrogation of every law which makes a distinction in treatment between citizens, based on religion, creed, color, or national origin.
> 2. Legislation to reinforce the constitutional guarantee that no person shall be deprived of life, liberty, or property without due process of law.
> 3. Legislation to end lynching.
> 4. Enactment of the Pepper Poll Tax Bill, so that all barriers to the exercise of the right to vote are eliminated.
> 5. Abolition of segregation and discrimination in the armed forces.
> 6. Withholding of federal funds from any agency which discriminates in the use of the funds.
> 7. An end to discrimination in jobs and job training.
> 8. Representation for Negroes on all missions, political and technical, which will be sent to the peace conference.

A program of this character obviously means social equality. The masses of Negroes are supporting it with their money, time, and energy. The Negro press has flatly demanded social equality. Said the Baltimore *Afro-American*, 'We believe in social equality if it is anything other citizens have!' It remains to be seen whether this development in the Negro's thinking will continue as aggressively racial, or eventually become absorbed in some sort of proletarian revolt. If Randolph has his way, 'Negroes will continue to hammer on this evil of Jim Crow until the monster is buried for all time.'

Chapter XVIII

These men are demonstrating that they are no appeasers, no Quislings who are set up to beguile their people into complacency in this crucial time of war and mounting prejudice.

— MICHIGAN 'CHRONICLE'

THE BLACK CABINETEERS

A LITTLE–KNOWN force in the drive to bring democracy to the Negro community is the 'Black Cabinet' — a corps of highly intelligent Negroes who hold key positions in Washington. As a liaison group, sometimes called the 'Black Brain Trust,' it functions as racial adviser to the government heads, and as such is one of the realities of government today. It is, as well, an integral part of the organized movement to end color distinctions. The men and women who form this influential body are determined, one of them told me, 'to secure for Negroes *all* the rights, privileges, and benefits now enjoyed by whites.'

This group, which forms the Washington arm of the national Negro leadership, is opposed to anything that smacks of race separatism — they are aggressively for integration. Indicative of this is the vigor with which it opposed the creation of a 'Super-Negro Bureau,' which was a plan being considered by the Washington administration to deal with all problems affecting Negroes. Members of the Black Cabinet fought the whole idea because they felt that such an agency would tend to make the Negro a ward of the government, and thus would subtly extend and perpetuate segregation.

Alert to trends, the Black Cabinet has managed to make definite strides in advancing the Negro's cause — always with the formidable aid of the mass-organization leaders — and Negroes count carefully the gains made.

The Black Cabinet has trained its heaviest guns on the employment of Negroes in government and war industries. I was frankly surprised when I was in Washington recently to see the thousands of Negroes who were working for the government and to see the variety of jobs they were doing — jobs hitherto beyond wishful thinking. Many held positions of authority and influence, and others were patiently solving technical problems as economists, lawyers, chemists, and consultants of various sorts. Hundreds were operating office machines and a few worked as secretaries to both white and Negro officials.

The number of Negro employees of the federal government jumped in recent years by more than one hundred thousand — with others being added daily. Negroes frankly say that a large factor in the Negro's integration in government service has been due lately to the vigorous way the Civil Service Commission kicked the bucket of tradition — photographs have been banned, designation of race on applications has been abolished, and the rule permitting a selection of one out of three eligible people — which once allowed discriminations — has been shelved. Working conditions also have improved. Today, many of the government cafeterias have been opened to Negro workers, separate rest-room accommodations eliminated, and in offices Negroes and whites work at adjoining desks.

These are the trends. . . .

Much remains to be accomplished.

The delicate task of negotiating further gains is the business before the Black Cabinet. But the very limitations of their rôles as 'advisers' is a clear impediment. Though their abilities are unquestioned, they deal only with 'Negro' problems. This fact caused George S. Schuyler, the *Courier's* columnist,

to call the group 'Porkbarrelensis Africanus.' He held that,
'While they are appointed as advisers, they actually give little
or no advice at all and have no part in shaping policy. What
advice they give is usually when outraged Negroes squawk
against some particularly unpalatable discrimination.' Some
Negroes are unkind enough to say that the Black Cabineteers
are salesmen for the New Deal. But in the summer of 1942,
the Washington *Tribune*, a Negro newspaper, proudly published a long list of Negro federal employees, detailing their
duties, with this head: 'These Represent Special Race Consideration.'

To some people the idea of a Black Cabinet may have a
curious ring. In reality, it is one of the Negro's methods of
exercising his 'right to petition' the government. As a matter
of fact, similar groups have been an anonymous feature of
American life since Booker T. Washington took the pulse of
the Negro, hurried to the White House to report, and returned
with reassuring antidotes. He headed a group called the
'Kitchen Cabinet,' which more or less functioned as adviser
to the government. Its members held three jobs mainly —
which came to be known as 'Negro jobs' — Register of the
Treasury, Auditor of the Navy, and Recorder of Deeds. Lack
of accomplishment by this and similar groups was due mostly
to the fact that their members were largely political hacks, who
had been put on the government payroll for services rendered
the Republican Party, and they had little influence in the
Negro community or within the government. Its modern
counterpart — the Black Cabinet — which rode to power on
the smooth pavement of the New Deal, is a streamlined edition,
but with vastly different objectives, and with vastly more
influence.

The group's immediate objectives include (1) an increase in
the number of Negroes in government service, at least as many
as they are entitled to by population percentage; (2) the giving
of jobs to Negroes according to their ability and training, and

not confining most of them to work as charwomen and to messenger and janitorial service; (3) appointment of Negroes to
policy-making positions and to the diplomatic and consular
service; and (4) to secure jobs for Negroes in private industry
to forward the war effort.

The Black Cabinet is a product of economic compul-
sions . . .

In the early days of the Roosevelt administration, intelligent
and well-educated young Negroes just out of school were meeting tremendous hardships in getting private employment.
Naturally they turned to government service for jobs, but
again found barriers. A long series of protests by Negroes and
liberal whites against discrimination in the government, which
they said gave comfort to private employers with discriminatory policies, brought about the appointment of Negro racial
advisers to secure better treatment for Negroes. No mere
window-dressing, they almost immediately sought equality of
employment for their people.

Help came from unexpected sources. Without much publicity, their aspirations received warm support from President
and Mrs. Roosevelt, and almost overnight things began to
happen. Heading a régime committed to change, the President issued orders against discrimination by government —
later to reaffirm this policy with his historic Executive Order
8802, which strongly urged both government administrators
and private employers 'to examine their employment and
training policies to determine whether or not these policies
make ample provision for the full utilization of available and
competent Negro workers.' Meanwhile, Mrs. Roosevelt, beloved by Negroes, championed the Negro's cause, kept in
touch with Negro thought, and by her own acts encouraged
the acceptance of Negroes on the same level as whites. This
attitude was implemented through the office of Harold L.
Ickes, Secretary of the Interior; Wayne Coy, the President's
liaison with department heads; and Doctor Will W. Alexander,
W.P.B. consultant on minority groups.

The Negro racial advisers who form the Black Cabinet are young men who have been trained as analysts, economists, educators, professors, labor organizers, newspapermen, and research and social workers. Many of them have been educated at the finest universities both here and abroad. Yet they do not regard themselves as an educated élite, but rather as 'intellectual workers.' Permeated with the bold thinking of the New Deal, slanted to meet the peculiar needs of the Negro, they help to unravel the knotty problems of racial relations in the government which crop up from time to time.

By and large they are cut from the same college-bred cloth, and although temperamentally, sharply vivid differences exist among them, as to objectives they are as close as white on rice. They do their thinking and talking together. Studies are initiated by them, Negro sentiment tested frequently, abstractions harnessed, and eventually mature programs formulated. Much constructive work thus has been accomplished. The effectiveness of the group stems from the fact that it usually operates as a cohesive unit, with well-defined objectives unencumbered by rigid party lines. In collaboration with liberal white government officials and Negro leaders, they advance the Negro's cause.

Late in the summer of 1940, with war threatening, A. Philip Randolph, president of the Brotherhood of Sleeping Car Porters; Walter White, executive secretary of the National Association for the Advancement of Colored People; and Doctor Channing H. Tobias, Negro Y.M.C.A. executive, among others, conferred with President Roosevelt on the status of the Negro in the armed services and war industries. They presented a memorandum whose intent sought integration of Negroes in the national war program. Sometime later Stephen Early, the President's press secretary, issued an ambiguous White House statement outlining the segregation policy to which the United States Army intended to adhere — 'not to intermingle colored and white enlisted personnel' —

and, worse, intimated that such a policy had been requested by Negro leaders. The ink had hardly dried on Early's release when Randolph, White, and Doctor Tobias wired the President, 'In a written memorandum we submitted we specifically repudiated segregation.' The Negro press rose in all its inflammatory might and denounced the President. Headlines shouted, 'WHITE HOUSE BLESSES JIM CROW.' Statements of the Negro leaders were quoted in full, accompanied by much critical comment. The Negro communities were incensed by what they termed a 'trick.'

To top this off, with the 1940 elections only a few days away, Early was charged with kicking a Negro policeman assigned to Pennsylvania Station in New York. The New York *Herald Tribune*, opposing Roosevelt's re-election observed in its story of the encounter that Early was the 'son of a Confederate general.' Negro press and pulpit denounced the indignity as reflecting the attitude of people close to the President. This threw the White House advisers and Democratic campaign strategists into something of a dither. A hurried call was put through to assemble the racial advisers, to offer views on how to counteract the situation. Some White House advisers thought the President, or a ranking cabinet member, ought to deliver a strong speech on the general Negro question, nicely outlining all that the administration had done for Negroes. The Negro advisers felt differently. 'Since the Negro's whole resentment is directed at the Army,' they argued, 'the situation can only be counteracted by some concrete and favorable development there.' Doctor Robert C. Weaver, spokesman for the Black Cabinet, then suggested as a means of stimulating Negro morale, that there be some Negro representation in the military councils of America's expanding war effort. Although the Army officials were opposed to it, the President, a few days before elections, finally took the bull by the horns and elevated Colonel Benjamin O. Davis to brigadier general, appointed Judge William H. Hastie as civilian aide to Secre-

tary of War Stimson, and made Lieutenant Colonel Campbell
C. Johnson executive assistant to Brigadier General Lewis B.
Hershey.

As it turned out, these appointments proved to be key spots
in a developing war program. The two men chosen to perform
the civilian tasks have sharply contrasted personalities. Tall,
wiry Judge Hastie is the younger man, and today an important figure in the Black Cabinet. Lieutenant Colonel
Johnson is a silent, graying veteran of the last war who hardly
speaks above a whisper. Though he lacks the scintillation of
most members of the Black Cabinet, he nevertheless has a
quiet aggressiveness which is much admired by his white colleagues. His sober influence often acts as a check on the more
impatient young men. Every inch the soldier — erect, commanding, decisive, and with simple dignity — his concern is
primarily in getting Negroes into the Army with a minimum of
racial hitches.

Judge Hastie, who recently resigned, was concerned with
the morale of the Negro soldiers. What he advised as to their
welfare eventually had far-reaching effect upon thousands.
His job was made extremely difficult by clashes between Negro
soldiers and white civilians — for he not only had to suggest
possible solutions, but had to explain to an uneasy Negro
public what efforts were being made to correct such conditions.

A typical situation developed at Camp Huachuca, planted
smack in the middle of the Arizona Desert near the Mexican
border. Except for a couple of squatter villages, the nearest
town (Tombstone, population eight hundred), is twenty miles
away — and Negroes are none too welcome. Darkness covers
Huachuca early, for the camp is situated in the shadow of a
high mountain. Almost devoid of recreational facilities, the
Negro soldiers stationed here had a hard time finding things to
do after nightfall. Once they pooled seven hundred dollars of
their wages to bring a Negro name-band from the West Coast.

Beyond this there was nothing. The boys were plenty salty about it all — and this situation culminated in clashes with the white townspeople near-by.

When Hastie caught wind of the situation, he swiftly went into action. After conferences with Army officials, a recreational program was put into operation inside and outside the cantonment. Hostesses were brought in, baseball teams were set up, and arrangements were made for regular week-end trips to the big towns. A number of U.S.O. men are now established in the population centers around the camp, preparing programs of civilian-soldier cooperation in entertainment. Today, Camp Huachuca is well on its way to live down its once bad reputation.

Nothing in Hastie's manner suggests the aggressive executive. He is reserved, professorial, even a bit other-worldly, yet he has a crisp, businesslike mind. He has a fascinating coffee-and-cream complexion which shows off strikingly against smooth black hair and a thin, trim mustache. 'The Jedge,' as he is called off the record, is a graduate of Amherst College (with Phi Beta Kappa honors) and Harvard Law School. Formerly dean of Howard Law School, he came into the government as assistant solicitor of the Interior Department. He is the first Negro to be appointed to a federal judgeship, a post in the Virgin Islands which he resigned because, as he put it, 'no one has a right to personal security in these times.' Negroes have considerable confidence in him — his zealous integrity being a strong factor.

Early in 1943, Hastie became fed up and resigned his job, charging the War Department with an anti-Negro bias that made his work there a travesty. He held that it was almost impossible to get things done, and, moreover, no one in the department seemed disposed to correct the flagrant Jim Crow policy against Negroes. He particularly flayed the Air Forces for maintaining a discriminatory policy which almost entirely excluded Negroes from the service. His resignation produced a sensation in the Negro community — and indeed elevated him to something of a hero.

Let's take a look at a few other figures in the Black Cabinet.

Top man today is handsome Doctor Robert C. Weaver, racial adviser to Paul V. McNutt, chairman of the War Manpower Commission. He has the vastly important job of keeping an alert finger on the pulse of the Negro labor supply. He must devise means and techniques of getting Negroes into war industries — and this, without upsetting the racial apple-cart and thereby retarding production. How to utilize a million Negro workers, either unemployed or underemployed, was the first big problem he had to wrestle with when he was made chief of the Negro manpower service — now defunct. Negro morale was at a low ebb. Negroes saw, he observed, white neighbors with no better or even poorer qualifications rapidly absorbed in war industries. To meet this problem, he approached factory-owners and persuaded them to consider the employment of Negroes. 'It is not enough,' he said, 'for management to have an *inclination* to use Negro labor; it must have a *conviction*, and transmit this conviction to supervisors, foremen, and workers.' Where there was a strong labor organization, he sought the active cooperation of the union. Finally he attempted to work out harmonious relations between labor and management for the easy introduction of the new Negro workers.

Weaver, who wears his clothes with a stylish flare, is of very light complexion — Negroes call him 'high yaller.' He is possessed of a refined intelligence, but is coolly aloof to acquaintances, and critics have pointed to this as a defect. Nicknamed 'Bob,' he is not one of the boys in the hail-fellow-well-met sense. Essentially, he is the student, discerning, deliberate, and removed. He is the first Negro to earn a Ph.D. in economics from Harvard University, and he entered the government in the early days of the New Deal — a protégé of

Ickes. As racial adviser in the Interior Department, he procured promotions for long-neglected Negro employees, job opportunities for Negro technical men, and other benefits for colored citizens from the programs under the jurisdiction of the Interior Department. Though there has been much rank-and-file criticism scoring his lack of aggressiveness on behalf of Negroes, his associates regard him as a sound and resourceful leader.

The most picturesque member of the Black Cabinet is noisy, flamboyant Ted Poston, racial adviser to Elmer Davis, head of the Office of War Information. As head of the Negro press relations, he provides Negroes with an account of how the war is proceeding and a basis for judging how well or ill the fortunes of Negroes fare. His task is to stimulate the energy of Negroes, through their press, and imbue them with a will to win the war. Beyond his job, he is famed in Negro circles as a master of the tall tale, and wrote that delightful *New Republic* piece, 'Revolt of the Evil Fairies,' in which he pictured himself as assaulting a Prince Charming! As an active participant in Harlem's *Amsterdam-News* strike during 1934, he helped throw into discard the tradition that Negro workers would not act against Negro bosses. He has an agile mind, and is alert to seize opportunities. His chief facetious boast is that he put his birthplace, Paducah, Kentucky, on the map.

A key man in the Black Cabinet is Frank S. Horne, shrewd, with a sly sense of humor, who is chief of the racial relations office of the Federal Public Housing Administration. He is ever alert to see that Negroes are not overlooked, and has been successful in getting many projects erected for them. Today, with large-scale migration of Negroes to the industrial centers, the importance of his work has expanded considerably. Horne studied at the Northern Illinois College of Ophthalmology, attended New York City College and Columbia University, and then taught school. A New Yorker by birth, he smokes innumerable cigarettes and likes an occasional drink. He is a poet of some distinction, but no long-haired intellectual, and is trained to look a problem squarely in the eye.

The women in the Black Cabinet have vastly different backgrounds. Only two figures are prominent. Mrs. Mary McLeod Bethune, director of the Office of Negro Affairs in the National Youth Administration; and Crystal Bird Fauset, racial relations adviser to Dean Landis, head of the Office of Civilian Defense. They are a contrast in early training, previous occupation, and personality. Mrs. Bethune is an educator. Mrs. Fauset is a politician. The former is a very dark woman, who is possessed of extraordinary charm and dignity, with a fine talent for winning friends, both Negro and white. Mrs. Fauset is very light in complexion, wears modish clothes, and is easy-on-the-eye. A consummate politician hailing from Philadelphia, she tiptoed tactfully over the prostrate forms of dancers, athletes, and thespians to survive the early purges of O.C.D. A competent, friendly woman, with exceeding resiliency under pressure, her job is to activize Negroes in the civilian defense programs. She is a rare type to be found in influential government circles today — a Negro Republican, and, as such, the only politician in the Black Cabinet.

Her colleague, Mrs. Bethune, is the self-taught founder and president of Bethune-Cookman College, which she 'prayed up, sung up, and talked up' into an outstanding institution for girls. Today, she is a leading spirit in youth and women's movements, and is president of the National Council of Negro Women, a powerful organization. Ida M. Tarbell once named her as one of the fifty outstanding American women. To her intimates, however, she is simply 'Ma Bethune.' Despite her advanced age and inclination to take on weight, she moves about with the vigor of a much younger woman. Her influence in the Black Cabinet rests on her link with the past, wide contacts among whites, mature judgment, and a willingness to 'go to the front' in critical situations.

An incident which occurred in the summer of 1942 will illustrate her forthright attitude on questions affecting her people. One of the most critical situations the Black Cabinet had to face was the execution of a Negro sharecropper, Odell Waller, who had killed his white landlord in Virginia. The case was brought forward by the Workers' Defense League. Acknowledging extenuating circumstances, the liberal opinion of the country had clamored for clemency. Negro leaders had attempted to prevail upon government officials to step in, but had little success.

Finally, Mrs. Bethune made a last appeal . . .

At one o'clock in the morning, a few hours before the scheduled execution, she called the White House by telephone and succeeded in talking with Mrs. Roosevelt — one of her keenest admirers. Mrs. Bethune pleaded fervently for a stay. Mrs. Roosevelt's response was immediate. She awoke the President and stated the case to him. Attorney General Biddle was called and asked his opinion. He closed the affair by saying the federal government had no jurisdiction. Next morning the Negro sharecropper went to his death — but Mrs. Bethune's status as a leader was secure.

The Black Cabinet, to accomplish its ends, often employs much of the positive features of the lobby — it arouses public interest through the press and pulpit, approaches influential white persons, puts the heat under congressmen with large Negro constituencies, and frequently goes directly to the White House. Sometimes it plants ideas in persons whose support would be helpful, and prods key public figures into assuming leadership of new programs, while the Black Cabinet itself does the in-fighting within the government arena. The source of its power and inspiration is undoubtedly the prevalent aggressive temper of the Negro people — to which the Black Cabinet is alertly responsive.

Sharp cognizance was taken of the Black Cabinet on the issue of the Detroit race riot early in 1942 — an occurrence which shocked the nation, and also brought the activities of this group into the open. The situation in Detroit seemed clear enough to members of the Black Cabinet. Before the completion of Detroit's Sojourner Truth Homes, a government housing project erected with public funds, the Washington housing authorities notified the Detroit Housing Commission to certify Negroes for occupancy. White people in the area protested, and led by Congressman Tenerowicz of Michigan, the issue was taken to the top officials. Twenty-four hours later the decision was reversed, and the project was opened for whites only.

Members of the Black Cabinet met and decided on a course of action. Before the Washington housing authorities could readily be approached, it was decided that public interest would have to be aroused. Within a short time the Negro press began blasting the housing officials, decrying in particular their weak-kneed policy. Negro organizations — the N.A.A.C.P., the National Urban League, and others — sent representatives to Washington to protest. Housing officials were deluged with telegrams and letters, and a march on Washington was staged by Detroit Negroes, who called on government officials and visited congressmen. No opportunity for publicity was overlooked. Negro demands were kept at a fever pitch by press and pulpit. With the barrage thus laid down, the Black Cabinet presented the demands of a united Negro community, taking the issue to the White House. The order was rescinded again, in favor of Negroes, reportedly upon White House intervention.

White people began a day-and-night vigil before Detroit's City Hall in protest. When the Ku Klux Klan entered the picture, the picket lines were shifted to the project's location — and the racial explosion occurred when Negroes sought to move into the buildings. Without government protection,

Negroes were blocked from entering the project for months. Meantime an F.B.I. investigation turned up links with Axis agents among the agitators. Soon a large section of the liberal white public took up the issue and supported the Negroes' right to live in the houses. Pressure by Negroes was again applied to make the Washington officials stand firmly by their decision, and the Sojourner Truth Homes were finally turned over to Negroes.

The Michigan *Chronicle*, a Negro newspaper, afterward declared that 'It was clear that the government [Negro] advisers put the welfare of their people above their jobs.' This view was expressed somewhat by Congressman Tenerowicz when he rose in the House of Representatives, observed that the affair had 'reverberated throughout the country,' and demanded to know whether 'the membership of the House must consult this new agency, the Black Cabinet, regarding any and all racial questions.'

Chapter XIX

. . . Some Americans fail to recognize the distinction between righteous advocacy, and what is called impolitic agitation. The Negro press is fundamentally an advocate.

— NORFOLK 'JOURNAL AND GUIDE'

FREEDOM OF THE BLACK PRESS

FROM Harlem to Tougaloo, the Negro press is the most loudly impatient agency for immediate, fundamental change in the status of the race. Possessed of no talk-softly policy, it is the Negro's most potent weapon of protest and propaganda, which, perhaps, is an aspect of its voracious appetite for sensationalism. At times, in its honest fury against injustice to black men, it is a kibitzer on the sidelines of American life; and at other times, especially in periods of moral inertia, it is a noisy wailing-wall. But always, it is a vigorous organ, maintaining a policy of 'race-angling' the news which affects Negroes directly. Today such a policy appears to certain white people as inflammatory, and sometimes as having an anti-war, defeatist ring. Consider these headlines which appeared after Pearl Harbor:

WARNS U.S. OF RACE WAR
U.S. 'FORCES' BRITAIN TO JIM CROW TROOPS

— New York *Amsterdam-Star News*

FIENDISH MOB OF TEXAS WHITES LYNCH
INNOCENT NEGRO ACCUSED OF ATTACK

— Pittsburgh *Courier*

NEGRO PREACHERS PUT OUT
OF SENATE AT GUNPOINT!

— Harlem's *People's Voice*

Westbrook Pegler, who later recanted, began the attack on the Negro press by charging that it resembled the Communist Party's *Daily Worker* and Father Coughlin's *Social Justice* in its 'obvious, inflammatory bias in the treatment of the news,' a treatment he also compared with Hearst's sensationalism. The federal government, too, became acutely aware of the Negro press in the early part of 1942, so much so that Archibald Mac-Leish, as director of the Office of Facts and Figures, called an informal conference of Negro editors and attempted to persuade them to lay off the rough racial stuff — for the duration of the war, at least. He offered no tangible evidence that Negroes would be accorded the privileges as well as the penalties of citizenship, so they refused to stop in their militant crusading efforts. Shortly thereafter — perhaps a coincidence — the Negro press came under the scrutiny of the Department of Justice. Two papers reported visits by F.B.I. agents — the provocative California *Eagle* and the aggressive Pittsburgh *Courier*.

'This sort of thing,' the *Courier* complained editorially, 'is an obvious effort to cow the Negro press.... Instead of trying to frighten Negro editors into silence, we suggest that the F.B.I. investigate those forces and institutions within America that are fostering and spreading Fascism and disunity by treating Negroes as second-class citizens.' To the insinuation that Negro newspapers receive subsidies from German or Japanese sources, the *Courier* replied with characteristic vigor. 'For anybody to think,' it declared, 'that Negro editors need prodding from abroad to castigate and condemn the undemocratic practices to which their people are subjected, is to reveal an appalling ignorance of the intelligence and temperament of colored people.'

This press-from-across-the-tracks makes no bones about its policy of protest and propaganda — a line from which it rarely two-steps. But the solid importance of this agency to the Negro community lies not in its editorial harangues alone, but in the fact that it provides a vast platform for the Negro leaders, serves as the coordinator of any mass action the race is impelled to take, and is an instrument of public education. Moreover, it is edited by ordinary men and women (not pundits above the crowd) who articulate the aspirations of the black rank-and-file. Above all, it keeps the Negro public exceedingly well informed (and indeed sometimes misinformed) of day-to-day happenings of particular concern to the race. Finally, its commentators discuss the implications and meanings of events in terms of their effect upon the Negro community.

Said Harlem's *People's Voice*, in its own self-conscious estimate of the Negro press: 'The daily is essential, but the weekly Negro paper is indispensable because of four exclusive virtues. The Negro newspaper is the medium of unabridged militant and ofttimes brilliant expressions of the Talented Tenth; it molds public opinion in the Negro's behalf and creates more race consciousness; it presents contemporary history better than any other institution, and it is the spokesman for racial rights.'

Negro newspapers are honest, faithful, and indeed biased to the Negro's cause, making no pretense at objectivity whatsoever — in fact, the logic of their very existence compels them to be such organs. They have an influence in American life far beyond the imagination of most white people. As a matter of fact, the Negro press has been a vital though largely unseen force for more than a hundred years. It has rivaled the Negro church in influence, and today has pretty much stolen the show, unencumbered as it is (and was) by religious dogma; or, for that matter, by rigid party lines. But its most positive influence has been felt mainly in periods of great social upheaval. What should be of acute interest to white people is the fact that the Negro press, whatever its virtues or shortcomings, is a faithful reflection of the Negro mass mind.

The oldest Negro newspaper is the *Christian Recorder*, organ of the African Methodist Episcopal Church, begun in 1848. The first Negro newspaper published in the United States, *Freedom's Journal*, made its appearance in New York City in 1827 — four years before the famous *Liberator* of the abolitionist Garrison, and at a moment when high-minded people began to gather forces for a mighty assault on slavery. It was a four-page weekly which served, as the editors expressed it, 'to hook together, by one solid chain, the whole population so as to make it think, and feel, and act, as one solid body.' Fighting to destroy a backward institution, it was of necessity an organ of propaganda. Its editors frankly explained that only 'strange necessity' compelled them to emphasize the racial aspects of the Negro's problems. Impatient to end human bondage, it reprinted the pamphlet of David Walker, an articulate Bostonian who later was assassinated. This tract shocked the country by calling upon the slaves to rise in revolt against their masters. Coming as it did a few years after the Denmark Vesey slave insurrection in Charleston in 1822, and just before the Nat Turner revolt in Virginia in 1831, its influence upon public opinion, North and South, was considerable.

When the agencies of emancipation found themselves without a cause toward the close of the Civil War, the end of the Negro press — then numbering about thirty publications — was clearly in sight. But the assassination of Lincoln brought new problems to the black population in the years that followed. Meantime, the white Northern leaders, consumed by the mighty rush for dollars, forgot about the progressive character of the war and left Negroes high-and-dry, and thus to shift for themselves in a hostile community. As Negroes sized up the situation, a Negro press was an urgent necessity to combat the rapidly mounting anti-Negro sentiment and to unify the black population for aggressive counter-action.

By the close of the century, the Negro press had become a

formidable entity, and in 1891 I. Garland Penn, a Negro editor, wrote its history in a thick book called *The Afro-American Press*. With America's entry into the first World War, the Negro press took on a sharp change in character. A number of radical publications appeared, the names suggesting something of their temper: *Challenge, Crusader, Emancipator,* and *Messenger*. So outspoken were they that the Department of Justice took steps to suppress them. Attorney General A. Mitchell Palmer, who conducted the investigations, solemnly reported that the utterances of the Negro editors were 'not the ignorant vaporings of untrained minds,' but the sober declarations of intelligent men who were 'defiantly assertive of the Negro's equality.'

Yet, contrary to Palmer's evaluation of radicalism, they were not at one in their social philosophy — though 'left' of any previous position that Negroes had taken. The New York *Age*, for example, acknowledged that change was necessary, but held that it should come through orderly democratic processes and by grace of the Republican Party, while the influential *Messenger* magazine demanded fundamental change by revolutionary action, inaugurated by united white and black labor. All, however, wanted change of some kind. But the most important development was that the Negro press broke out of its limited orbit of concentrating on injustices to the American Negro only, and began to concern itself with the plight of oppressed colored peoples elsewhere in the world.

Most widely circulated, and in general typical of the radical publications, was the *Messenger*, edited by A. Philip Randolph and Chandler Owen, lecturers at the Rand School of Social Sciences. The Lusk Committee, a body appointed by the New York State Legislature to investigate radicalism, declared it to be 'by far the most dangerous of all the Negro publications.' It was, according to its prospectus of 1917, 'the only Magazine of Scientific Radicalism in the world published by Negroes,' in which its editors aimed to lift their pens above 'cringing demagogy of the times and above the cheap peanut politics of the old, reactionary Negro leaders.' The *Messenger* denounced those leaders who, while holding lucrative federal war jobs, indulged in rhetoric and bombast to 'lull Negroes into a false sense of security.' It particularly took to task W. E. B. Du Bois, who, in its view, fought lynching but failed to grasp the causes underlying it, and who spoke for harmony between whites and blacks yet encouraged scabbing by Negroes against white strikers. The *Messenger* did not confine its attacks to Negro leaders. It took slaps at white labor leaders like Samuel Gompers, who was 'selling out both white and Negro labor's interests.' The unity of the white and black rank-and-file was frankly urged, as 'capitalism knows no color line.'

If not openly hostile, the *Messenger* was certainly indifferent to Negro businessmen, holding that Negro workers must organize and protect themselves against exploitation by Negroes as well as by whites, for a few successful Negro businessmen would bring no change to the status of Negro labor. Later it had a change of heart, which dovetailed with the split in the radical ranks. In 1925 it published a 'Negro Business Achievement Number,' in which very little was said about the radical movement or the struggles of laboring men. The *Messenger* had lost its voice of thunder and greeted January, 1928, with 'Hail! A Prosperous and Happy New Year.' This issue was decidedly racial in tone, with inspirational pieces by Negro business people. The next year it quietly passed into oblivion, along with the other radical publications of its day.

Only a shade less militant were the two established newspapers of the community — though the *Age*, today one of Harlem's three local weeklies and frankly Republican in outlook, was cautious. The oldest journal in the community, it was first published in 1880 as a little tabloid called *Rumor*. Its expensive woodcuts and scant sale of advertising space created too heavy a burden for its publishers, and it was taken over by T. Thomas Fortune and Jerome B. Peterson. Under this management — from 1887 to 1907 — the paper was renamed the New York *Age*, and gained a national circulation. It led demands for the abolition of separate schools in New York, fought for the adoption of a civil rights bill, and finally carried on an effective crusade to obtain the right for Negroes to serve in the Spanish-American War. It had a large hand in the organization of the National Negro Business League and the National Afro-American Press Association.

T. Thomas Fortune, its editor, was a writer of considerable ability and was regarded by his contemporaries as the dean of Negro journalism. He once had been an assistant to Amos Cummings on the *Evening Sun* and later a contributor to the New York *Sun* under Charles A. Dana. He was the most widely read Negro editor of his time; his editorials in the *Age* drew repeated comments from the white dailies. Theodore Roosevelt, when police commissioner of New York, once said, 'Tom Fortune, for God's sake, keep that pen of yours off me.' When Roosevelt became President, he sent the Negro journalist to investigate conditions in the Hawaiian and Philippine Islands. As friend and adviser to Booker T. Washingon, Fortune assisted the Tuskegee educator in the preparation of his autobiography. In his declining years Fortune joined the Back-to-Africa Movement of Marcus Garvey, perhaps because he had seen so many other plans fail. He died before the final collapse of the Pan-African dream.

About 1907 Fred R. Moore, later to become an alderman, purchased the *Age* and became its editor and publisher. He continued the independent and challenging policy started by Fortune. When, for instance, the Ku Klux Klan was revived after the First World War, the *Age* exposed its aims and methods, having secured a copy of its creed and ritual — this campaign antedated the one launched by the old *World*. In 1919 the *Age* joined the exodus to Harlem and established its

offices at 135th Street. Today it sells for five cents a copy, re-
tains its old format, and appeals to the conservative people of
Harlem, and has a circulation of about twenty thousand. In
more than fifty years of existence, the *Age* has shown a keen
sense of social responsibility, a policy underscored by its
owner's adherence to the philosophy of Booker T. Washington.
Besides Fortune, the paper's most distinguished editors have
been James Weldon Johnson and Lester A. Walton, who later
was appointed as Minister to Liberia by President Roosevelt.

The *Age's* chief competitor in Harlem started its career in
1909, when James H. Anderson took six sheets and a pencil
and published the *Amsterdam News* — the name came from the
street on which he lived. Later Edward A. Warren became its
publisher, and after his death his widow, Sadie Warren, a
former dancer, and her daughter entered into a partnership
with Anderson, whom they later bought out. The paper was
sold to the Powell-Savory Corporation in 1935, and its name
was changed to the New York *Amsterdam-Star News*. Today it
is ranked as one of the largest Negro papers in the country.
Besides giving information about local events, it extends its
coverage to national and international affairs, as it did when it
sent a reporter to the 1936 Olympic Games in Berlin. The
Amsterdam-Star News, which sells for ten cents a copy and has a
circulation of about thirty-four thousand, speaks out trucu-
lently. Many of its contributors, like Du Bois and Roy Wilkins, are nationally known figures. Politically, through the
years, it has leaned heavily on the Republican Party — though
since the New Deal it has supported the Democratic Party
nationally. Somehow, it also has managed to support all
other parties and movements for the betterment of the Negro,
and has unceasingly campaigned for his rights and the improvement of Harlem. Beyond this, its chief aim seems to be
the development of a wealthy Negro business class.

A third paper stepped into the field in 1942 — the *People's
Voice*, a *PM*-ish tabloid edited by Adam Clayton Powell, Jr.

Initially, it was said to be partially financed by Marshall Field, millionaire owner of *PM*. From the take-off, *PV* pledged itself to be a non-partisan, working-class paper, and the spearhead of all movements that worked toward 'the full emancipation of the people.' To build circulation the editors conceived the idea of running serially Richard Wright's novel, *Native Son*, a story of poverty and crime in Chicago's Black Belt. So vehemently did Negroes protest that it was discontinued after four installments. The editors explained that *PV's* readers, many of whom were not 'hep cats,' objected to the story's 'profanity.' I suspect that the protests had deeper meaning — and, incidentally, is a marked comment on the Negro people's reaction to this book. In sharp departure from established journalistic practices, *PV* boasts that it accepts no advertising that preys on superstition. Lately, with financial troubles about to down the paper, Doctor Max Yergan, president of the National Negro Congress, was brought in as a publisher. This fact, plus the paper's support of Ben Davis, Jr., Negro Communist candidate for congressman-at-large from New York State in the 1942 elections, suggests in the minds of some people that the paper has associations with the Communist leaders.

The Black Metropolis is the chief news center of Negro America. Besides the three local weeklies, Harlem offices are maintained by the larger Negro publications published elsewhere in the country. Altogether, there are some two hundred and thirty Negro newspapers in the United States, and a news-gathering agency which services most of them — the Associated Negro Press with main offices in Chicago. These papers have a combined circulation well above two million. Twelve papers are members of the Audit Bureau of Circulation — the *Courier* leading the field with a circulation of 225,000 (in 1942). To snatch the Negro circulation, some white newspapers in the South publish 'special colored editions.' Recently, the Negro press has made a bid for a white public. Any success in this endeavor is proudly hailed. When Henry Ford, the automobile manufacturer, bought a year's subscription to the *Courier*, his check was reproduced with this head: 'FORD SUBSCRIBES ... HERE'S THE PROOF.'

The largest and most influential papers, besides those already mentioned, are the Baltimore *Afro-American*, Norfolk *Journal and Guide*, and Philadelphia *Tribune*. There are also the Chicago *Defender*, Kansas City *Call*, Cleveland *Call and Post*, Oklahoma City *Black Dispatch*, and California *Eagle*. Down South, where the bulk of the Negro population lives, there are only two papers of real merit: the Houston *Informer* and Atlanta *Daily World*. For their mutual interests the owners formed the Negro Newspaper Publishers' Association, which held its fourth annual conference in Chicago in the spring of 1942. They adopted a war resolution which pledged their papers to campaign for 'victory at home and abroad.'

Together, these papers employ about two thousand workers, and own equipment worth considerably more than a million dollars. When, as has happened on occasion, the ownership of one of these papers changes from Negro to white, there is not necessarily any modification of that organ's aggressive racial policy.

There are, as well, two hundred and thirty-nine religious, fraternal, literary, and labor journals, school and college publications, and a few theatrical, picture, and fashion periodicals. The quality magazines, calmly edited, non-profit organs, include The Crisis, organ of the N.A.A.C.P., edited by Roy Wilkins; *Opportunity*, magazine of the National Urban League with Harvard-bred Elmer A. Carter at the helm; *Journal of Negro Education*, a quarterly of opinion published by Howard University, and *Journal of Negro History*, edited by Carter G. Woodson, a well-known historian. There also is one literary publication, *Phylon*, a quarterly edited by W. E. B. Du Bois and published by Atlanta University. These publications have distinct prestige in American life and are often looked to for authoritative opinion about the Negro.

Early in its modern career, in the preparation of a style sheet, the Negro press attempted to settle a knotty problem — the issue being whether the race should be referred to as 'Negro,' 'Colored,' 'Afro-American,' 'Aframerican,' 'African,' 'Race,' or plain 'Black.' One Negro scholar, William H. Huggins, devoted a whole chapter of his book to 'that word Negro.' The battle still rages in certain quarters. If white people are in doubt as to the acceptable term — the Negro writer and public speaker is in no less a quandary. I doubt very much that every Negro will be satisfied with my own use of the terms 'Negro' and 'Black' throughout this book.

For two centuries American Negroes called themselves merely 'people of color,' and even whites so designated them in the very earliest documents I have examined. The Dutch, Spanish, and English settlers leaned toward 'black' — hence the term 'Negro,' which means black. In 1786, Jupiter Hammon, a slave on Long Island and the first Negro poet in America, addressed himself to 'Negroes,' but this term did not have real currency until the years before the Civil War. Absence of color made one *white*, obviously. Sometimes 'African' was used by Negroes, but this term was discarded when schemes were advanced to colonize Negroes in Africa. Today's fine distinctions of color and terms were not yet in vogue.

The issue finally came to a head in this century — coincident with talk about race pride. T. Thomas Fortune, editor of the *Age*, excluded 'Negro' from his vocabulary because of the disagreeable connotation with the word 'nigger' — which perhaps is the clue to the whole business. He is credited with being the originator of the term 'Afro-American,' which was adopted by the Murphy clan, founders of the Baltimore *Afro-American*. In Marcus Garvey's heyday, 'African' and 'Black' supplanted 'Afro-American' for a time. The Chicago *Defender* meanwhile had a style sheet which excluded 'Negro,' 'Afro-American,' and 'Black' altogether, and instead used 'Race,' as it does today — for example, one is a 'Race man,' or it is a 'Race paper.' The *Age*, since Fred R. Moore's régime, has used 'Colored,' which, of all the terms, has the nice sound of respectability and refinement. In recent years, the *Daily Worker's* discussions of the Negro problem have helped somewhat to popularize the description, 'the Negro people,' among certain intellectuals.

The *Voice of Ethiopia* — with eyes lifted toward an African utopia — complained that the word 'Negro' signified nothing beyond the connotation of enslavement, and was an invention of white men to degrade the race. Every other race, it said, is known by the continent, land, or nation whence it came; therefore Negroes should be called 'African' or 'Ethiopian.' For years many literary folk liked 'Aframerican,' which has a melodious lilt, but this term has a derisive meaning to Negroes. H. L. Mencken and George S. Schuyler, the Negro satirist and *Courier* columnist, did much to give it this bad reputation, and today they are practically the only writers who use it. Many Negroes are indifferent to the whole matter. Yet I would say that generally the adjective 'colored' and the generic designations 'Negroes,' 'the Negro race,' and 'the Negro' are acceptable — but the use of 'Negress,' 'Negra,' and of course 'nigger' are considered unforgivable. However, the term 'nigger' is used by Negroes quite freely when out of the earshot of whites, sometimes having a good deal of affectionate meaning to them.

Once this business was fairly settled, Negroes launched a campaign in the late twenties to persuade the white publications to capitalize the 'N' in Negro. Were it not for certain events in American history, this would appear to be an extremely trivial thing; there is in fact no logical reason why the name of any race should be capitalized. In some languages, as for example the French and German, it is not. But Negroes held that in our language the names of races are capitalized, and that in the United States the Negro race alone should be designated by a small letter could hardly be the result of accident. It seemed to reflect, in the Negro's view, the conviction of the white man that the Negro was in some way inferior to other races.

The campaign bore fruit. Today nearly every large and reputable newspaper and magazine has adopted this form. 'So doing,' the old *World* commented editorially, 'they have contributed in a quiet but enormously effective way to the racial pride of the Negro. . . . It is merely one more sign that the effort of many to ease the acuteness of the racial problem is thoroughly sincere.' Despite this wisp of recognition, I can't help making the observation that, socially and economically, Negroes still remain in a *lower-case* category.

Most of the Negro newspapers are weeklies, the one exception being the Atlanta *Daily World*. Once the stuff of racial idealism is cut away, they are operated primarily for profit, and in this sense are like their white contemporaries. What is good business in the judgment of the owners, rarely is hampered by the nonsense about race.

A few Negro papers employ white men as solicitors. Today the *Courier* maintains a Fifth Avenue office in New York — distinct from its Harlem office — staffed by white advertising people. But still there is little profitable advertising in Negro newspapers. The chief revenue comes from the sale of the papers themselves, which usually sell for ten cents a copy and are circulated nationally. What advertising there is consists largely of sucker items, such as lodestones, zodiacal incense, books on unusual love practices, and products that purport to turn black skin to white or straighten kinky hair. About this phase of its operations, the Negro press is very sensitive. It has made determined efforts to eliminate such advertising from its columns — but, for the present, it is either such advertising or none! It would hardly be an exaggeration to say that without sucker items, many papers would probably have to close shop.

In recent years, the papers have turned to soliciting the advertising of nationally sold products — with profit to themselves. Big, noisy advertisements of Philip Morris cigarettes suddenly appeared in three papers in the summer of 1941 — Harlem's *Amsterdam-Star News*, the Chicago *Defender*, and the Washington *Afro-American*, papers which are located in areas with very large Negro populations. The cigarette advertiser, succumbing to steady blandishments, sought to test Negro smokers in these cities to see if they would respond to a direct appeal made through the Negro press. This experiment was watched eagerly by the other papers. 'If that campaign goes over,' the *Courier* remarked editorially, with a sharp eye on the cash register, 'not only those newspapers but many Negro newspapers will be used by cigarette companies who are interested in the Negro market.' An appeal was forthwith made to the 'race loyalty' of its subscribers. Unblushingly, the *Courier* said, 'Philip Morris Cigarette has had the courage and the nerve, even in the face of competitive criticism, to give the Negro market a chance through its newspapers; and it is up to every Negro who smokes cigarettes to consider this appeal.'

It is only fair to say that this venturesome advertiser cashed in handsomely on his meager investment — for such appeals do get tangible results. Yet this very lack of advertising has its positive features. It often permits Negro newspapers to speak out boldly on social and racial questions, and explains in a measure why they are almost radical in their economic outlook. As small enterprises, for example, they are anxious to see government control of big business extended. As organs that cater to working people, they strongly support the worker's right to enter trade unions, and to be represented by them. But, again like their white contemporaries, they are opposed to the unionization of their own employees. Thus the successful strike of the editorial workers of the *Amsterdam-Star News* in 1935, the first open dispute between Negro workers and a Negro employer, was unique in the history of the Negro press, and really alarmed the other publishers.

The management declared that the strikers had been 'misled by Communists,' and characterized the American Newspaper Guild as an 'outlaw dues-collecting organization.' Heywood Broun, the late Scripps-Howard columnist and president of the Guild, was criticized for having become involved in a quarrel among Negroes. 'It would be cheaper for the Guild to obtain jobs for these men and women now walking the streets,' the publishers said, 'than it is going to be for the Guild to support them in their attempt to wreck a Negro business.' Mayor La Guardia took a hand in the situation and attempted unsuccessfully to bring together the strikers and the management. Financial troubles finally downed the paper and it was purchased by the Powell-Savory Corporation and a union contract was signed with the new management. By 1942 only *one* of the original twenty-odd strikers was still employed by that paper.

Though mainly concerned with the stern affairs that affect black men, Negro newspapers are not by any means mere crêpe-hanging sheets of woe. Most every paper contains a few comic strips, humorous cartoons, and a gossip column — no doubt to soften the blows dealt by a tough front page. The most distinguished, certainly the most original, contribution is the well-executed and widely syndicated feature, 'Bootsie,' a delightful Harlem character created by Oliver Harrington, a graduate of the Art School of Yale University. Nowhere in art or literature has Negro humor been more engagingly presented. A typical Harrington cartoon, which kept Negroes laughing for days, showed the affable Bootsie, a fat, sleepy-eyed fellow in baggy pants, about to depart from a sumptuous party. Effusively shaking the hand of his beaming hostess, he saluted her with: 'Bon soir, *Madamemoiselle* Brown, the chitterlin's sho' was dee-vine!'

Nearly every large publication has a column titled 'Harlem,' in which the doings of colored café society are recorded for the edification of those in the hinterland. Much of this output is done in the manner of the Broadway gossip columns. Thus so-and-so in the Negro press becomes the 'Black Walter Winchell,' the 'Black Danton Walker,' or, at the very least, the 'Black Ed Sullivan.' In the flavorsome vernacular of jive talk, these boys reel off the names of the various 'reet guys' and 'mellow chicks' who were involved in this divorce case or that switchblade fracas. Competition among the gossip-vendors is keen to scoop the field with a choice morsel about a 'medico,' a tidbit about a footloose 'gray' (white person), or a juicy item about a bedroom farce. The boys call it feuding!

Let's dig the jive in Dan Burley's 'Back Door Stuff,' a popular feature of the *Amsterdam-Star News*. 'A portly social nobleman of some financial stability,' he writes, 'was reportedly given the boot by his waitress tootsie-wootsie the other night and the portly one, they say, went into the tavern where she works and gave her gray boss a piece of his mind about trotting around on the q.t. with his chick. And the gray boss did not say one word. The scene shifts to the Mighty Dome [Washington], where a certain hubby is copping a righteous slave with Uncle [Sam] and who didn't like the idea of his girl (she rooms with the waitress) running around with a gray. Owoo, such goings on!'

Yiddish-speaking Eustace Gardner, short, bland, and age-less, who has been pounding the Harlem beat for a quarter of a century or more, is perhaps the most enterprising of the free-lance boys. 'Chappy,' as everyone knows him, combines a genial temperament with a tough hide which refuses to allow the critical stabs of outraged editors to penetrate his heart. He has in succession been a brickyard worker, machinist's helper, basketball player and manager, football coach, fancy ice-skater, professor of psychology, press agent, theatrical promoter, newspaper publisher — and in between he spent two amiable years on the W.P.A. When asked about his newspaper experience, Chappy says, 'That's a great question — great; I'm proud to answer that . . .'

Ambition burns in him with rare brilliance. In the midst of the Ethiopian-Italian War — Chappy had an inspiration. He disappeared from his Harlem haunts for about a week or so and everyone figured the worst had happened. Not until the New York *Times* revealed his whereabouts in a full-column story did Harlem learn the facts. He had performed the truly remarkable stunt of pulling the leg of the metropolitan press. Chappy, in a monstrous hoax, palmed off a plain Miss Islin Harvey, Harlem relief recipient, as the 'Princess Heschla Tamanya, cousin of His Majesty, Emperor Haile Selassie of Ethiopia.' He had ensconced her in a suite of the Broadway Central Hotel, the *Times* reported, done over in primitive lavishness, and attended her with two ladies-in-waiting. The *Daily News*, in its account of her 'arrival,' observed that 'the princess disdains the chairs and sofas of white civilization.' Unable to resist the magnificence of his own staging, Chappy promptly became the impeccable beturbaned 'Monsieur Chappie Gardner, Le Président of the Ethiopian Press Association.' The hoax leaked out when Harlem recognized Chappy and Miss Harvey from pictures published in the *News*.

Chappie says his motives were the purest. He wanted to help the despairing Miss Harvey get off the relief rolls. With the little publicity she would get, he hoped to launch her on a singing career — and thus see her gainfully employed as the 'Ethiopian Thrush.'

Many Negro newspapers could not exist without extensive coverage of society news — actually, social notes are second only to racial issues. Indicative enough is the great number of social clubs in a Negro center like Harlem — but Harlem has by no means the corner on the society market. Discriminating society editors faithfully report the names of all who attend an outstanding affair, describe the women's apparel in detail, and publish pictures. In a burst of enterprise, the *Afro-American* dispatched its star reporter to England post-haste to cover the coronation of George VI. Not, however, to record the historic event alone, but to report the who's who among the colored people who attended.

Much space is also devoted to lively articles on fashion, art, music, the theater, sports, spot-news photography, and shopping hints. But the meager operating capital precludes any staffs or coverage (or indeed salaries) that approximate those of the white dailies. The larger Negro publications have underpaid correspondents in the principal news centers of the world. Before the war, the *Afro-American* had Chatwood Hall in Moscow and Ollie Stewart in Rio de Janeiro. The *Courier* had J. A. Rogers in Addis Ababa, and later in Paris. *The Crisis* receives regular dispatches from George Padmore from London. Such free-lance writers as Roy De Coverly, stationed in Copenhagen, corresponded with a number of papers here. Today, alert to the Negro's concern about the Negro troops, the *Courier* has a competent reporter, Edgar T. Rousseau, 'Somewhere' at the African front to cover the exploits of America's black warriors; and the *Afro-American* has Stewart in London. Widening the horizon of the Negro's thinking on the color problem, the *Courier* recently added two columnists new to Negro journalism: Kumar Goshal, an East Indian; and Liu Liang-Mo, a Chinese.

In one sense, Negro newspapers are the Negro affairs supplements of the white dailies — for nearly every Negro who reads a white daily also subscribes to at least one Negro newspaper. Something akin to the unique rôle of *PM*, Negro papers print considerable news and features which can find no place in the white press, either because of its taboos or squeamishness. The *Amsterdam-Star News*, for instance, published a feature with the provocative head, 'English White Woman and Colored Husband Under Heel of Hitler.' Two installments, blatantly illustrated, had a blonde refugee relate her cruel experiences as a white woman married to a Negro in Nazi-dominated France. This is somewhat in line with the fact that the Negro press maintains vastly different standards from the white press for the handling of material involving interracial participants. Crime stories illustrate the point well. When an insanely jealous Chinese cut his Negro spouse and left her to die in the lobby of Harlem's fashionable Rochambeau Apartments, the incident was dismissed by the Negro press with a routine account on its inside pages and no follow-up appeared.

This affair was not quite so sensational as it sounds — though an obvious analogy to the white press would be for a Negro to stab a socially prominent white woman to death in the lobby of the Hotel Waldorf-Astoria. Yet, if a similar deed were committed by a white man with the victim a Negro woman, the story would certainly get banner headlines in the Negro press and bring down the wrath of the entire Negro community on his luckless head. The *Amsterdam-Star News*, following racial conflicts in the South, carried these three streamers in one edition:

TEXAS MOB LYNCHES DYING MAN
GEORGIA MOB GOES FOR DRAFTEE
COURT UPHOLDS SOLDIER'S LYNCHING

As a rule, crimes against whites by Negroes are generally found to have extenuating circumstances, viewed as they are against the whole social background.

There is, however, some parallel with the white press in a Negro editor's sense of reader interest. If the delightful limbs of the actress Marlene Dietrich are worth more columns of space in the white press than, let us say, a significant scientific development, who is to quarrel with the Negro press because the devastating limbs of Joe Louis or a display of bulky high-yaller cheese cake commands more attention than the discoveries of the late Doctor George Washington Carver, the Tuskegee scientist?

The Negro press is extremely race-conscious and works to foster race-consciousness in Negroes — some people indeed charge that it reeks with prejudice against whites. The racial

patriotism of the Negro press is beyond doubt its salient characteristic; and such patriotism often inclines toward black
chauvinism. This negative aspect may be the result of its
noisy pummeling of every form of racial discrimination, proscription, and double-dealing by whites. Actually, the Negro
press has the tremendous task of beating down insinuations of
Negro inferiority, which creeps into schools, newspapers, magazines, and radio. Today, the war — complicated by racial
factors — has given sweeping force and appeal to the black
nationalism of Negro newspapers. Since Pearl Harbor, this
aggressive racial policy is said to contribute to the doubt and
apathy in the minds of the Negro military and civilian population toward the war. This has caused grave concern to many
people in the white community. The blatant advertising of
racial inequalities in the United States by Negro newspapers
is of undoubted propaganda value to the Axis. But a development which has apparently escaped the notice of the white
community is that the Negro press has declared *war* against
the American Fascist dictator, Jim Crow, as well as against
the Axis dictators, and therefore can impute no good to the
enemy.

Viewed on its broadest plane, this is in fact a crusade for
democracy! The Negro press is, in effect, serving the fundamental of all peoples — white and black — by its insistence
upon the extension of democracy. A case in point is the
'Double V' campaign — for victory at home and victory
abroad — launched in the spring of 1942 by the *Courier*, to
which nearly every Negro newspaper and pulpit has lent support. The program includes the purchase of war bonds and
stamps, contributions to blood banks, participation in civilian
defense, and conservation of waste materials; educational
equality; and equal opportunity in war industry, as well as
a fight against all forms of discrimination based on race, color,
creed or class, the poll tax, and political disfranchisement.
The *Courier* has been successful in enlisting the support of

many prominent white and Negro leaders as well as the black rank-and-file.

In short, the editorial line of the Negro press today is the urgent need of extending democracy to the American Negro, and the profoundly positive effect it would have in galvanizing Negroes into action, as well as the reassuring effect it would have upon the colored peoples elsewhere in the world.

If the Negro press seems impatient, it is because the improvements in the Negro's status are so imperceptible as to be hardly noticed — particularly to those who know where the shoe pinches.

Chapter XX

We cannot stop tanks with squads of janitors.
We cannot blast the enemy with buckets of char-
women.

— ROBERT WEAVER

EXECUTIVE ORDER
NUMBER 8802

SIX months before the Japanese attack on Pearl Harbor, Negro communities in the urban areas were seething with resentment. This was reflected by the outspoken utterances of ordinarily conservative Negro leaders, by the pointed editorialized reporting in the Negro press, and, as well, by the inflammatory letters-to-the-editor. Responsible observers were manifestly worried, fearing that the resentment would burst into a social holocaust, perhaps to rival anything the nation had known. Harlem's *Amsterdam-Star News* described the situation in this language: 'Where there was once tolerance and acceptance of a position believed to be gradually changing for the better, now the Negro is showing a "democratic upsurge of rebellion," bordering on open hostility.'

Among other things, this unrest had been brought to a head by the frustration Negroes were experiencing at being barred from jobs in the defense industries. One million and more Negroes were unemployed — but no longer did the Negro have the cold comfort of the Depression when white men too were unemployed. His had become a black fate. According to the 1940 census, there were 5,389,000 Negroes in the labor force, 3,582,000 of which were men. A government survey found that, of 29,215 employees in ten war plants in the New

York area, only 142 were Negroes. In fifty-six war-contract factories in St. Louis, each employed an average of three Negroes. Outside the N.Y.A. and W.P.A., there were practically no provisions for Negroes in the program of defense-employment training, despite the need for manpower and the increasing number of Negroes on the W.P.A. rolls. The United States Employment Service sent out an inquiry to a selected number of defense industries as to the number of job openings and whether they would employ Negroes. More than fifty per cent stated flatly that they would not. In Texas, of 17,435 defense jobs, 9117 were barred to Negroes — and in Michigan, the figure was 22,042 out of 26,904. Moreover, contrary to the assumption that Negroes are barred only when they seek skilled work, no less than 35,000 out of 83,000 unskilled jobs were declared closed to Negro applicants.

Is the Negro as competent a worker as the white? Here is what *Fortune* magazine says, quoting a survey made by the National Conference Board, were the experiences of those managements which have Negro personnel. One hundred and two selected managements of industries employing Negroes had been requested to rank Negro and white employees on comparable skilled and semi-skilled work. As to ability, seventy managements graded Negro workers equal to their white colleagues, thirty-one poorer, one better than whites. As to production, eighty-five managements found Negroes equal to, twelve poorer, five better than white workers. As to regularity in attendance, sixty-four managements reported Negroes to be equal to, thirty-two poorer, five better than white labor.

Yet Negroes were being shuttled between employer and union — each claiming that the other discriminated. In a statement to the President, the N.A.A.C.P. argued that 'equitable employment of racial groups in defense industries was more than an issue of racial policy' — the nation's production was at stake! The White House replied, 'It is the policy of the War Department [letting contracts] that the services of Negroes will be utilized on a fair and equitable basis. ...' However, it soon was apparent that the President's wish was not taken literally by those responsible for carrying it out. No real effort was made to integrate Negro labor.

A great Negro push was mobilized to dramatize the situation. Early in 1941, A. Philip Randolph, president of the Brotherhood of Sleeping Car Porters, called for a 'Negro March on Washington!' In the midst of the mobilization campaign, he told me, 'The administration leaders in Washington will never give the Negro justice until they see masses — ten, twenty, fifty thousand Negroes on the White House lawn!' The Baltimore *Afro-American* concurred. In calling for mass action, it said: 'One individual marching up and down Pennsylvania Avenue in front of the White House denouncing race prejudice is arrested as a crank. Ten thousand persons get respectful attention!' In short order, buses were hired, special trains chartered, and a demonstration of upwards of fifty thousand Negroes was planned to take place on July 1, 1941. Certainly the rank-and-file of Negroes were in the mood. Both the N.A.A.C.P. and the National Negro Congress supported the march actively, and Walter White brought his influence and prestige to the movement. Thousands of dollars were spent. Press and pulpit played decisive rôles in whipping up sentiment. And those efficient couriers — the Pullman porters — carried the word to Negro communities throughout the country.

The prospect of thousands of determined Negroes in the nation's capital alarmed white Washington, a city with a Negro population of two-hundred-odd thousand restive Negroes. Some people recalled the race riot which occurred in the capital following the last war. When it became apparent, not only that Randolph and White were in earnest, but that the number of marchers was likely to be very large, Fiorello La Guardia, mayor of New York and then boss of the Office of Civilian Defense, pleaded with them to abandon it. Mrs. Roosevelt journeyed to New York and personally asked that the march be called off, and was politely refused. The President was also refused.

What made the Negro leaders so determined is revealed in a letter Walter White wrote John Temple Graves, and made public only recently. White said:

> We had pleaded with the President to break his silence and to speak out against discrimination which not only was doing an injustice to the Negro, but was definitely jeopardizing our national security.... But for five months we were given the run-around. Appeal after appeal was made to Washington with little tangible results. Conference after conference was held, and nothing happened.... Discontent and bitterness were growing like wildfire among Negroes all over the country. It was only then that Mr. Randolph and several others of us planned the March as a last resort....

Four days before the critical day — with the nation rapidly approaching war — Randolph, White, and others were called to Washington. They went demanding the issuance of an executive order forbidding discrimination. Sitting with the President were ranking members of his cabinet and representatives of the Office of Production Management, predecessor of the War Production Board. The conversations took place at a time when the government could ill afford to risk a demonstration which might further crystallize the antagonism of Negroes. The Negro leaders were shown a first draft of an order which outlawed discrimination in industry, but said nothing about government. They rejected it. Finally Mr. Roosevelt wrote his famous Executive Order 8802, and the march was canceled. But the masses of Negroes were bewildered. Even Randolph's colleagues were disappointed by the easy conclusion of the affair.

As it turned out, Randolph and White displayed considerable statesmanship, for the President's proclamation — the first presidential order affecting Negroes directly since Lincoln's day — created the Committee on Fair Employment Practices, an agency which may very well prove to be the opening wedge to the economic equality that Negroes seek. Certainly it commits the government to opposing racial discrimination in jobs. Moreover, its broad democratic implications affected, as well, five million Jews, five million aliens, six million foreign-born citizens, one million Orientals and American Indians, and five million Spanish-speaking peoples. The order declared:

> ... the policy of the United States [is] to encourage full participation in the national defense program by all citizens of the United States, regardless of race, creed, color, or national origin, in the firm belief that the democratic way of life within the Nation can be defended successfully only with the help and support of all groups within its borders.

The original personnel of F.E.P.C. was representative of those elements in our society which were expected to attack with vigor the problems of discrimination. Included were two whites and one Negro representing organized labor, liberal whites representing an influential Southern newspaper and a large manufacturing concern, and an able Negro lawyer holding an important elective office in Chicago. Malcolm S. MacLean, president of Hampton Institute, was made chairman, and Lawrence W. Cramer, former governor of the Virgin Islands, executive secretary. Essentially, the committee's job is to investigate complaints of discrimination and to take steps to redress grievances. Its most effective method is to hold public hearings.

Almost immediately, F.E.P.C. was thrown into a clash with organized labor's established policy of excluding Negroes from unions. For instance, Negro plumbers and steamfitters in Chicago complained that they were unable to get jobs at the Great Lakes Naval Training Station and at the Francis Cabrini Defense Housing Project. Two American Federation of Labor unions had agreements with the contractors on these projects providing that only union members could be employed, but these unions did not admit Negroes as members. F.E.P.C. investigated the charges, and finding them to be true, ruled that the agreement was 'illegal and inoperative' because it barred Negro workers. Soon afterward Negroes went to work.

When white labor in the South has dealings with black labor, the inferior status of the Negro must be conceded in front. Moreover, white labor in the South not only has used every form of trickery and violence to drive the Negro out of the labor movement, but has resorted to legislation to accomplish its aims. Theoretically, though, white and Negro workers should be natural allies. Yet union troubles over Negro employment go back a long way. At the close of the Civil War, there were some two hundred thousand Negro artisans, many of whom sought membership in union organizations. Faced with strong color barriers, a group of Negro workingmen met in Union League Hall at Washington as early as 1869, with one hundred and sixty-one accredited delegates present, to form their own organization. The question of fraternizing with white labor was frankly met, and a delegation was elected to appear at the white National Labor Union which was meeting the next month in Philadelphia. Faced with a put-up-or-shut-up situation, the white men attempted to create a conference of white and Negro delegates, representing Negro and white unions. This proposal met with Negro opposition, which finally broke out in racial discord and made cooperation between the races almost impossible.

A more liberal policy was shown by the Noble Order of the Knights of Labor, which attempted to assume leadership of the working class in 1880. The ambition of the order was to organize all workers, skilled and unskilled, without regard to nationality, sex, or color. But six years later the Federation of Organized Trades and Labor Unions, which had been formed in 1881, withdrew from the Knights of Labor, declaring its independence and its interest in skilled craft workers only. Thus the American Federation of Labor was created. Its policy naturally militated against the unskilled laborers, and particularly against Negroes, who were almost 97 per cent unskilled. Though the Federation came out abstractly against color discrimination, clauses in the constitutions of many of its unions permitted admittance of white men only. The leadership was not long in realizing that this policy was a bar to its expansion. After the problem was brought before the 1900 convention, Samuel Gompers is quoted as saying, 'To insist... upon a delegation... of colored workers being accorded representation in a central body would have meant the dissolution of that organization.'

This was the beginning of an historic retreat...

Under the plea of autonomy, the various national unions introduced different types and methods of segregation. Negroes were chiefly organized in auxiliary locals, usually in subordination to the nearest white local. They could not transfer to white locals, even if there were no Negro unions in the vicinity. They were declared ineligible for skilled work, could not hold office, and could not be represented in conferences and conventions except by whites. Many unions limited their membership by putting up prohibitive initiation fees and allowing new members to come in only on the recommendation of their friends already within the ranks. In 1902, separate charters were issued to unions composed exclusively of Negro workers. These never prospered, and by 1906 only five per cent of the two million organized workers were Negroes, and even their numbers were steadily declining.

With the signs, 'FOR WHITES ONLY' seemingly hanging everywhere, the Negro's employment situation became desperate. In the fall of 1910, an important organization, the National Urban League, was established to provide facilities for Negro employment, as well as for improved home life, education, and social work. Its leaders made direct efforts — as they do today — to lift trade-union racial barriers, because they believed that if the Negro could get into the white unions, he would be able to improve his living standard. The formation of the league followed a meeting called by Mrs. Ruth Standish Baldwin, a white woman of wealth and position, whose purpose was to help the Negro improve his condition. Among those who took part in its founding were Edwin R. A. Seligman, Miss Elizabeth Walton, L. Hollingsworth Wood; and the Negroes, George E. Haynes, Eugene Kinckle Jones, and Fred R. Moore, editor of the New York *Age*. Today, with Lester B. Granger at the helm, the league has forty-five local branches, each with an industrial relations department to secure jobs for Negroes in all lines; these branches form powerful pressure groups. The organization provides vocational guidance for Negro youth, reaching yearly more than seventy-five thousand students of high school and college. With its magazine, *Opportunity*, the league — though generally cautious — is a force in movements which have as their purpose the full utilization of Negro workers.

Twenty-four international unions, ten of them affiliated with the American Federation of Labor, exclude Negroes from membership. The United Mine Workers of John L. Lewis, however, long ago discarded this anti-Negro policy, because its leader was an exponent of industrial unionism — everyone in the mine belongs to the same union. It was the Congress of Industrial Organizations that introduced this form of unionism on a mass scale. Since its constitution contains no color bar, thousands of Negroes have entered the labor movement for the first time. By 1935 there were fifty thousand organized Negro workers in New York City alone. But this does not mean that some C.I.O. unions do not draw the color line. In Birmingham, Alabama, the A.F. of L. acted as champion of Negro ironworkers, merely because the local C.I.O.

did not. In two Ingalls Iron Works plants, the C.I.O. local was the bargaining agent, but had done little to improve the situation of the Negro workers — about a third of the personnel. Negroes remained in the low-paid categories, and they complained of unfair treatment. Negroes offered to bolt the C.I.O. when and if the A.F. of L. would promise to right their grievances. Once assured, they shifted *en masse* to the A.F. of L., and indeed had the promises lived up to when the next contract was negotiated.

Union antagonism toward Negroes is largely a result of the past practice of employing Negroes as a reserve labor force to depress the wages of white workers and as strikebreakers. But the national leadership of labor — particularly the C.I.O. — has recognized the problem and has been quick to assist governmental agencies in ironing out local difficulties where employees have gone on strike or used other methods of protesting the employment of Negroes. The unions have not licked the racial problem by any means, but they have given management and Negro employees better protection against difficulties arising from Negro employment. When Detroit workers at the Hudson Naval Ordnance Arsenal went out on a 'wildcat strike' because eight Negro employees, in accordance with their union seniority rights, had been assigned to machines formerly operated by white workers, the officials of the United Automobile Workers, a C.I.O. local, told them they would be expelled from the union unless they returned to work at once. This firm stand closed the matter and the strikers went back to work.

Paul V. McNutt, head of the nation's manpower program, tells a story which is illustrative of a new and growing spirit among the rank-and-file of white workers. A Negro janitor was upgraded in a plant in Long Island, New York, and when a number of white workers threatened to quit, a foreman made a short speech before their departure:

> You see that bridge over there and those docks? Who do you
> think is guarding them? And who is guarding all of the vital

areas in New York? *Negro soldiers.* Do you kick about that?
No! Then why have you got so much nerve as to walk out
when a Negro is put on a machine the same as you are?

We can't help it if his skin ain't white. But he is an American
citizen, and if Negroes are good enough to guard this city and
keep you safe, then Negroes are good enough to work and earn a
living the same as you men.

Every worker was back at his machine the next morning.
Yet Negroes are often forced to play power politics in the
labor ranks today, for they are dealing with hard-bitten politicians. When the nasty mess started between John L. Lewis
and Philip Murray to control the C.I.O., which incidentally
has approximately five hundred thousand Negro members, Negroes began jockeying for position. They took inventory of their
gains, but held that in spite of their numbers they did not hold
enough positions of leadership. The business of bargaining was
in prospect when Horace R. Cayton, Negro labor historian and
labor editor of the Pittsburgh *Courier*, advised an opportunistic
course. 'The thing to do,' he said, 'is to realize that either way
it goes — Lewis or Murray — there will be a fundamental re-
alignment in the labor movement of the country. Now is the
time to make both sides bid for Negro support and now is the
time to formulate the things which the Negro workers really
want. Instead of waiting to see which side will offer what,
black workers should state what they want and make the labor
unions meet the price.'

Backed against the wall, white labor often heaves the buck
to management, saying, 'Employers raise the objection to
Negro workers.' In theory, an employer should have fewer
objections than the white worker. He seldom is forced to have
social contact with his workers. Yet management has been
notoriously anti-Negro in its hiring policies. However, one
interesting development since Executive Order 8802 is the fact
that not one employer has flatly said: 'I refuse to employ
Negroes. So what!' If this is his attitude, he certainly has been

much more tactful than the diplomats of labor. While the employment of Negroes today is still on a small scale, here and there pressure has made employers give way in their traditional policies.

A notable example is the Lockheed-Vega Aircraft Corporation which has made determined efforts to integrate Negroes in one of its plants. The officials began by developing a comprehensive plan in which foremen and supervisors were charged with responsibility for its success. Not only were the company's foremen and supervisors sent a memorandum announcing the company's intention to abide by the President's executive order banning discrimination, but a similar memorandum was sent to Aeronautical Lodge 727 of the International Association of Machinists, bargaining agent for the company's employees. Notices also were posted on all employee bulletin boards. Finally, one Negro after another was introduced into the plant — Joe Louis introduced the one hundredth with much cheering by the white workers. Today almost a thousand Negroes, women among them, are employed at Lockheed-Vega in classifications ranging from sheet metal, drill press, and foundry to wing and tail assembly, material control, plumbing, and plant maintenance.

Here are the four major objections raised by white employers and the facts used by the government agencies to refute them:

Objection: 'Negroes and whites just won't work together.'

Fact: Negroes and whites do work together. They are working together in plants like Ford, Kelsey Hayes, Murray Corporation, Bethlehem Shipbuilding, and the Denver Ordnance Plant — in the shipyards of Virginia and North Carolina — in the iron and coal fields of Alabama — in all parts of the country.

Objection: 'Negroes just can't do the work.'

Fact: The Newport News Shipbuilding and Dry Dock Company employs more than six thousand Negroes as machine operators, outside machinists, stage-builders, riggers, bolters, drillers, regulators, chippers, caulkers, blacksmiths, and as skilled, semi-skilled, and unskilled workers in a dozen other categories. When the defense program was launched, there had been sufficient employment of Negroes by American industry to convince most people that Negroes, as individuals and when subjected to the usual processes of training and selection, can do any and all types of production jobs.

Objection: 'We're interested only in production.'

Fact: The employment of Negroes is a production factor. Unless American industry uses qualified Negro workers and trains thousands of additional Negroes, just as we train white men and women, we cannot have full production.

Objection: 'The unions won't let us hire Negroes.'

Fact: Fewer than two dozen of the more than two hundred major unions in this country have constitutional bans against Negro workers today. In many cases of union discrimination, the government has stepped in to get for Negroes full membership or work permits. An employer who meets union resistance to his attempts to hire Negroes may invoke the full support of the federal government, the President of the United States, and the heads of both major labor groups.

If signs mean anything, Negroes are beginning to make headway along the economic front, through the efforts of rank-and-file white workers. In New York City the Railway Mail Association, an A.F. of L. local, smashed a twenty-nine-year color bar by voting into membership seven Negro mail clerks, an action that was taken in open defiance of the union's 'lily-white' national constitution. These advances have their social implications as well. The United Electrical, Radio, and Machine Workers, a C.I.O. affiliate, wired the hotel proprietors of Indianapolis to alter their anti-Negro policies, which bar Negroes from registering at the city's hotels and eating in the hotel dining-rooms, or lose the union's annual convention. From church quarters have come statements like that of the National Catholic Committee, which demanded that Negro workers be treated like any other worker. Twenty-two labor unions and locals recently pledged themselves, in a formal statement to the government, to fight anti-Negro discrimination in war industry by helping to place Negro workers. Even down South, there are encouraging signs. The North Carolina Federation of Labor elected its first Negro vice-president recently. He is thirty-two-year-old Haywood Williams, a line-setter employed by the Liggett & Myers Tobacco Company, of Durham, North Carolina. A distinctly heartening development is the C.I.O.'s formation of an Anti-Discrimination Committee to combat racial bias within its own ranks, with George Weaver, a Negro, as its executive director.

The bulk of Negro labor is still unskilled, a fact that Negroes have shouted from the housetops as one of the results of discrimination. Whereas every third gainfully working white American belongs to the skilled or semi-skilled groups, only one out of each eight Negroes belongs to these groups. Even where training is possible for Negroes, they are among the missing. In the pre-employment and refresher-training courses supervised by the United States Office of Education in the District of Columbia, an area where Negroes form 22 per cent of the population, only 3215 Negroes were enrolled — less than 4 per cent of the trainees. Out of 4630 training sources only 194 accepted Negroes. *Fortune* magazine's reporters found 12,472 persons training for war production in Texas. These included exactly 206 Negroes. Yet there was provision to train more than 23,000 workers. A New Orleans shipyard, reprimanded by the Maritime Commission for falling behind schedule, complained of not enough local skilled labor. Some seven hundred additional trained workers would have caught up the slack. Yet some 7000 local Negroes had registered for training without getting a tumble!

From its beginning, the F.E.P.C. was deluged with complaints of racial discrimination. More than six thousand were filed with the committee in one year's time. Today it receives an average of eight hundred complaints a month. The job ahead appears to be a tremendous one — for at present less than three per cent of the employees in war industries are Negroes. Many more complaints, significantly enough, come from the North and West. The explanation offered by responsible observers for this situation is that Negroes in the Southern areas are intimidated. Long experience has taught them that to tell Washington about their grievances is to invite the wrath, and eventual reprisal, of the local white folks.

The Birmingham, Alabama, hearings illustrate the point well. When the F.E.P.C. scheduled investigations for this city, the Gadsden, Alabama, *Times* made the announcement in this fashion: 'A bunch of snoopers, two of whom are Negroes, will assemble in Birmingham, June 18 [1942], for a three-day session to determine whether the South is doing right by Little Sambo.' Some papers referred to the committee as a 'group of black-and-tan investigators,' 'halo-wearing missionaries of New Deal socialism,' and 'Roosevelt racial experts.' One writer characterized the affair as an 'inquisition,' and another spoke of 'dat cummittee fer de purteckshun uv Rastus & Sambo.' The F.E.P.C., in the view of one paper, was 'an instrument for political and social reform operating under a vicious disguise.' Though no untoward incidents occurred, there was much head-shaking and more apprehension. During the excitement, one white man, while on the witness stand, was heard saying, 'Yes, sir,' to a Negro questioner.

To the South, Executive Order 8802 is — in the words of Governor Dixon of Alabama, who refused to accept on behalf of his state an Army contract for tent cloth because there was a clause in the contract against race discrimination — 'meddling with the racial policies of the South' and 'a crackpot reform.' Other Southerners talk in stronger language. Horace C.

Wilkinson, a Birmingham lawyer and politician with a reputation for race-baiting, called from retirement to make a speech to the Kiwanis Club of Bessemer, Alabama, soon after the hearings, said indignantly that Negroes 'are now being given jobs that have always been filled by white men.' He defended the exclusion of Negroes from certain trades unions. He related instance after instance of employers being forced by the United States Employment Service to hire Negroes against their will. He viewed with alarm Negroes working alongside of white workers in offices and factories. The Alabama politician had a solution for all this. He proposed the organization of a 'state-wide, South-wide, nation-wide League for White Supremacy.'

'The time to act is now,' he said. 'An organization should be formed, so strong, so powerful, so efficient, that this menace to our national security and our local way of life will rapidly disappear. It can be done. It should be done. Alabama must lead the way.'

Those are the words of a demagogue. Listen to an acknowledged 'liberal' of the South. Before hearings in Birmingham, Mark F. Ethridge, a member of F.E.P.C. and managing editor of the Louisville *Courier-Journal*, declared that he would not have accepted membership on the President's committee if he had thought its purpose was to destroy segregation, further contending that the executive order was 'not a social document.' He boldly said, 'He [the Negro] must recognize that there is no power in the world — not even in all the mechanized armies of the earth, Allied and Axis — which would now force the Southern white people to the abandonment of the principles of social segregation.' Earl B. Dickerson, a Negro member of F.E.P.C., promptly answered Ethridge. 'I am unalterably opposed to segregation, whether in the South or North,' he said. 'Concessions should not be made to the South, which after all is still a part of the geographical boundaries of the United States. There should be "no pussyfooting" on segregation by members of the committee.'

The grim truth is, the South has thrown down the challenge to the federal government. It regards Executive Order 8802 as the initial assault on its way of life. As a matter of fact, the South itself has declared war on the North — that is, in so far as the Negro and his rights are concerned. Backward elements in that section seek to choke off the Negro's livelihood, as a means of halting his advance. Apparently they don't believe with Mrs. Roosevelt that 'We have probably come to a point where we have to make up our minds either to live in a democracy and make it a reality or to accept the fact that we are not capable of meeting the challenge.'

Executive Order 8802 may or may not be a social document of tremendous import, but it certainly is a significant stride in the Negro's advance. Negroes already are asking that F.E.P.C. be made a permanent government agency with enlarged powers. What the committee eventually will be rests with its members — as well as with Negroes and their progressive white friends and allies! If they are aggressive in supporting the order's intent, most certainly it will be something meaningful. Big, jovial George M. Johnson, a former Howard University professor and assistant executive secretary of the committee, tipped his mitt on what he regards as the real meaning of the President's order. 'The President,' he said recently, 'must have recognized that carrying out the purposes of the order would lead inevitably to social advance for the Negro.'

At the moment, however, the F.E.P.C. is subject to the strains and stresses of politics. During the summer of 1942, Mr. Roosevelt dropped the committee — a political hot potato — in the lap of Paul V. McNutt, head of the War Manpower Commission. A. Philip Randolph, in a wire to the White House, said the shift would make the committee utterly useless in its fight against job discrimination. The executive order transforming the F.E.P.C. from an independent agency responsible to the President himself to one which may find itself dependent for funds on Southern politicians in Congress has discouraged Negroes considerably. They view it as an attempt to silence the committee.

Ironic, to say the least, is the fact that the War Production Board was charged with widespread anti-Negro discrimination in its operations and control section by the United Federal Workers, a C.I.O. affiliate. Much, indeed, has been made of the fact that the F.E.P.C. has not washed the dirty linen of the federal government, where Negroes say, despite gains, racial discrimination still is rife. But F.E.P.C. can complain, with justice on its side, that it is inadequately equipped with personnel to run down the thousands of grievances. What apparently is most needed is further clarification by the President of the intent of Executive Order 8802, a statement so plain that few will misunderstand, thus enabling F.E.P.C. to carry out its enormous task with vigor.

The F.E.P.C. has stirred up much heat. Actually, its gains have been negligible compared with the job to be done. But its total accomplishments will, in a measure, determine the place Negroes will have in the economic life of the country after the war.

Chapter XXI

*If I were a Negro I would live in constant fury
and probably would batter myself to death
against the bars inclosing my condition.*

— WESTBROOK PEGLER

NEGROES ARE SAYING...

LISTEN to the way Negroes are talking these days!

Gone are the Negroes of the old banjo and singin' roun' the cabin doors. Old Man Mose is dead! Instead, black men have become noisy, aggressive, and sometimes defiant. Actually, this attitude is a reflection of a cold enthusiasm toward the war brought on by what the Pittsburgh *Courier* calls 'The War Against Negroes.' The fact is, there still is considerable doubt and apathy in the minds of the Negro civilian and military populations, which seriously hampers the war effort, particularly among those who are unable to lift their eyes to the hills. This is not the idle speculation of irresponsible observers, but an implacable fact that is revealed by the casual remarks dropped daily by the Negro man-in-the-street, and by his overt acts as well.

Recently a Harlem physician was summoned to court for driving about with a large sign tied to the rear of his automobile. It read:

IS THERE A DIFFERENCE?

JAPS BRUTALLY BEAT
AMERICAN REPORTER

GERMANS BRUTALLY BEAT
SEVERAL JEWS

AMERICAN CRACKERS
BRUTALLY BEAT
ROLAND HAYES & NEGRO SOLDIERS

JOIN THE AUTO CLUB PLACARD BRIGADE

A picture of this inflammatory display was reproduced on the entire front page of Harlem's *People's Voice*, with a story applauding the doctor's daring and denouncing his arrest by the police. Such attitudes are by no means sectional. During a quarrel with her white employer in Raleigh, North Carolina, an unnamed Negro woman retorted, 'I hope Hitler does come, because if he does he will get you first!' She was sent to prison for three years. Charles Steptoe, a Negro, twenty-four years of age, was sentenced to ten days in the workhouse because he refused to stand while 'The Star-Spangled Banner' was played in a Harlem theater. When, in another instance, a young Georgia-born Negro, Samuel Bayfield, came before the federal court for sentencing on an admitted attempt to evade the draft, he was asked where he was born. Bayfield told the court, 'I was born in this country against my will!' A Philadelphia Negro truck driver, Harry Carpenter, was held on charges of treason. He was accused of having told a Negro soldier: 'You're a crazy nigger wearing that uniform — you're only out fighting for white trash. This is a white man's government and war and it's no damned good.'

A story is going the rounds in Washington's Negro circles of

an old Negro woman who boarded a streetcar and sat in the
only available seat — one next to a white sailor. He instantly
jumped to his feet and angrily stalked off. The Negro woman
calmly spread into the vacancy, and, in mock humility, said,
'Thanks, son, for the whole seat.' Then she slowly appraised
the white-clad figure. 'Nice suit you're wearing that Joe Louis
bought!'

Sterling Brown, a Negro poet and gifted reporter of South-
ern life, heard a Negro bragging at a gas station: 'I done regist.
Expect to be called soon. That Hitler. Think he can whup
anybody. I'm gonna capture Hitler. I'm gonna deliver him to
President Roosevelt. At the front door of the White House.'
The white bystanders applauded — but froze when he added,
'Then I'm gonna fight for some rights over here.'

A reporter for Harlem's *Amsterdam-Star News* interviewed
James Miller, a Negro aged sixty-two, who had served thirty
years in the Navy, concerning Negroes enlisting in the Navy —
'a branch of our military service where they are apparently
not wanted,' so one question ran. 'Unless they get the same
opportunity as white men,' he said, 'I don't think it fair to mis-
lead them.' A veteran of both the Spanish-American War and
the first World War, he was bitter because he recalled how two
of his uncles had served the Navy with distinction. It was not
until 1922, he recalled, that the Navy set up a Jim Crow
policy restricting Negroes to certain branches of the service.
The Negro seaman added: 'We're the most loyal race in the
world. We're supposed to be citizens of this country and our
integrity as soldiers remains unquestioned, but they still don't
want us.'

A fairly typical attitude is that of the Negro soldier who said,
'Sometimes I feel very proud of being a member of this big,
huge army, until I pick up a paper and see where a Negro
soldier was lynched and it makes me feel like, "What am I
doin' here!"' Other soldiers are disappointed with their own
treatment by the Army. One stationed at a camp deep in the

South complained in a letter to a Harlem friend that the post restaurant — where he was stationed — was divided with one side marked 'Colored' and the other 'White.' According to his report, two Negro soldiers went into the 'Colored' section and, finding it crowded, went across into the 'White' one. A white officer was called and ordered them to leave, and when they refused, he had them arrested. 'This,' the letter concluded, 'is just one of the milder insults that we go through down here. It will not be long before the [Negro] boys here will resent these un-American practices. . . .'

This sort of attitude is heard in other quarters. A group of rural Negroes living outside Richmond, Virginia, were having a heated argument over what difference there was between the *old* and *new* Negro. 'Well, as I sees it,' drawled an octogenarian finally, 'when the old Negro was insulted he shed a tear; today, when these young ones is insulted they sheds blood.'

This extravagant talk is perhaps wishful thinking on the old man's part. What is a fact, though, is that events since Pearl Harbor have stirred a sorely driven people. While Nazi spies and saboteurs went to trial one after another in an atmosphere of judicial fairness and public calm — six Negroes were lynched! One of these, Cleo Wright, was burned, his body mutilated and tied to an automobile, and dragged through the streets of Sikeston, Missouri. Right on the heels of this, a Negro sharecropper, Odell Waller, was executed in Pittsylvania County, Virginia, for the killing of his white landlord, though the liberal opinion of the country, acknowledging extenuating circumstances, clamored for clemency. Yet a week or so later a white man, Eugene Ekland, who vowed to exterminate the Negro race and in the process murdered five Negroes in the nation's capital, was sentenced only to fifteen years in prison! A sort of melancholy footnote was the discovery of two fourteen-year-old Negro boys hanging from a bridge in the town of Meridian, Mississippi. They had been taken from a jail, where they had been confined for reportedly confessing to an attempted rape.

When Southern gentlemen take the law in their own hands, Negro women too are victims. An Army nurse, Lieutenant Nora Green, stationed at the Tuskegee Army Air Corps School, received orders to prepare for overseas service. Before sailing, she went on a shopping tour in Montgomery, Alabama. On her return trip to Tuskegee she boarded a bus, and the white driver pummeled her into unconsciousness following a dispute over the denial of a seat she had reserved in advance. Afterward a Negro editor was heard to say, 'Something like that makes you wonder if Montgomery isn't still the capital of the Confederacy.'

Even before the United States entered the war, disturbing reports were tumbling out of the Army camps. There were race riots at Fort Oswego. Fighting between races at Camp Davis. Discrimination against Negroes at Fort Devens. Jim Crow conditions were prevalent at Camps Blanding and Lee. Stabbings occurred at Fort Huachuca, killings at Fort Bragg, and the edict 'not to shake a nigger's hand' at Camp Upton. Nearly every day reports were heard of Negroes going A.W.O.L. So moved was Harlem's *Amsterdam-Star News* that it described the situation with this headline:

TERROR REIGN SWEEPS
NATION'S ARMY CAMPS
NEGROES GO A.W.O.L.

One morning in the summer of 1941, the New York *Times* calmly reported that following friction with the white population near Little Rock, Arkansas, forty-three Negroes of the Ninety-Fourth Engineers (labor) battalion, stationed at Camp Custer, had departed from the maneuver area. Actually, they had run off to seek safety from violence of the white citizens and state police. 'As we were walking along the highway,' one of the soldiers said afterward, 'we saw a gang of white men with guns and sticks, and white state troopers were with them. They told us to get the hell off the road and walk in the mud at the side of the highway. One of our white lieutenants walked up to a state trooper and said something. I don't know what. Anyway, the trooper told him to get them blacks off the highway "before I leave 'em laying there." Then out of a clear blue sky the state trooper slapped the white lieutenant. . . . Some of our men began to talk about returning to Camp Custer for protection. That night they left by bus, train, and walking. Three of us hopped freight trains after walking forty-two miles to avoid white people, who we felt would attack us because of our uniforms.'

A Negro who has lived in the freer atmosphere of the North and has become aware of his rights will not relinquish them or put up with abuse because he happens to be in the South. That he wears the uniform of the United States Army increases his self-respect. To some Southerners such a man is a dangerous 'nigger' who must be made to 'know his place' — with violence and terror, if necessary. The prejudiced Southerner refuses to accord even the ordinary decencies to the Negro and is not impressed by the statements of the federal government about this being a war for democracy. In his view, democracy is not a way of life for all, but a luxury for better-class white people only.

'Make way for that *white* Lord God Jehovah!'

Senator John D. Bankhead of Alabama expressed the Southern viewpoint in a letter to General George C. Marshall, Army Chief of Staff. He suggested that Northern Negroes be quartered in Northern states only. 'Our people feel,' he said, 'that the government is doing a disservice to the war effort by locating Negro troops in the South in immediate contact with white troops at a time when race feeling among the Negroes has been aroused and when all the energies of both the whites and blacks should be devoted to the war effort.' If Negro soldiers must be trained in the South, he said finally, 'as a re-

sult of social and political pressure, can't you place Southern
Negro soldiers there and place the Northern Negro soldiers in
the North, where their presence is not likely to lead to race
wars?'

The South proposes to be unbending in extending even the
simple dignities to an Army uniform — if a Negro wears one.
Negroes are equally insistent that, if they must die as equals,
then they must be treated as equals. These sharply differing
views met head-on in a flare-up at Fort Bragg, North Carolina,
the result of an affray in which a Negro soldier and a white
military policeman were killed. In this instance, however, the
killing of the white man was the act of a Southern Negro whose
resentments against injustice mounted to a desperate thrust
for human dignity. The soldier, Ned Turman, had voiced objections to an attack on a fellow Negro soldier and, for his
pains, was clubbed over the head by two white M.P.'s. In
wrestling to protect himself, the Negro managed to snatch the
gun of one of his assailants. Brandishing it, he stepped back
and cried, 'I'm gonna break up you M.P.'s beating us colored
soldiers!' And with that he fired the fatal shot. The other
white M.P., standing near-by, shot the Negro to death. After
the shooting, whole companies at Fort Bragg not involved in
the affair — their Negro officers included — were forced to
stand all night with their hands above their heads while armed
military policemen patrolled the camp.

This affair occurred before the war. Today, with national
unity desperately needed, racial tensions have increased rather
than abated. The N.A.A.C.P. urged the War Department to
include in its military instructions courses on the racial implications in the war, believing that such instructions were
greatly needed to counteract racial bigotry. The suggestion
was courteously but firmly turned down. Meanwhile, friction
between white and Negro troops reached a critical stage at
Fort Dix, in New Jersey, which certainly suggests that the
problem is not sectional. Three soldiers were killed and five

wounded in a fifteen-minute gun battle. According to the
official Army version, the trouble started when a soldier
stepped out of a telephone booth in the Waldron Sports
Palace, an amusement center across a highway from a Negro
barracks, and two other soldiers in the waiting line outside the
booth made a simultaneous rush for it. A scuffle ensued, the
military police were called, and they attempted to separate
the participants. A Negro lunged for the M.P.'s pistol, but
only ripped the holster and then ran out of the tavern.

The M.P. ran after him, commanding him to halt, and
fired a warning shot into the air. This was the signal for a
fusillade of rifle shots from the Negro barracks across the road.
One of the M.P.'s fell mortally wounded at almost the first
volley. White and Negro soldiers began pouring out of the
tavern and the barracks. The military police were called
out, and a battle began from opposite sides of the highway.
The M.P.'s were armed with pistols and the colored soldiers
with rifles. At the height of the battle, two white officers came
running up the highway, yelling the order to cease firing, and
both sides obeyed. By then about fifty shots had been fired.
Fifteen Negroes were involved and fifty white military policemen.

There was more to this affair than met the eye. Underscored by smoldering resentments, the gunplay had climaxed
a series of Negro-white clashes, caused mainly by an influx of
a detachment of Southern M.P.'s. Until that time relations
between Negro and white troops were on the whole good, and
were steadily getting better. A Negro officer told a *PM* reporter that soon after the arrival of the M.P.'s, 'they immediately started kicking the Negro troops around. They'd flare
up at the drop of a hat. Things were especially bad on buses
to and from camp. If the bus was filled and Negro soldiers
had seats, those Southern M.P.'s would order them to stand
up and surrender their places to whites.' Fights became frequent. Race friction increased. Morale declined noticeably.

The Negro regiment, it should be mentioned, was the same unit whose commanding officer, Colonel Riley E. McGarragh, posted a particularly offensive notice at temporary regimental headquarters at Marcus Hook, Pennsylvania:

> Any cases between white and colored males and females, whether voluntary or not, is considered rape and during time of war the penalty is death.

This order was later rescinded following protests from Negro organizations. 'I've been at Fort Bragg, where things were bad enough,' said the Negro officer. 'But this is worse. Hell may break loose unless something's done quick.' He felt the situation could be improved by removing the Southern M.P.'s because 'the colored man gets on well with Northern soldiers, and even with many Southerners who've learned that we've got to fight against a common enemy, not against each other.' Evidently the authorities paid him no mind. A few months later, Fort Dix was the scene of another fatal brawl in which a Negro soldier was killed.

'It is all right to be loyal if it is encouraged,' ran a letter to the editor of Harlem's *Amsterdam-Star News*. 'But I fail to see where America is doing anything to encourage the loyalty of black men.... Remember, that which you [Negroes] fail to get now you won't get after the war.' That comment appeared one week after Pearl Harbor. The issue of the paper that published this comment contained twenty articles by staff writers which dealt critically with the treatment of Negroes. Two weeks later, sixty prominent Negroes met in New York City in a conference called by the N.A.A.C.P. and the National Urban League to consider the Negro's part in the war effort. The group passed with only five dissenting votes a resolution introduced by Judge William H. Hastie, then civilian aide to the Secretary of War, that 'the colored people are not wholeheartedly and unreservedly all out in support of the present war effort.' Walter White, executive secretary of the N.A.A.C.P., attributed this country-wide apathy of Negroes to discrimination in the Army, Navy, and Air Corps, and especially in the war industries.

This situation has its roots in the very immediate past. In the first World War Negroes at once sought to participate as soldiers. With full consciousness of their duties as citizens and with the desire to act the rôles of men, they gladly bore their share of the war effort. W. E. B. Du Bois, then the acknowledged leader of the Negro community, articulated the race's view toward the conflict in his now famous 'Close Ranks' statement to the nation as well as to certain skeptical Negroes:

> We of the colored race have no ordinary interest in the outcome. That which the German power represents spells death to the aspirations of Negroes and all dark races for equality, freedom, and democracy. Let us not hesitate. Let us, while this war lasts, forget our special grievances and close ranks shoulder to shoulder with our own white fellow-citizens and the allied nations who are fighting for democracy. We make no ordinary sacrifice, but we make it gladly and willingly with our eyes lifted to the hills.

This stirred Negroes in 1918. The conditions facing Negroes did not cause any lag when the call for volunteers was heard. Also, more than two million Negroes were registered under the Selective Service Law, and more than three hundred thousand were called. To the number drafted throughout the country were added 37,723, representing the Negro regulars and National Guard members. About two hundred thousand saw service in France, fifty thousand in actual combat. The fighting units constituted the 92d and 93d Divisions. To the 92d was attached the 367th United States Infantry, popularly known as the 'Buffaloes,' while the 15th Regiment (the New York National Guard) was part of the 93d. Two Negroes, Henry Johnson and Needham Roberts, were the first American privates to receive the *Croix de Guerre*, the French award for bravery.

Not until the war was over did the full measure of ill-treatment meted out to the Negro troops come to light and then only after Du Bois had visited Europe in 1919 to attend the Pan-African Congress. Documentary evidence of the discriminatory conditions faced by Negro troops was published by *The Crisis* magazine. One section alone will illustrate the attitude of the American high command, a memorandum called 'Secret Information Concerning Black American Troops.' It began with this statement:

> It is important for French officers who have been called upon to exercise command over black American troops, or to live in close contact with them, to have an exact idea of the position occupied by Negroes in the United States. The information set forth in the following communication ought to be given to these officers and it is to their interest to have these matters known and widely disseminated. It will devolve likewise on the French Military Authorities, through the medium of Civil Authorities, to give information on this subject to the French population residing in the cantonments occupied by American colored troops.

Here are a few typical passages:

> We must prevent the rise of any pronounced degree of intimacy between French officers and black officers. We may be courteous and amiable with these last, but we cannot deal with them on the same plane as with the white American officers without deeply wounding the latter. We must not eat with them, must not shake hands or seek to talk or meet with them outside of the requirements of military service. . . .

> Make a point of keeping the native cantonment population from 'spoiling' the Negroes. [White] Americans become greatly incensed at any public expression of intimacy between white women and black men. . . .

> The increasing number of Negroes in the United States (about 15,000,000) would create for the white race in the Republic a menace of degeneracy were it not that an impassable gulf has been made between them . . .

> This indulgence and this familiarity are matters of grievous concern to the Americans. They consider them an affront to

their national policy. They are afraid that contact with the French will inspire in black Americans aspirations which to them [the whites] appear intolerable....

It developed that the Negro soldiers had themselves found a way of showing resentment. In a field near Metz on Thanksgiving evening in 1918, the regiment whose bravery in combat in the great offensive at Champagne had only a month before earned it the *Croix de Guerre* (their casualties were eleven hundred) was ordered to sing 'My Country, 'Tis of Thee.' The music boomed and the soldiers, the black warriors from America, some three thousand of them, stood silent with grim and sober faces. From all that great assemblage rose only the voices of the regiment's six white officers!

While these were the conditions abroad, the Negro civil population was the victim of some of the bloodiest race riots in American history. Even regiments in training in the United States were forced to undergo indignities and violence. One regiment was sent to Spartanburg, South Carolina, and at once the men were beset by Jim Crowism. The white population was no less considerate. The proprietor of a local hotel ordered a Negro officer named Noble Sissle, today a well-known band leader, to remove his hat when he entered the lobby — contrary to Army regulations — and kicked him into the street when he refused. A riot was averted only by the restraining influence of Lieutenant 'Jim' Europe, the regiment's popular band leader. On another occasion fifty Negroes marched on the city to 'avenge' two missing buddies and only the efforts of a sympathetic white colonel prevented bloodshed.

At the close of the war, administration leaders began a campaign to convince Negroes that no great change in their traditional position in America could be expected. With such a government policy, Negroes became the victims of new outrages throughout the country. Even the Ku Klux Klan was revived. In view of these events, Du Bois was forced to confess that he was less sure today than then of the soundness of his war attitude. 'I did not realize the full horror of war and its wide impotence as a method of social reform,' he wrote sadly. 'I doubt if the triumph of Germany in 1918 could have had worse results than the triumph of the Allies. Possibly passive resistance by my twelve millions to war activity might have saved the world for black and white....'

Today, the prejudice shown by Army officials seems very little different from that of yesterday. Reports have trickled back from England — to illustrate — that the American high command is attempting to impose various forms of segregation and discrimination on the Negro troops. The British liberal *New Statesman and Nation* reports examples of discrimination and even assault against Negro soldiers. A British soldier wrote to complain that in a certain English port, Negroes were barred from a well-known restaurant. He said English soldiers were instructed not to eat and drink with Negroes, and restaurant employees were told to bar them. 'I have met [white] Southerners,' an English writer said, 'who seemed rational enough until the Negro problem was mentioned, and who would then show a terrified, lynching spirit, which was about the ugliest thing imaginable.' He also noticed that they 'took it for granted that it is their duty to interfere if they see black troops with white girls.' A most recent episode involves a Southern white soldier who was invited to an English home, and created a scene when he discovered that a fellow guest was an American Negro soldier. He attacked the Negro in the presence of the guests, ruining the evening for everybody.

The *New Statesman and Nation* made this significant comment:

What is to be done? The American government must face the problem itself. It must use every device of persuasion and authority to let white Southern troops know that it is against discipline to treat Negro soldiers in the way to which their training and education has accustomed them.... If things are left to drift, unhappy incidents will occur ... and the British will instinctively take the side of the Negroes against their white assailants.

One interesting fact about these reports is that they were passed by the British censor, which may suggest the emergence of a new British policy on race. Even the conservative elements in the House of Lords have been stirred. The Lord Chancellor, Viscount Simon, is quoted as attacking a proposal to accept the American segregation pattern with the indignant retort: 'I do not suppose Lord Shaftesbury is proposing that any distinction should be drawn between white and colored soldiers. That is the last thing the British Parliament would tolerate for a moment.'

From all reports, Negro troops are very popular with the English people, who have arranged many entertainments for them — much to the disgust and indignation of some white Americans. This very spirit in certain unrelaxing whites is what caused a bloody race riot in the United States, when two thousand whites engaged in pitched battle with five hundred Negroes to prevent them from occupying the Sojourner Truth Homes, a Detroit housing project built with public funds for Negro war workers. Immediately, this occurrence was seized upon by Axis agents to stir up racial strife and disrupt war production. Mob rule gripped one of the country's principal arteries of war industry, and demonstrated the federal government's weakness on the race issue.

A firm stand by the government on racial questions, would be translated into acts by the humblest white citizen in America — not to mention the white troops abroad. More important, though, is the fact that native Fascists, prodded by Axis agents, defied the government in Detroit. This riot was perhaps one of the most successful acts of sabotage during this war. At secret meetings, Ku Kluxers received orders to keep the Negro workers from entering their new homes. The F.B.I. investigation revealed surprising scope to Ku Klux Klan activities in Detroit, even to boring from within labor's ranks, and to links with Axis agents. The National Workers' League, a pro-Nazi group whose officials were later indicted, cooperated with the Klan in preparing and staging the subsequent riot in which scores of people were injured.

Today, however, the importance of millions of Negroes is being increasingly recognized in administration circles — to wage total war, a total population must be set in motion. The President wrote the N.A.A.C.P. convention in the summer of 1942: 'I note with satisfaction that the theme of your significant gathering read, "Victory Is Vital to Minorities." This theme might well be reversed and given to the nation as a slogan. For today, as never before, "Minorities Are Vital to Victory."' The status of the Negro in 1942 is considerably different from that of 1917. For one thing, his opportunities are definitely broadening, but only under public pressure. For example, an aviation unit was established at Tuskegee, though there is provision to train only a dozen Negro pilots a year. With few exceptions, the officer personnel is Negro. The ranking administrative officer is Lieutenant Colonel Benjamin O. Davis, Jr., a graduate of West Point in 1936, son of Brigadier General Benjamin O. Davis, first and only Negro general. This fact, incidentally, reminds me that in the last war, to prevent the promotion that was rightfully due him, the ranking Negro officer, Colonel Charles Young, was retired on the pretext that he suffered from high blood pressure. To prove that he could withstand the rigors of a military campaign, he rode horseback from Chillicothe, Ohio, to Washington, D.C.!

Decidedly on the credit side of the ledger has been the partial removal of a long-standing discrimination in the Navy. It recently agreed to enlist Negro 'reservists,' a step forward, since it hitherto admitted Negroes only in the most menial capacities. Unfortunately, this development was marred by official Jim Crow, Negroes having been placed in distinct units separate from the whites. At the outbreak of the war abroad, there were about fourteen thousand Negro soldiers in the Regular Army, whereas only about four thousand of some hundred and forty thousand enlisted men in the Navy were Negroes. The draft brought many hundreds of thousands into the Army. The War Department has announced that at full strength there will be three hundred and seventy-five thousand Negro soldiers in the Army. However, the Army's more liberal policy toward Negroes has not been duplicated by the Navy — This is, however, somewhat like a choice between the frying pan and the fire. The Army is training several thousand Negro officers, but the Navy has made no provision for training officer material. A high degree of morale has been attained at the Army's Officer-Candidate Infantry School at Fort Benning. Here — on Talmadge's Georgia soil — white and Negro candidates attend the same classes, eat in the same mess hall, sleep in the same barracks, and generally fraternize together. There have been no racial incidents. Encouraging too was the launching of the merchant ship *Booker T. Washington*, with a mixed crew of Chinese, Filipinos, Negroes, and whites, and with a Negro captain, Hugh Mulzac, in full charge of operations. Incidentally, a former British seaman, he sailed his first ship in the United States under the colors of Marcus Garvey's Black Star Line.

These things represent progress. Witness the acts of Negroes. During a drive in Austin, Texas, three Negro brothers — Arthur, Felix, and Osle Jackson — each bought twenty thousand dollars' worth of war bonds. Eddie Anderson, the Negro comedian known as 'Rochester,' invested his earnings in a San Diego parachute factory — and significantly enough, employs Negro, Mexican, and white workers. Two song writers, Andy Razaf and Eubie Blake, turned out a patriotic song called 'We Are Americans Too,' which is currently popular in Negro communities. While pro-Axis agitators shout, the masses of Harlem seek to be included in the war program and confidently carry out the tasks assigned them. For instance, the Negro community has shown better discipline during the city-wide blackout tests than any other area, according to the city officials. Said Newbold Morris, President of the City Council, 'If you give Harlem a chance, the people will respond.'

Listen to the simple faith of a Negro youngster. Alice Godwin, a Harlem high-school student, wrote the following composition in her French class:

> I am a member of a race without a chance to do what it wants to do and without liberty in the whole world. I have been told that this war is a war for liberty for everybody. That is the reason this war is important to me.... It is with great fear that I consider my future under the heel of Hitler. He has said, hasn't he, that I am only half of a human creature?... I shall be glad to wear old shoes not in style. These things are very little compared with the suffering in a world under Hitler. Each little sacrifice I make, I make joyously. It is for a new world, tomorrow, isn't it?

Hope among Negroes rides high. But a minority of vocal whites are determined that the Negro shall not advance. When white liberals and the federal administration appease such elements, the Negro's thinking is confused and his morale lowered. The almost insurmountable prejudice of employers and backward labor unions is no abstraction — but a solid fact the Negro faces day after day. He well knows there are white men in America who would rather lose the war — even their own freedom — than see any change in the racial *status quo*. This attitude has received provocative encouragement from Axis sources.

One of the curious paradoxes of this war, despite its notorious ballyhoo of racism is the fact that Nazi agents have attempted to capitalize on the dissatisfaction of Negroes as well as whites. Adolf Hitler himself seems to have set the pattern. Back in the spring of 1932, he entertained a Georgia-born

Negro, Milton S. J. Wright, in a dinner party at the Europäisch Hof, a fashionable hotel in Heidelberg. The Nazi leader had invited Wright, then a student at Heidelberg University, to talk with him about life in the United States. 'As I recall,' says Wright, today a professor at Wilberforce University, 'he mentioned the names of Booker T. Washington, Paul Robeson, Jack Johnson, Florence Mills, W. C. Handy, Josephine Baker, and the Scottsboro boys.' He spoke loudly, long, and with air of authority on American affairs, but stung his Negro guest with this:

'Negroes must be definitely third-class people,' Hitler said slyly, 'to allow the whites to lynch them, beat them, segregate them, without rising against their oppressors!'

A report of this incident was printed in the Negro press. Obviously handicapped by loud pronouncements of 'Aryan' racial superiority, the Nazi agents — Negro and white — have made some amazing détours. Both in the French colonies and the United States, they have tried to rouse the black man against the Jew. Sometimes they have baldly tried to convince Negroes that the Nazis are not anti-Negro. Mercer Cook, a Negro professor at Atlanta University, tells the story of a German professor in a Negro college who invited Jesse Owens to his class to counteract what he called 'the charges of the Jew-financed American press.' He informed his students that the Nazis had treated the colored athletes with every consideration during the 1936 Olympic Games, and that Hitler had not refused to shake the hands of the 'black auxiliaries.'

The Berlin incident once came up in my conversations with Jesse Owens. When he arrived in New York from abroad, I was one of several hundred newspapermen — Nazi and Japanese correspondents included — who met the boat on his return. The American reporters showered him with questions as to how the Nazis had treated the Negro athletes. He was evasive — at least so I felt. After this mass interview, Owens and I, along with two other Negro Olympic competitors, rode up to Harlem in a taxi and I again put the question to him point-blank. He told me candidly — as one Negro to another — that the Nazis bent backward in making things comfortable for them, even to inviting them to the smartest hotels and restaurants. If the Nazis disapproved of the American Negro athletes' associations with the German girls, the athletes said, nothing in what they said or did suggested it. But we know now that that was a shrewd bit of propaganda by the Nazi leaders, for the story was widely if naïvely told in Negro circles!

Negroes in America have even received reports that the Nazis have cleverly postponed the application of Hitler's anti-Negro dictums in France — perhaps because of the increasing importance of Africa in the war. Mercer Cook, a student of French life, received a report of a Negro soldier from Guadeloupe, demobilized in June, 1940, and about to return to his native land, who was convinced that he had nothing to fear from the Nazis and was persuaded to continue his work on the *agrégation* at the Sorbonne. Even Negroes married to 'Aryans' have been permitted to remain in business in the Paris area. The French Negro author, René Maran, whose *Batouala* won the Goncourt Prize in 1921 and was widely read by American Negroes, was forced to go into hiding in 1940. Yet, after a year of ominous silence, he was again published. Today he is believed to have returned to his apartment in the rue Bonaparte, and in the summer of 1942 received the Grand Prix Broquette-Gonin, awarded by the French Academy. Perhaps to offset the acts of the Negro Governor Félix Eboué, who brought French Equatorial Africa to the side of democracy and gave the Free French movement a territorial base, Hitler allowed Marshal Pétain to name a Martinique Negro, Senator Henry Lémery, as Minister of Colonies! Actually, though an admitted descendant of slaves, he espoused the Rightist cause and openly admired Léon Daudet. Last reports have dispelled this short-lived illusion. In a reshuffle of the Pétain cabinet, Lémery disappeared on Hitler's order.

Negroes today boldly look beyond the horizon of the Negro community, even beyond the borders of the United States, and are concerned with the condition and future of colored peoples elsewhere in the world. Harlem's *People's Voice*, in a long editorial, observed that 'The United Nations must immediately rethink the entire Colonial Problem,' and concluded with the remark, 'The Axis can only be beaten by a free world.' The recent outbreak of rioting at Nassau in the Bahamas, which assumed the proportions of a labor revolt, was not lost on American Negroes. Native despair and unrest in Jamaica, in the face of increasingly serious food shortages, which are being felt throughout the Caribbean, have brought Negroes to voice their indignation to the British and American governments.

Negroes sometimes suspect that there is a tacit understanding among English and American leaders to limit democracy to white men only. Observations of this character are suggested by the demand of the British government that the United States send no American Negroes to work on the West Indian bases; and, what is more important, the fact that the American administration quietly acquiesced. Nor are such feelings dispelled by revelations of wage differentials. Congressman Vito Marcantonio called attention to conditions existing at Borinquen Field, Puerto Rico, where skilled white workers received a dollar and fifty cents per hour and native skilled workers only forty cents per hour.

Negroes are keenly conscious of the ironic fate which has thrown Africa into the vortex of struggling empires. The war's objectives of freedom and democracy are ardently desired by American Negroes for the Africans, who are playing no small part in the contribution of men and resources for the defense of democracy. Du Bois, in a recent lecture at Yale University, expressed the general attitude of American Negroes. He stressed the fact that the white world had millions of dollars invested in Africa, which obviously makes that continent an important part of the world economy. Yet in current plans and discussions, nothing is said about its future. If white America is little concerned, certainly such groups as the African Students' Association in the United States are keeping the issue alive among American Negroes.

These issues are of undoubted propaganda value to the Axis. The unyielding attitude of Britain in India, with the American government's tacit support of this policy, has been the subject of much discussion in Negro circles. To Negroes, these issues are tied to the ultimate objectives of the war! Said the *Courier* editorially, 'The rule of India, like that of other colonies, is based on military force, and when that force remains in the hands of alien rulers there can be no real independence nor successful defense against foreign invaders, as recently demonstrated in Malaya, Burma, and Java.' Pearl Buck, very much admired by Negroes, has expressed the view that the progressive character of the war changed when Indian freedom was rejected.

What all this adds up to in the minds of Negroes is a pattern of continued white domination of colored peoples. Therefore conflicts between the races are regarded as inevitable — that is, without cooperation and desire by whites to see that freedom is the desire and right of all peoples. These, and manufactured issues, are daily dinned into the ears of black men by the Axis. From Berlin, of all places, a broadcast was heard commenting upon the announcement of a new all-Negro United States infantry division. Said the announcer: 'President Roosevelt stated recently that he was against race discrimination. One might ask the President why he was segregating Negroes in a special troop.'

Chapter XXII

One of the most disturbing of the Axis propaganda campaigns in America has been, naturally, an attempt to split our war effort asunder on a racial basis...

— ROBERT TALLMAN

MADE IN JAPAN

RACIAL conflicts in the United States are propaganda meat to the Japanese, who would persuade the darker millions of the world that Japan is fighting a war to liberate oppressed colored peoples. To Berlin and Rome, otherwise cynical about such matters, race riots are likewise useful exhibits to hold before the world as proof that America cannot win because it is a nation paralyzed by internal quarrels. Following the riot in Detroit, the Nipponese lost no time in making short-wave broadcasts from Manchukuo, charging the United States with being 'stained with the bloody guilt of racial persecution.' In the wake of a clash between Negro and white soldiers at Alexandria, Louisiana, a Tokyo radio reported 'racial trouble fomenting within the United States Army,' and observed slyly, 'This proves the disunity of the American Army.'

The Japanese are old hands at using ugly truths to propagandize Negroes. For years Japanese scholars and journalists, even houseboys and chefs, traveled all over the country, gathering surprisingly accurate information about the American race problem. Even before the present World War, the Japanese groped about for an effective method of reaching black men. They tried two approaches. One failed miserably. The other succeeded partially. The first experiment was directed at the intellectuals. When the Pan-African Congress assembled in Paris in 1919, they thought they saw a real opportunity. Black men from various parts of the world, disillusioned by the events of the war, had gathered to formulate a world policy under W. E. B. Du Bois's leadership. Closely collaborating with the American leader were at least four of the six Negro members of the French Chamber of Deputies. The Japanese made friendly advances to these men, inviting them to visit Japan. But the idea of winning over the American Negro masses through Du Bois somehow evaporated in the late twenties with his tour of Japan.

The Japanese did, however, make some considerable impression upon some few Negro intellectuals. James Weldon Johnson, for one, reported the excellent treatment he received while visiting Japan some years back. Negro travelers were unanimous in applauding the Japanese hospitality to black men. The highly literate magazine, *Phylon*, edited by W. E. B. Du Bois, as late as 1940 was remarking that the 'contemptuous insulting and bulldozing attitude toward Japan has driven Japan into the arms of Hitler.' One writer declared that 'The economic encirclement of Japan by British and American capital as well as by the psychology of the color line has long threatened Japan with industrial starvation.'

The next phase of Japanese attempts to win Negroes bag-and-baggage came to something of a blossom after the Depression, when for the first time they made some inroads with the rank-and-file. They sought out discouraged elements among the teeming thousands of the urban areas. Through the Ministry of Propaganda, they found a few radical nationalists, fiercely anti-white, who would lend an ear to talk of an all-colored utopia. Besides, a number of Japanese of attractive manners and sound knowledge of American affairs came to the United States and posed as menials, seeking social ties with

Negro domestics and professing inviolable racial kinship.
Leon W. Taylor, writing in the Baltimore *Afro-American*, recently recalled conversing at length with Japanese chauffeurs
at Saratoga, at Belleair, Florida, and with other Japanese
domestics in Lexington, Kentucky, who revealed this line of
talk. From a Negro girl, who had a Japanese friend, he
learned of propagandizing among the Negro help at summer
resorts as late as 1940. W. C. Handy, composer of 'St. Louis
Blues,' told me of a cook who traveled about the country for
five years as a member of his vaudeville troupe, and who later
turned out to be an eavesdropping Japanese Army officer.

By assiduously cultivating contacts, these people insinuated
themselves into the Negro community, and, in time, some
Negroes came to look upon the Japanese as belonging to a *mes-
sianic* race, which would lead black men out of bondage. A
few Negroes traveled in Japan on grants and subsidies; others
in Washington, Pittsburgh, New York, and Los Angeles entertained distinguished Japanese like Yasuichi Hikida, a graying,
animated little man who always showed up at Negro social
functions accompanied by a Negro woman.

A word about Mr. Hikida, whom I knew as a suave and
genial scholar, will illustrate the manner in which Nipponese
characters threaded their way through Negro life. This
gentleman made good-will tours to Black Belts throughout the
country, often traveling 'Jim Crow' to survey the condition
under which the American Negro lived and worked. He was a
guest at Tuskegee and Hampton Institutes. During these
busy years — some ten of them — he translated Walter
White's documentary study of lynching, *Fire in the Flint*, into
Japanese and wrote an unpublished biography of Toussaint
L'Ouverture, black leader of the Haitian Rebellion, which,
Mr. Hikida explained, was 'an Oriental viewpoint toward the
Negro problem in the United States.'

As late as 1941 he appeared at a debate in Harlem in which
the Sino-Japanese conflict was the subject. He ably supported

the arguments of two Japanese correspondents of *Nitchi Nitchi*, a powerful Tokyo daily newspaper, who made a forthright declaration of Japan's 'Monroe Doctrine.' He decried, among other things, the establishment of international settlements in China, where as he put it idiomatically, 'Chinese were Jim Crowed by whites.' He defended his country's aggression as an effort to drive out the whites and modernize China in the interest of an 'Asia for Asiatics,' and wound up his talk with a nice reference to 'our darker brothers' — the American Negroes. Though he lived in Forest Hills, a swank white neighborhood where it seems he was employed as a servant, he maintained a Harlem address at the colored Y.M.C.A., and every year unfailingly he sent his Negro friends Christmas cards — usually a picture of Japan's Rising Sun. He once was employed by a Westchester County Army colonel, for whom he worked three years as a servant. The F.B.I. picked him up after Pearl Harbor. The net result of his associations with Negroes was that those who knew him came to feel that the Japanese were very cultivated people with respect for Negroes. Nipponese figures have disappeared from Negro life, but not altogether the impression they made, nor the operatives they set in motion.

Negroes and Japanese, for the most part, live in the same areas, except on the eastern seaboard, where the Japanese are very few in numbers. On the West Coast the Japanese numbered more than one hundred thousand before evacuated. As neighbors, they were rather warm toward Negroes. The Japanese, who operated many business enterprises and pretty much controlled truck farming and the vending markets, employed considerable Negro help. Particularly did friendships spring up between Nisei (second-generation Japanese) and young Negroes, and intermarriage was frequent.

The wealthy Japanese had little to do with Negroes, some indeed adopting the prejudice of white people. About four years ago the Japanese came into possession of a tract of land in Los Angeles on which they planned to build homes. The white people living in the immediate vicinity raised objections and even went to the city council and asked that the tract be set aside for a park, hoping thereby to forestall a Japanese housing development. The Japanese, many of them unable to vote, appealed to Negroes for political support. Opposed to racial discrimination, Negroes soon put the heat on their councilmen and were thus successful in defeating the proposal to exclude the Japanese. The pay-off — almost poetic in its irony — came when Negroes discovered that the Japanese had restricted the tract against occupancy by Negroes!

Negroes generally deplored evacuation of the Japanese from the West Coast. The authorities apparently had little knowledge of the numbers of intermarriages that existed. But since the first days of evacuation, the authorities have relaxed the rules for exceptional cases. The American Civil Liberties Union made an appeal that affected Negro, Filipino, and Caucasian husbands with Japanese wives. Today such persons may apply at the civil control stations for 'temporary certificates for mixed racial family groups.' A friend of mine who visited the main evacuation center in Los Angeles frankly reports that he was amazed to see that almost a fourth of the visitors were Negroes.

Relations between Japanese and Negroes on the West Coast were wholly on a personal basis. Responsible observers say that the resident Japanese did not attempt any international propaganda among Negroes. Moreover, Negroes here took little stock in Japan's claim of leadership of colored peoples, partially because a very small but vocal Korean group — bitter Japanese-haters — were always blasting Japanese claims.

In the East and Midwest the situation was found to be something else again. Take the case of a Georgia-born Negro named Gulam Bogan. Away back in 1931 he met Allah in the streets of Detroit — at least so he said — and was told that

Negroes were Moslems, and that they should cast aside their 'slave names' and assume new ones. Somewhat of an intimate God, Allah told Bogan that the Japanese would attack the United States in 1941, and that when it happened Negroes must not fight for America because the Japanese would liberate them. Gulam Bogan listened attentively. Soon afterward he shed his 'slave name' and took the name Elijah Mohammed, and sometimes Mohammed Rassoul. The task of delivering Negroes from the white man's yoke became his mission. He established a number of Temples of Allah and Universities of Islam in Washington, Detroit, and Milwaukee. Membership was said to run into the thousands. The creed was simple and attractive to some: the ultimate destruction of the white man, with the Japanese as liberators.

This sounded like sheer nonsense until the F.B.I. looked into the matter. What apparently was another fantastic cult was revealed as a first-rate hate organization. A white reporter, Robert Ruark, was startled by the 'cold viciousness of the cult's hatred for the whites.' In court, contemptuous evasion characterized its dealings with the opposite race. The American flag's colors were explained thus: the blue stood for untruth, and the white represented the white man's complexion — impure. Red symbolized justice, but only to the healthy and wealthy, while the stars were governors of the states which had persecuted Negroes. The Christian Bible was referred to as 'that poison book.' One speaker was heard to say, 'We praise Allah every time an Allied ship is sunk.' Several hundreds of Bogan's followers refused to register for the draft, on the ground that they were already registered with Islam, as represented by Prophet Bogan. Fifty were sentenced to three years in prison.

Following raids on three Negro cults in Chicago, the F.B.I. picked up eighty-one Negroes, members of the Peace Movement of Ethiopia, the Temple of Islam, and the Brotherhood of Liberty for the Black People of America. Eleven of the men, reputed to be leaders, were charged with sedition and the others were accused of violation of the Selective Service Act. It developed that these cults once had the support of Major Satakata Takajashi, a Japanese official, who was described as the leader of Japanese espionage in the United States for ten years preceding Pearl Harbor. The Negroes involved claimed to belong to the same race as the Japanese. The F.B.I. revealed the whole business as a plot to create a force of American Negroes and Orientals faithful to Japan which could be utilized by Japanese armed forces in the event of an invasion.

Some months later, when twenty-one Negroes, members of the International Reassemble of the Church of Freedom League, Inc., were arrested by the F.B.I. in connection with a conspiracy to encourage evasion of service in expeditionary warfare, it was discovered that definite links existed between Japanese and Nazi propaganda. For letters were sent by the league to draft boards, saying that its members would not report for induction unless assured they would not serve in overseas combat. The members claimed that their religion did not make them conscientious objectors — but it taught them not to fight outside their own country! One Ethelbert Anselm Broaster, a forty-year-old Negro native of British Honduras, was 'general messenger' of the movement.

In Harlem, meantime, a group was formed called the Ethiopian Women's Work Association, ostensibly for the purpose of protesting against lynching. Somehow, along the way, the members formed a special conscientious objectors' committee which advocated refusal to fight unless the federal government insured to Negroes justice under its Constitution. They adopted the motto, 'Justice, like Charity, begins at home. Remember Crispus Attucks.' At the organization's headquarters other groups met, such as the Crispus Attucks Mission Foundation, advising its audiences not to bear arms, and the African-Asiatic Historical and Folklore Society, with a program designed to 'educate' children.

Police stenographers, assigned to report the speeches of Harlem street-corner orators, recorded the utterances of 'Captain' Carlos Cook, a noisy anti-Semite. He was charged with having said: 'Hitler is a good white man. Personally, I admire any white man who can organize white people to kill each other. The white race should produce more Hitlers. If there were more Hitlers we [Negroes] wouldn't have a damn thing to worry about!' He was the 'administrator' of the African Nationalist Pioneering Movement, a pro-Axis organization. Actually, he was without any visible following and merely harangued idlers along Lenox Avenue. He was convicted and sent to jail.

One of Harlem's scores of soapbox speakers held forth for a disagreeably long time, but the law finally caught up with him. He was black and bellicose Harry Fredericks, a former Garveyite and executive vice-president of the Pioneer Negroes of America, Inc. He added to his notoriety by writing a signed article, which was published by the *Amsterdam-Star News* and irresponsibly headlined, 'IS ADOLF HITLER THE NEGRO'S ENEMY?' In it, Fredericks declared that

> This white 'Beast of Berlin' so-called, is the greatest friend of the black man today, for he is splitting up the world-agreed system of economic, cultural, and political oppression of the black man fostered by the British Empire, the French, Belgians, Dutch, Italians, and others.... Let these white people fight right down to the last man, so we black folks can take over the world again!

Fredericks peddled a vicious magazine, *Negro Youth*, which contained chunks of items like this: 'They [whites] try to frighten black people about Hitlerism or a "Nazi Plan" for Negroes. There is no difference between Hitlerism and democracy. Both are white!'

The arrest by the F.B.I. early in 1942 of Policarpio Manansala, a Filipino known variously as 'Doctor O. Takis' and 'Mimo De Guzman,' brought to light a full-dress movement to organize the dark-skinned races for armed uprisings should Japanese forces invade United States soil. Short, rather solidly built, and well dressed, with, as one man said, 'a suit for every day in the week,' he was linked to Japan's militaristic Black Dragon Society. From 1932 to 1938 he had been active in establishing units of the society in New York, St. Louis, Indianapolis, Kansas City, Cincinnati, Pittsburgh, and Philadelphia. His operatives formed groups in Cleveland, Detroit, and Chicago. The organization devoted itself to building an all-colored world, in which the yellow and black races would predominate.

Policarpio first appeared in Negro life sometime in 1932, when he showed up at the home of a Negro named Burt F. Cornish, an elevator operator in St. Louis who was active in fraternal affairs. He was accompanied by a Mr. M. Liang. Policarpio introduced himself as 'Doctor Oshima Takis,' and his friend as a Chicago importer. Liang, a tall thin man, immaculately dressed, was attended by a huge Negro valet, and gave the impression that he was associated with the Japanese consulate. These men lived at Cornish's home for several months, met his friends, and formed the Pacific Movement of the East World, which ostensibly was a proper fraternal organization. Several thousands St. Louis residents joined the movement, captivated by its florid promises of a world in which colored Americans would be 'truly emancipated.' In time, though, the leaders of the movement began to preach that colored peoples had no stake in America — 'where they are segregated and discriminated against, where they are lynched and barred from labor unions and institutions of higher education.'

Eventually Policarpio, as 'Mimo De Guzman,' came into association with Robert O. Jordan, a Negro known as the 'Harlem Hitler' who was seized by the F.B.I. and sentenced to ten years in prison. This Jordan, who worked closely with German and Japanese agents, had had a checkered career of intrigue and conspiracy. A former Marcus Garvey follower, he was born in Jamaica, B.W.I., in 1900, and at fourteen years of age went to England. Four years later he shipped out on the *Nippon Yusen Kaisha*, a ship belonging to the Japan Mail Steamship Company, Ltd., largest steamship company in Japan. He later served as quartermaster on the Japanese ship *Singapore Maru*. In 1920 he turned up in Harlem by jumping ship. He remained here except, for visits to Costa Rica, England, France, and Germany. Once he was detained in Glasgow, Scotland, for declaring in a public speech that England was doomed because she could not win a war against Germany. Mysterious sources produced the money for his release. In the United States, he had affiliations with the Christian Mobilizers. He attempted to join the America First Committee, but his offer was turned down because of his obvious anti-Semitic activities.

A small, nattily dressed man, with a passionate flare to his nostrils, which dilated when he spoke, Jordan organized the Ethiopian Pacific League, sometimes called 'Tojo's Movement,' during the heat about Ethiopia in 1935. It was launched in cooperation with Policarpio, alias 'Guzman,' and the ingratiating Yasuichi Hikida, as the 'Eastern Division' of the Pacific Movement. The F.B.I. estimated that at the peak of its influence the organization had five thousand members. A more accurate figure would be five hundred. Jordan's Sunday evening meetings at 113 Lenox Avenue attracted crowds of three and four hundred. An accomplished rabble-rouser, his speeches frequently dealt with the Jews and he urged his militant followers to take over Harlem from the 'aliens.' In his indoor meetings, as well as on street corners, he made no bones about his liking for Hitler and the Japanese. In Holy-Roller manner, he would shout: 'I'll cut my throat if Hitler doesn't win this war!' or he would murmur sweetly, 'Hitler has a plan all drawn up; it's a beautiful plan and it was made with the agreement of the Japanese.' He always leaned heavily on emotionalism and knew well how to drive a point home. He would first prepare his audiences by hitting upon the sore spots of discrimination and segregation — 'There is no democracy in America because of discrimination against the Negro!' A favorite climax to his oratory was to shout at his frenzied audience: 'England has spoken. America has spoken. Germany has spoken. Japan has spoken. Now Africa speaks!'

The night of October 22, 1941 — to illustrate a typical meeting — he held an audience of three hundred Negroes and several Japanese spellbound. They sat on hard benches in his Lenox Avenue headquarters and listened to him lambaste America. He opened with:

> I am here to bring you the word of the Fuehrer. I am his ambassador, and I have been sent by him to prepare you for the coming of the greatest man of all times, Adolf Hitler. . . .
>
> You Negroes think that Japan doesn't like you. That is not so. You think that they don't like you because the Americans and English have made you think the Japanese are our enemies. But the Japanese do like you. They want to help you and give you back your culture, as they have done to the Chinese. In China today there is no famine and there are no floods because the Japanese know how to take care of the Chinese. The Japanese cleaned up the waterfront of China, built homes for the Chinese, established schools and hospitals and made them a new people, a credit to the New Order. . . .

He concluded his talk by calling for a 'whispering campaign' to persuade every Negro that Hitler is the greatest blessing the Negro ever had and is opening the way for a 'true democracy for Negroes.' Then he took up a collection 'to help carry on the good work and spread the word for the Axis Powers.' Seated on the platform were the Negro officers of the league, and two white men. They said nothing, but appeared to be vastly interested spectators. Meanwhile, the audience applauded wildly, and even answered each mention of Hitler's name with cheers of 'Heil Hitler!'

Armed with considerable funds, Jordan headed a group of zealous race missionaries and skilled agitators, described as agents provocateurs, who, when the F.B.I. began its drive against pro-Axis elements, were swept into the dragnet. His lieutenant was Eugene Holness, a tall fellow with long shiny hair and a small mustache, who spoke so softly as to seem abashed. Joseph Hartrey, a sallow-complexioned fellow who wore green suits and snapped out his words belligerently, was the contact with the Christian Front Movement. He sought to escape arrest by enlisting in the Army, but was brought back for trial. He is quoted as saying, 'I will fight for Japan with every drop of my blood, and I wouldn't ask a penny, for I realize that when the war is over I will be rightly paid and looked upon not as an inferior, but looked upon as an equal man of the Japanese people, and the dark people of the world.'

For such knock-down-drag-out affairs — for indeed some spoke of murder — a disarmingly mild little man found his way into the organization. He was the Reverend Ralph Green Best, a rather short black man with a sprinkling of gray in his closely cropped hair. The image of what Uncle Tom should look like, he was the one who used to lead the tiny audiences in prayer — but followed it up with terrific tirades against the United States! He was a contrast to James Thornhill, a bitter anti-Semite who frequently presided at the meetings. He publicly declared on one occasion that if the government were 'foolish enough to give him a gun,' he would shoot his own commanding officer.

After several weeks of investigation, the *Amsterdam-Star News* reported that the Ethiopian Pacific Movement was not only active in Harlem, but had followers and sympathizers throughout the country. 'Supported by foreign capital,' said this paper, 'the movement in certain areas is reported to have taken a deep-seated root not only among colored residents but also in the ranks of the Christian Front.' On the heels of this report, the Pittsburgh *Courier* revealed that the campaign in the

Midwest had gathered so much momentum that 'Negro leaders are becoming anxious over the growing attitude that the race would be better off if Japan won the war.' Intelligent and technically trained youth, it said, were bitter because in spite of their training they were denied jobs and therefore felt a Nipponese régime would be no worse.

Jordan and his men were small-time racketeers compared with a white man who wheedled his way into Negro life, and acquired status with the smart set of Harlem. He was Joseph Hilton Smyth, a tall, sallow man with a long forehead, an unkempt mustache, and a thick mop of brown hair dangling over his right ear. He was well known in literary and publishing circles. Negroes were dumbfounded when the fact came to light that he was a paid propagandist for the Japanese, and he was convicted in the fall of 1942 and sentenced to ten years in prison. This answered the question of his sources of money, which he splashed about wildly.

Smyth, a Bohemian of pre-Depression vintage, was born at Plymouth, Massachusetts on December 4, 1901, of irreproachable Yankee stock. According to his autobiography, *To Nowhere and Return*, he had lived a full life, marrying at random and drinking until he was 'reeking of stale whiskey.' After attending several preparatory schools he wound up at Harvard, where he attended a few classes and was dropped at the end of the year. He did better at Boston's New School for Design, picking up enough art to illustrate his autobiography years later. He helped film *Down to the Sea in Ships*, acquired a limp after receiving wounds in an abortive revolution in Guatemala, worked on the copy desk of the New Orleans *Times-Picayune*, and drifted to France, where he fraternized with Frank Harris and other expatriates.

He returned to the United States and began writing for the magazines. 'Slowly,' he wrote, 'I became aware of the devious workings of various pressure groups, political and religious, and social organizations intent on coloring or suppressing the news.' In 1938 he acquired ownership of one of America's oldest and most reputable magazines, *The Living Age*. In his autobiography, Smyth said that his earnings as a writer enabled him to buy the magazine. Actually, the purchase price of fifteen thousand dollars was supplied by Shintaro Fukushima, Japanese Vice-Consul in New York, in charge of press relations. Together with two other white men, he received a total of one hundred and twenty-five thousand dollars. Almost immediately the magazine began publishing articles defending Japanese aggression in China, and suggesting not too subtly that American stakes in the Far East were not worth a tangle with Japan. Soon after obtaining *The Living Age*, he founded *The Foreign Observer*, a weekly news forecast of domestic and foreign events, which also adopted a Japanese line, and later bought the reputable *North American Review*.

Smyth's relations with Negroes began in 1938. He was introduced to the Negro community by the handsome Annastean Haines, whom he met while she was a singer at Leon and Eddie's, a Broadway night club. In 1936 she had successfully sued Duncan McMartin, Canadian multimillionaire, for forty thousand dollars after she was injured while riding in his car. Smyth married her and moved to Harlem. They lived in the fashionable Roger Morris Apartments on Sugar Hill. He was to all appearance devoted to his wife, and lavished gifts upon her, including a pair of pedigreed Siamese cats. He made her a stockholder in all his magazine ventures. Wearing furs worth thousands of dollars, she rode about Harlem in a smart cream-colored roadster. He also gave her a home in Old Lyme, Connecticut.

Not until 1940 did Smyth actually attempt to disseminate pro-Japanese propaganda among Negroes. In the early part of that year, he founded the Negro News Syndicate, a press service national in scope which was intended to reach Negro publications. He employed three Negroes, and established offices in Harlem in his wife's maiden name. He frequently sent out articles under her signature. On one occasion, to make the releases attractive to the Negro editors, he wrote them thus: 'Because of our singular contacts with foreign correspondents abroad and in Washington, and because of our contacts with the large press associations, we are able to furnish you with vital news, *without charge*.' Few papers accepted the offer, though the syndicate remained active up to Pearl Harbor, losing considerable money every week. Here are a few samples of the sort of stuff he distributed:

> The white press in America has never properly understood or interpreted the current conflict in Asia.... The racial issues involved have been utterly disregarded. Hence the current clash over the status of the Netherlands Indies. Japan maintains that they should be considered a part of the new East Asian economic union, in which the other countries of Asia should have rights *at least equaling* that of the white Western Powers...

> The Pacific War will impoverish Negroes. Since 1930 Japan has been the largest foreign buyer of American cotton, importing in recent years considerably more than a million bales annually, or over ten per cent of the total United States cotton crop. Any drastic break in this trade — such as is currently being provoked by British attempts to enlist United States support in protecting Britain's Pacific possessions — would have an immediate and disastrous result on a considerable portion of the American Southland. Millions of Negroes now dependent, directly and indirectly, on cotton for their livelihood would suffer....

Smyth's activities made no impression on Negroes. Almost to a man they were outraged by the treacherous assault upon the United States at Pearl Harbor — not having digested whole-cloth Nipponese propaganda. But as a result of significant infiltration of ideas emanating from Japanese sources, there is today little active anti-Japanese feeling prevalent in the Negro community. A survey of the leading Negro newspapers since the war began reveals no letters-to-the-editor

condemning Japanese treachery and few editorials castigating
the Japanese foe, a fact which might suggest that many Negroes have been neutralized. A reporter for the Baltimore
Afro-American told Mrs. Roosevelt, during an interview with
the Negro press, that he had attended Negro meetings 'where
Japanese victories were slyly praised and American defeats at
Bataan and Corregidor brought amused and knowing snickers.'

The Negro's attitude toward the war is directly a product of
his condition. And his condition is no longer a purely domestic question in which one section of the white population ac-
cuses the other of a lack of righteousness, and lets the matter
drop there. Actually, the color problem, underscored by
events abroad, is an element in the larger strategy of defeating
the Axis. The condition of the black man in the United States
has become the barometer of 'democracy' to the colored
leaders of the world, and even suggests to them — should
certain Fascist-minded elements here have their way — the
sort of 'democracy' which may dominate the new world
a-coming. Did Gandhi not say, 'The [white] Allies have no
moral cause for which they are fighting, so long as they are
carrying this double sin — the sin of India's subjection and
the subjection of Negroes'?

The Japanese are acutely aware that the problem of color
is one of the pivotal questions in the war. They know that
there are millions of colored peoples who want to see the last
of the white man's rule — witness India, Singapore, Burma,
and Malaya!

Chapter XXIII

... It is high time to awake out of sleep: for now is our salvation nearer than when we believed. The night is far spent, the day is at hand: let us therefore cast off the works of darkness, and let us put on the armour of light.

— FROM THE EPISTLES OF ST. PAUL

NEW WORLD A-COMING

THE Negro stands at the door of a fretful future. What it will be no man can say — there are no blueprints. The Negro may not be able to predict his future, but he knows what he wants — liberty and peace, and an enriched life, free of want, oppression, violence, and proscription. In a word, he wants democracy — cleansed and refreshed. He wants to be able to feel, see, and smell, and get his teeth into it — democracy can be like that! Faced today with fascism or democracy, the Negro's choice is simple. He is against fascism, finally and inexorably, both at home and abroad. For few men understand its dangers better than he. Its lash has already cut him deeply, savagely.

But men — white or black — do not rally to negative slogans!

It is cold comfort to tell the Negro his lot will be worse if the cause of democracy falls. Negroes want tangible assurances that the loud talk of democracy is in fact meant to include them. They need assurances desperately. But by no means will they be satisfied with mere high-sounding platitudes.

They want concrete safeguards of their rights. Without them, they will lose faith. For they have been treated too long as pariahs, despised, neglected, and left to despair, in a country whose soil their blood, tears, and sweat have nurtured. Too long have they been denied the right to vote in the South, faced with blind alleys of opportunity everywhere in the nation, and even denied the right to die for their country as equals.

Tradition must be overturned, and democracy extended to the Negro. These are hardly the times to fumble about with abstractions. We are in a titanic life-and-death struggle with ruthless and efficient foes. Negroes, as well as colored peoples elsewhere, must be galvanized into decisive action on the side of democracy.

The color problem has become a world-wide issue to settle here and now. Should tomorrow the Axis surrender unconditionally, Negroes say, the capitulation would provide only a brief interlude of peace unless the white world believes and acts without reservation to make true the words of Sumner Welles, that 'Our victory must bring in its train the liberation of all peoples. Discrimination between peoples because of their race, creed, or color must be abolished.' Millions of black, brown, and yellow peoples still do not believe that the white world believes in or intends to put into effect democracy for all once the danger to themselves has passed.

This belief is what accounts for the depths of passion that underlie the Negro's struggle today.

There is nothing mystical about the Negro's aggressive attitude. The noisy espousal of democracy in the last war gave stimulus to the Negro's cause, and set the race implacably in motion. By advancing it in this war, democracy has become an immediate goal to the Negro. His rumblings for equality in every phase of American life will reverberate into a mighty roar in the days to come. For the Negro feels that the day for talking quietly has past. Moreover, he knows that America can be recharged with progressive vitality. Few nations have this country's flexibility to change. In spite of vocal opposition, Negroes have hope. For they have an abiding faith in the eventual rightness of things. When they sing '... on solid rock I stand!' this is no illusion, for the foundation of their aspirations comes directly from the nation's great promise contained in its Constitution.

But the path to glory is a thorny one. Not the least will be the discussions pundits will indulge in to determine how and when a people should be free, discussions which will revolve around the 'Negro problem.' What is generally referred to as the Negro problem is in fact a set of phobias, prejudices, and fictions, which unscrupulous men — both Negro and white — exploit for their own gain. Today, as a result, black men and white in America do not face human beings; they face a straw man, an entity built out of the imagination which they pummel daily. Unhappily, people believe what they want to believe. Moreover, the whole educational structure of American life — schools, radio, and motion pictures — supports false theories of race and contributes to a false picture of that man across the tracks. In essence, this is what makes it so difficult for white men and black to face each other frankly and to admit the truth about each other. Usually the inner foes of democracy stimulate antagonisms between them: the race missionary in the Negro world, the pro-Fascist and Ku Kluxer in the white world.

Can the South be persuaded to end its segregation and discrimination against the Negro? This is the crux of the matter in the minds of most people. To Negroes social equality — the issue in a nutshell — is something quite different from that in the minds of many white people. James Weldon Johnson once expressed the Negro's view. 'There should be nothing in law or public opinion,' he said, 'to prevent persons of like interests and congenial tastes from associating together if they mutually desire to do so.' However, Negroes are too realistic to expect any fundamental change in the Southerner's attitudes overnight, but he does believe that with the will to act the rôles of enlightened people, at least the economic and educational barriers can be lifted.

Whenever logic fails, inevitably the Southerner will ask the white man who supports this view, 'Do you want your daughter to marry a Negro?' Obviously this question obscures the real truth of the matter. For Negroes do not struggle for equal rights to marry white women. The question presumes, as well, that if a Negro is permitted to enter a polling place, a theater, a school, or a public conveyance, marriage between the races automatically follows. Listen to Langston Hughes:

> Nobody sleeps with or eats with or dances with or marries anybody else except by mutual consent. Millions of people in New York, Chicago, and Seattle go to the same polls and vote without ever cohabiting together. Why does the South think it would be otherwise with Negroes were they permitted to vote there? Or have a decent education? Or sit on a stool in a public place and eat a hamburger? Why they think simple civil rights would force a Southerner's daughter to marry a Negro in spite of herself, I have never been able to understand. . . .

Essentially, the masses of Negroes are concerned only with jobs — for they believe that fundamentally their problem is an economic one. They want the 'FOR WHITES ONLY' signs torn from every job in American life, for, barred from earning a living wage, they are kept at the bottom of the heap. And with them are millions of white men kept in a similar condition — with little beyond the luxury of being *white!* The integration of Negroes in our economic life would end differences and divisions between the races now perpetuated by what each fails to learn about the other, and accentuated by their separation.

The Negro believes that progressive leadership on the color question should come from the administration — from President Roosevelt himself. The fact is, he stands at one of those great crossroads in history. He has said that our generation has a 'rendezvous with destiny.' The colored world looks to him for that leadership. Some will say, in opposing this, that the public mind is not ready for the Negro in America to be a fully participating citizen. But neither, in a similar sense, was the public ready for the emancipation of the slaves during the Civil War. In those days white men certainly were not rallying to a banner of freeing the Negro race. Yet Lincoln rose magnificently and freed the slaves. While the Emancipator's name has been shaped in legend and song, the anti-Negro demagogues and timid souls have long since been forgotten.

This is the day for bold action. Mr. Roosevelt can serve the democratic way, and preserve the integrity of our Constitution, with a sweeping pronouncement that would set the colored peoples of the world on fire with enthusiasm for the war and give men — white and black — the hope they so desperately need. No man in history has faced a greater challenge. No people has faced a greater opportunity to serve humanity. The Negro's cause in America is the barometer of democracy. If it falls here, it falls everywhere, for colored men will lose hope, and the world will be plunged into a racial convulsion which may very well bring about the destruction of civilization. America is a great moral force. Its leader, President Roosevelt, must lift himself above the picayune racial concerns of Sikeston, Missouri, or Atlanta, Georgia, or Meridian, Mississippi, and view the color problem in its broadest international terms.

The Negro's cause will rise or fall with America. He knows well that his destiny is intimately bound to that of the nation. America stands today as a symbol of freedom! The loss of this symbol will mean the loss of hope for white and black alike. This war, undeniably, belongs to the Negro as well as to the white man. To this extent, it may be called a 'People's War' — for in spite of selfish interests a new world is a-coming with the sweep and fury of the Resurrection.

THE END

Bibliography

GENERAL REFERENCE WORKS:

Chicago Commission on Race Relations, *The Negro in Chicago*, 1922.

Dictionary of American Biography, 1936.

Eighth Annual Report, New York City Housing Authority, 1941.

'Food Costs More in Harlem,' *Report* by the National Association for the Advancement of Colored People (pamphlet), 1942.

The Mayor's Commission, *Report on the Conditions in Harlem*, 1936.

New York Committee of Vigilance. *First Annual Report for the year, 1837, Together with Important Facts Relative to Their Proceedings, 1837.*

New York State Temporary Commission, *Second Report on the Condition of the Colored Urban Population*, February, 1939.

Report on Economic Conditions of the South, made by the National Emergency Council (pamphlet), 1938.

Reports of the City-Wide Citizens' Committee on Harlem, 1942.

BOOKS AND PAMPHLETS:

Allen, Richard. *History of African Methodist Episcopal Church*. (No publication date.)

American Anti-Slavery Society, *Annual Reports*. New York, 1834–1841; 1855–1861. (No reports published between 1841 and 1855.)

American Convention for Promoting the Abolition of Slavery and Improving the Condition of the African Race. (Title variations.) *Minutes*, Philadelphia, 1794–1828.

An address delivered on the celebration of the abolition of Slavery in the State of New York, July 5, 1827, by Nathaniel Paul, Pastor of the First African Baptist Society in the City of Albany. (Pamphlet.)

An Oration Commemorative of the Abolition of the Slave Trade in the United States, delivered before the Wilberforce Philanthropic Association in the City of New York on the 2d of January, 1809. By Joseph Sidney. (Pamphlet.)

Asbury, Herbert. *The Gangs of New York*, 1929.

Baker, Paul E. *Negro-White Adjustment*, 1934.

Barnes, G. H. *The Antislavery Impulse, 1830–1844*, 1933.

Bayton, James A. 'The Psychology of Racial Morale,' *The Journal of Negro Education*, vol. XI, April, 1942.

Beaton, Cecil. *Cecil Beaton's New York*, 1938.

Boyer, Richard O. 'Councilman Powell of Harlem,' *New Masses*, vol. XLV, November 3, 1942.

Brawley, Benjamin. *A Social History of the American Negro*, 1921.

Brown, Earl. 'Colored Soldiers, U.S.A.,' *Survey Graphic*, vol. XXXI, November, 1942.

Brown, Earl, and Leighton, George R. *The Negro and the War*, Public Affairs Pamphlets, no. 71, 1942.

Brown, Henry Collins, Editor. *Valentine's Manual of Old New York*, 1916–1929.

Brown, Sterling A. 'Out of Their Mouths,' *Survey Graphic*, vol. XXXI, November, 1942.

Calverton, V. F. *Where Angels Dared to Tread*, 1941.

Catterall, Helen Tunnicliff, editor. *Judicial Cases Concerning American Slavery and the Negro*, 5 vols., 1928–1935.

Common Council of the City of New York. *Minutes*, 1675–1776, 1784–1831, 8 vols., 1905.

Cook, Mercer. 'The Negro Knows Fascism,' *Free World*, vol. IV, November, 1942.

Cornish, Samuel E., and Wright, Theodore S. *The Colonization Scheme Considered in its Rejection by the Colored People*, 1840.

Cromwell, John W. *Conventions of Free People of Color* (pamphlet), 1904.

Delany, Martin Robinson. *The Condition, Elevation, Emigration and Destiny of the Colored People of the United States (Politically Considered)*, 1852.

Detweiler, Frederick G. *The Negro Press in the United States*, 1922.

De Voe, Thomas Farrington. *The Market Book, a History of the Public Markets in the City of New York, from Its First Settlement to the Present Time*, 1862.

Donnan, Elizabeth, editor. *Documents Illustrative of the History of the Slave Trade to America*, 4 vols., 1930–1935.

Douglass, Frederick. *My Bondage and Freedom*, 1853

———— *Narrative of the Life of Frederick Douglass, An American Slave. Written by Himself*, 1853.

Du Bois, W. E. Burghardt. *Dusk of Dawn*, 1940.

———— *Black Reconstruction*, 1935.

———— *The Souls of Black Folk*, 1903.

———— *The Suppression of the African Slave Trade to the United States of America*, 1896.

Dummond, Dwight Lowell. *Roosevelt to Roosevelt*, 1937.

Egans, Pierce. *Every Gentleman's Manual*, 1845.

Evans, William L. 'Federal Housing Brings Residential Segregation to Buffalo,' *Opportunity Magazine*, April, 1942.

Farson, Negley. *Behind God's Back*, 1941.

Ferguson, Elizabeth A. 'Race Consciousness Among Negroes,' *The Journal of Negro Education*, vol. VII, January, 1938.

Flick, Alexander C., editor. *The History of the State of New York*, 10 vols., 1937.

Foster, G. G. *New York by Gas-Light*, 1850.

Fox, Dixon Ryan. 'The Negro Vote in Old New York,' *Political Science Quarterly*, vol. 22, 1917.

Franklin, Charles Lionel. *The Negro Labor Unionist of New York*, 1936.

Frazier, E. Franklin. *The Free Negro Family*, 1932.

—— *The Negro Family in the United States*, 1939.

Garnet, Henry Highland. *An Address to the Slaves of the United States*. Report of the National Convention of Colored Citizens, New York, 1843.

Garrison, Wendell Phillips, and Garrison, Francis Jackson. *William Lloyd Garrison: Story of His Life Told by His Children*, 4 vols., 1894.

Garrison, William Lloyd. *Thoughts on African Colonization: or An Impartial Exhibition of the Doctrines, Principles, and Purposes of the American Colonization Society, together with the Resolutions, Addresses, and Remonstrances of the Free People of Color*, 1832.

Garvey, Amy Jacques, editor. *Philosophy and Opinions of Marcus Garvey*, 1926.

Gosnell, Harold F. *Negro Politicians*, 1935.

Graves, John Temple. 'The Southern Negro and the War Crisis,' *The Virginia Quarterly Review*, vol. 18, Autumn, 1942.

Harap, Louis. 'Anti-Negroism Among Jews,' *The Negro Quarterly*, vol. I, Summer, 1942.

Harris, Abram L. 'The Negro As Capitalist,' *The American Academy of Political and Social Science*, vol. XII, 1936.

Haynes, George E. *The Negro at Work in New York City, a Study in Economic Progress*, 1912.

Headley, J. T. *The Great Riots of New York City, 1712–1873*, 1873.

Herskovits, Melville J. *The American Negro*, 1928.

High, Stanley. 'Black Omens,' *The Saturday Evening Post*, vol. 210, May 21, 1938.

Holland, Jerome H. 'The Role of the Negro Church As an Organ of Protest,' *The Journal of Negro Education*, vol. XI, April, 1942.

Horsmanden, Daniel. *A Journal of the Proceedings in the Detection of the Conspiracy Formed by Some White People in Conjunction with Negro and Other Slaves, for Burning the City of New York in America and Murdering the Inhabitants*, 1741.

Hoshor, John. *God in a Rolls Royce*, 1936.

Hubert, James H. *Urbanization and the Negro* (pamphlet), 1936.

Huggins, Willis N., and Jackson, John G. *An Introduction to African Civilizations*, 1937.

Hughes, Langston. *The Big Sea*, 1940.

—— 'What the Negro Wants,' *Common Ground*, vol. II, Autumn, 1941.

—— 'What Shall We Do About the South?', *Common Ground*, vol. III, Winter, 1943.

Johnson, Charles S. *The Economic Status of Negroes*, 1933.

Johnson, James Weldon. *Black Manhattan*, 1930.

—— *Along This Way*, 1933.

—— *Negro Americans, What Now?* 1934.

Kaskeline, Egon. 'Félix Eboué and the Fighting French,' *Survey Graphic*, vol. XXXI, November, 1942.

Kiplinger, W. M. *Washington Is Like That*, 1942.

Little, Arthur W. *From Harlem to the Rhine*, 1936.

Locke, Alain, editor. *The New Negro*, 1925.

Loggins, Vernon. *The Negro Author*, 1931.

McKay, Claude. *Harlem: Negro Metropolis*, 1940.

—— 'There Goes God,' *The Nation*, vol. XCL, February 6, 1935.

McKee, Samuel. *Labor in Colonial New York, 1664–1776*, 1935.

McKelway, St. Clair, and Liebling, A. J. 'Who Is This King of Glory?', *The New Yorker*, vol. XXII, June 13, 20, 27, 1936.

Michie, Allan, and Ryhlick, Frank. *Dixie Demagogues*, 1939.

Minton, Bruce, and Stuart, John. *Men Who Lead Labor*, 1937.

Mitchison, Naomi. 'Epiphany of Harlem,' *New Statesman and Nation*, vol. IX, June 29, 1935.

Moon, H. L. 'Thank You, Father, So Sweet,' *The New Republic*, vol. LXXVIII, September 16, 1936.

Morgan, Edwin Vernon. *Slavery in New York*, 1898.

Moton, Robert Russa. *What the Negro Thinks*, 1928.

Myers, Gustavus. *History of Tammany Hall*, 1901.

'The Negro's War,' *Fortune*, vol. XXV, June, 1942.

New York City Writers Project, Roi Ottley, Editor. *Negroes of New York* (unpublished).

Nicolay, J. G., and Hay, J. *Abraham Lincoln*, 10 vols., 1890.

O'Callaghan, Edmund Bailey, editor. *Documentary History of The State of New York*, 4 vols., 1856.

Odum, Howard W. *An American Epoch*, 1930.

Ovington, Mary White. *Half a Man, The Status of the Negro in New York*, 1911.

—— *How the National Association for the Advancement of Colored People Began* (pamphlet), 1914.

Owen, Chandler. 'Negro: Anti-Semitism: Cause and Cure,' *The National Jewish Monthly*, vol. 57, September, 1942.

Palmer, A. Mitchell, Attorney-General. 'Radicalism and Sedition Among the Negroes as Reflected in Their Publications' (Exhibit No. 10), 1919.

Parker, Robert Allerton. *The Incredible Messiah*, 1937.

Parrington, Vernon Louis. *Main Currents in American Thought*, 3 vols., 1927–1930.

Penn, I. Garland. *The Afro-American Press and Its Editor*, 1891.

Poole, William Frederick. *Anti-Slavery Opinions before the Year 1800*, 1873.

Powell, A. Clayton, Sr. *Against the Tide*, 1938.

Powell, Adam Clayton, Jr., *The Negro and the Present Crisis* (pamphlet), December, 1941.

Reddick, L. D. 'Anti-Semitism Among Negroes,' *The Negro Quarterly*, vol. I, Summer, 1942.

Reid, Ira De A. *The Negro Immigrant*, 1939.

Reuter, Edward Byron. *The American Race Problem*, 1927.

Savannah Unit Georgia Writer's Project, *Drums and Shadows*, 1940.

Sayers, Michael, and Kahn, Albert E. *Sabotage!* 1942.

Schuyler, George S. 'Dr. Jekyll and Mr. Hyde, and the Negro,' *Common Ground*, vol. I, 1941.

—— 'Who Is "Negro"? Who Is "White"?' *Common Ground*, vol. I, Autumn, 1940.

Scott, Emmett J. *Official History of the American Negro in the World War*, 1919.

Siebert, Wilbur H. *The Underground Railroad from Slavery to Freedom*, 1898.

Smith, James McCune, M.D. *A Lecture on the Haytien Revolution, with a Sketch of the Character of Toussaint L'Overture. Delivered at the Stuyvesant Institute (N.Y.) February 26, 1841*, 1841.

Smith, Samuel Denny. *The Negro in Congress*, 1940.

Smyth, Joseph Hilton. *To Nowhere and Return*, 1940.

Society for Promoting the Manumission of Slaves; and Protecting such of them as have been or may be Liberated. Minutes and Reports, 12 vols., 1785–1849.

Spero, Sterling D., and Harris, Abram L. *The Black Worker*, 1931.

Standing, T. G. 'Nationalism in Negro Leadership,' *The American Journal of Sociology*, vol. XL, September, 1934.

Stein, Clarence S. 'Investment Housing Pays,' *Survey Graphic*, vol. XXIX, February, 1940.

Still, William. *The Underground Railroad*, 1931.

Stokes, I. N. Phelps. *The Iconography of Manhattan Island*, 6 vols., 1915–1928.

Stolberg, Benjamin. 'Black Chauvinism,' *The Nation*, vol. 140, May 15, 1935.

Trollope, Mrs. Frances Minton. *Domestic Manners of the Americans*, 1828.

United States Congress. *Congressional Record, Proceedings and Debates*, 76th, 77th Congresses.

Valentine, David T., compiler. *Manual of the Corporation of the City of New York, 1841–1866.*

Van Deusen, John G. *'Brown Bomber,'* 1940.

Van Rensselaer, Mrs. Schuyler. *History of the City of New York in the Seventeenth Century,* 2 vols., 1909.

Wakely, Joseph Beaumont. *Lost Chapters Recovered from the Early History of American Methodism,* 1858.

Washington, Booker T. *Up From Slavery,* 1915.

———— *The Story of the Negro,* 2 vols., 1909.

Washington, H. A., editor. *The Writings of Thomas Jefferson,* 1853–54.

Wesley, Charles H. *Negro Labor in the United States,* 1927.

———— 'The Negroes of New York in the Emancipation Movement,' *The Journal of Negro History,* vol. 24, January, 1939.

White, Walter. 'The Right to Fight for Democracy,' *Survey Graphic,* vol. XXXI, November, 1942.

Wilkerson, Doxey. 'FEPC — The Alphabet Hope,' *New Masses,* vol. XLV, October 20, 1942.

Wilkes, Laura Eliza. *Missing Pages in American History,* 1919.

Williams, George W. *History of the Negro Race in America,* 2 vols., 1883.

Williams, Joseph J. *Hebrewism of West Africa,* 1931.

Wilson, Henry. *History of the Rise and Fall of the Slave Power in America,* 3 vols., 1873.

Wilson, Joseph T. *The Black Phalanx,* 1888.

Woodson, Carter G. *A Century of Negro Migration,* 1918.

———— editor. *The Mind of the Negro as Reflected in Letters Written During the Crisis, 1800–1860,* 1924

———— *The Negro in Our History,* 1928.

Work, Monroe, editor. *Negro Year Book,* 1940.

Workers of the Writer's Program of the Works Projects Administration in the State of Virginia, *The Negro in Virginia,* 1940.

NEWSPAPERS:

New York: *Amsterdam-Star News, Daily Worker, Herald Tribune, People's Voice, PM, Post, Times, World-Telegram.*

Baltimore *Afro-American,* Michigan *Chronicle,* Pittsburgh *Courier,* Chicago *Defender,* Norfolk *Journal and Guide,* Los Angeles *Tribune,* Philadelphia *Tribune.*

MAGAZINES:

The Crisis, Opportunity, Phylon.

Index

Abebe, Prince Lij Araya, 42
Abolitionists, 12–22
Abyssinian Baptist Church, 142, 225–27
Abyssinian Jews, 141–42
Advertising, in Negro press, 280, 281
African Grove, 12
African Methodist Episcopal Zion Church, 11, 13
African Negroes, 41–43
African Orthodox Church, 73–74
African Popes, 103
African Society for Mutual Relief, 12
African Students' Association, 42
Afro-American, 284–85
Afro-American Council, 23
Afro-American Realty Company, 32
Alexander, Cato, 30
American Anti-Slavery Society, 18
American Colonization Society, 77–78
American Democracy, 252–53, 287–88, 311, 325, 334, 336, 342, 343–47
American Federation of Labor, 250, 293–94, 295, 296, 297, 300
American Friends of Haiti, 50
American Pro-Falasha Committee, 141
American-West Indian Association on Caribbean Affairs, 48
Amsterdam-Star News, 47–48, 87, 132, 133, 134, 166, 178, 198, 201, 252, 263, 275, 281–82, 283, 285, 286, 289, 308, 310, 314, 334, 338
Anderson, Eddie, 321
Anderson, Marian, 240, 241
Anti-Semitism, 104, 118, 119, 121, 122–33, 135–36, 149–50
Anti-slavery, Quakers and, 9; Revolutionary War and, 9–10; northern, 9–11, 12; emancipation movement and, 12–22; Underground Railroad and, 13–14, 18, 30; Vigilance Committee and, 14–15; newspapers on, 17; American Anti-Slavery Society and, 18; Fugitive Slave Law and, 18–19; Dred Scott decision and, 19; Civil War and, 19–22; Emancipation Proclamation and, 20; Reconstruction Period and, 22; Negro suffrage and, 206

Armistead, Mme. V. D. S., 87
Armstrong letter, 230
'Articles of Cooperation,' 239
Asiatics, 53–56
Atlanta, 168, 176
'Atlanta Compromise,' 36
Atlanta *Daily World*, 280
Austin, J. C., 223
Azikiwe, Nnamdi, 42

'Back Door Stuff,' 283
Back-to-Africa Movement, 67–81, 102, 150
Baker, Ella, 126
Baker, George, 89. *See also* Father Divine
Baker, Newton D., 69–70
Baldwin, Mrs. Ruth Standish, 296
Ballot, the, 203–19
Bankhead, Senator John D., 311–12
Baptist Church, 221, 227
Barefoot Prophet, 64
Barrow, Joseph Louis, *see* Louis, Joe
Bassa Moona, 43
Batista, Colonel Fulgencio, 50
Bayen, Malaku E., 42, 110, 111
Beaton, Cecil, 175
Beck Shoe Corporation, 116
Beecher, Henry Ward, 13
Beethoven, Ludwig Van, 103
Beguine, 47
Beni Israel of India, 141
Bennett, James Gordon, 21
Benychuda, Yoseh Ben Moshea. *See* Matthew, Rabbi Wentworth Arthur
Bernadotte, Jean Baptiste, 103
Best, Rev. Ralph Green, 338
Beth Hatphala Number 1, 138
Beth-Israel, 139
Beth Israel Synagogue, 135
Beth Zekanim, 138
Bethune, Mrs. Mary McLeod, 264–65
'Big Five,' 237
'Black Bohemia,' 25–26, 27–28
Black Abyssinian Jews, 141–42
'Black Beautiful,' 33, 93
'Black Cabinet,' 237, 254–67
Black Cross Navigation Company, 80